genius series

MATHEMATICS Olympiad Excellence GUIDE

Salient Features of the Book

- All the questions are in MCQ format
- Meant for International/National Olympiads, Quizzes, Inter school competitions
- In-depth analysis of each topic, followed by relevant practical and illustrative examples
- Comprising questions prepared by teachers from various schools of India and abroad
- Comprising questions of various National and International Olympiads
- Model Test Papers with explanations
- Special emphasis on concept and problem solving skills

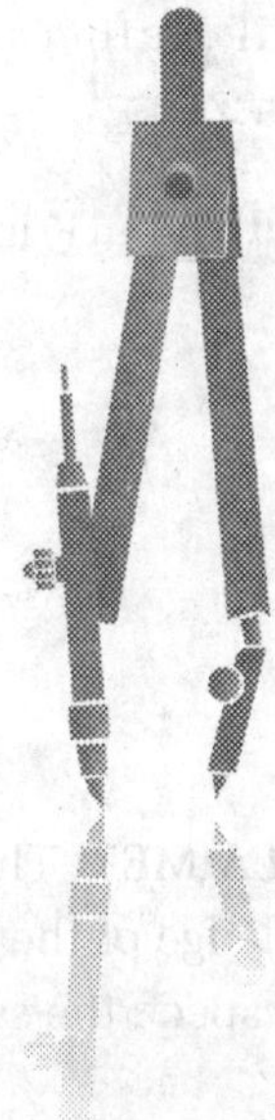

CLASS 3rd

Prepared & Published by: **Silverzone Enterprises India Pvt. Ltd.**
B-2|Ansal Chamber-II, Bhikaji Cama Place
New Delhi-110066(India)
E-mail : info@silverzone.org

Printed by: Tan Prints India Pvt. Ltd., Rohad, Haryana

DISCLAIMER: The text material of this book is completely based on the original self-ideas and knowledge of the author. In case, any part of this book is found similar with any other book in any respect, the same should be treated as mere coincidence only.

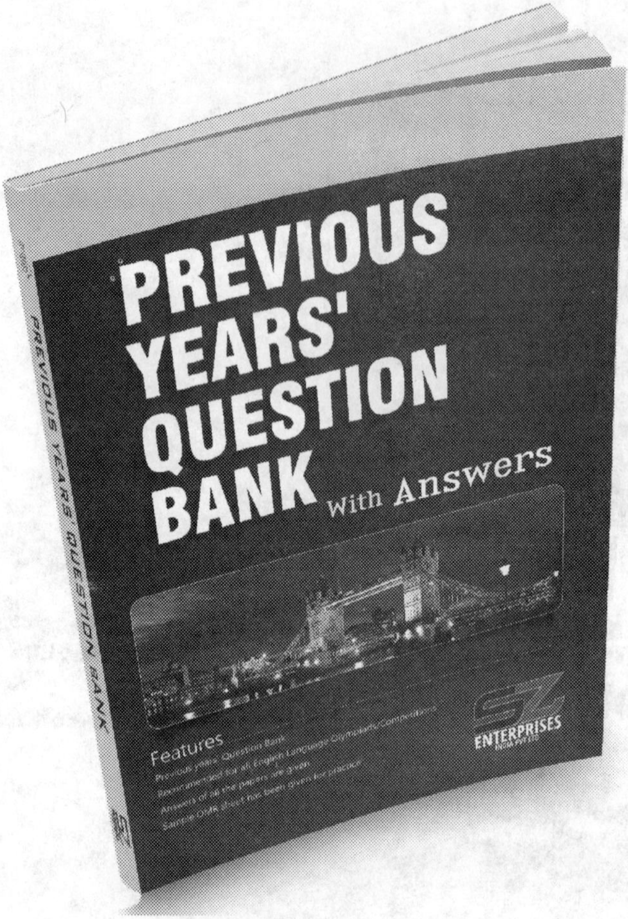

ALSO RECOMMENDED

Previous Year's Question Bank

National/International level competitions and Olympiads have made a major contribution to enhance the student's growth academically. These Olympiads serve as a boon for participants as these help in developing their confidence level to a great extent. The result of the exam does not indicate pass or fail for the participants so the fear of losing or failing in a particular exam does not bother the children and they give the exam without stress. This adds to encouragement of the children to participate in various competitive examinations as by studying Previous Year papers, their morale is boosted. These papers are of great help as by solving these papers the students are encouraged to give exams fearlessly as they are aware about the pattern of the exam conducted in previous year. These papers serve as a kind of rehearsal for participants to a certain level. These will also help you to understand the syllabus, pattern and how the pattern and difficulty levels have evolved over the years. By solving these papers the participant can find out your shortcomings and accordingly prepare for the current exam he/she wishes to crack this year. Thus, previous year papers are the best way to get a clear idea of the exam pattern and level of difficulty of questions as these contain all questions with answers and detailed explanation.

Olympiad Excellence Guide

genius series

Mathematics

TABLE OF CONTENTS

CHAPTERS

MODEL TEST PAPERS

10001

OMR - ANSWER SHEET

PLEASE SEE INSTRUCTIONS OVERLEAF BEFORE FILLING THE ANSWER SHEET

SILVER ZONE FOUNDATION

PARTICIPANT'S NAME

FATHER'S NAME

SCHOOL NAME

PARTICIPANT'S ENROLLMENT NUMBER

Column	Options
1	A B C D E F G H I J K L M N O P Q R S T U V W X Y Z –
2–9	0 1 2 3 4 5 6 7 8 9
10	A B C D E F G H I J K L M N O P Q R S T U V W X Y Z –
11–12	0 1 2 3 4 5 6 7 8 9

PARTICIPANT'S CLASS

WRITE CLASS
Exp. 06 for class 6th

CLASS 01
CLASS 02
CLASS 03
CLASS 04
CLASS 05
CLASS 06
CLASS 07
CLASS 08
CLASS 09
CLASS 10
CLASS 11
CLASS 12

MOBILE NUMBER

(10 digits, each: 0 1 2 3 4 5 6 7 8 9)

TEST PAPER TYPE

Check 'Type' on Question Paper

A B C D (two columns)

OLYMPIADS - SELECT YOUR SUBJECT

- (I) Informatics Olympiad (iIO)
- (M) Mathematics Olympiad (iOM)
- (S) Science Olympiad (iOS)
- (E) English Language Olympiad (iOEL)
- (G) GK Olympiad (SKGKO)
- (F) French Language Olympiad (iFLO)
- (T) Talent Hunt Olympiad (iTHO)
- (H) Hindi Olympiad (ABHO)

STREAM FOR CLASS XI & XII OLYMPIAD - iIO ONLY

- COMPUTER SCIENCE (C++) (S)
- INFORMATICS PRACTICES (JAVA) (J)
- COMPUTER SCIENCE (PYTHON) (P)
- MULTIMEDIA & WEB TECHNOLOGY (M)

STREAM FOR CLASS XI & XII OLYMPIAD - iOS ONLY

- PCB (B)
- PCM (M)

MARK YOUR ANSWERS WITH HB PENCIL/BALL POINT PEN (BLUE/BLACK)

Q	Options	Q	Options	Q	Options	Q	Options
1	A B C D E	11	A B C D E	21	A B C D E	31	A B C D E
2	A B C D E	12	A B C D E	22	A B C D E	32	A B C D E
3	A B C D E	13	A B C D E	23	A B C D E	33	A B C D E
4	A B C D E	14	A B C D E	24	A B C D E	34	A B C D E
5	A B C D E	15	A B C D E	25	A B C D E	35	A B C D E
6	A B C D E	16	A B C D E	26	A B C D E	36	A B C D E
7	A B C D E	17	A B C D E	27	A B C D E	37	A B C D E
8	A B C D E	18	A B C D E	28	A B C D E	38	A B C D E
9	A B C D E	19	A B C D E	29	A B C D E	39	A B C D E
10	A B C D E	20	A B C D E	30	A B C D E	40	A B C D E

SIGN. OF THE CANDIDATE & DATE OF EXAMINATION

SIGNATURE OF THE INVIGILATOR

Chapter 1 Number Sense and Numeration

Learning Objectives

- Introduction
- Number Types
- Ascending and Descending Order
- Face Value and Place Value
- Number Facts
- Number Patterns
- Problems Based of Numbers
- An Introduction to Roman Numerals

Introduction

Numbers are useful in counting quantities that we see around us in our daily life. Numbers can be found everywhere. Numbers are expressed in figures as well as in words. The group of figures representing a number is called numerals for that number. In this chapter, we will study upto 4-digit numbers and their names.

Number Types

Numbers are classified according to their type. The first type of numbers is the first type we ever learned about: the counting numbers or the natural numbers and the next type of numbers is the whole numbers, which are the natural numbers together with zero. Let us study the number types.

Natural Numbers and Whole Numbers

Natural Numbers

Counting numbers are known as **natural numbers**. There are infinite natural numbers starting from 1. Natural numbers are denoted by N. Therefore,

N = {1, 2, 3, 4, ...}

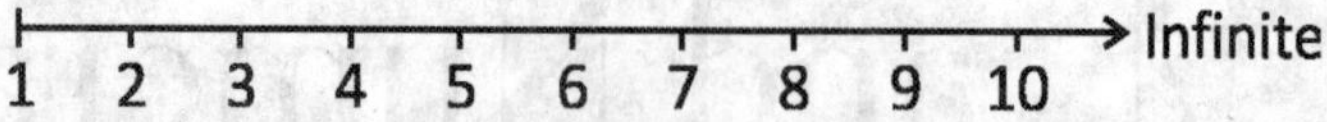

The arrow-head on the right side shows the natural numbers counting upto infinite.

Whole Numbers

Counting numbers including 0 are known as **whole numbers**. If the counting numbers start from 0, then they include the set of whole numbers. Whole numbers are denoted by W. Therefore,

W = {0, 1, 2, 3, 4, 5, ...}

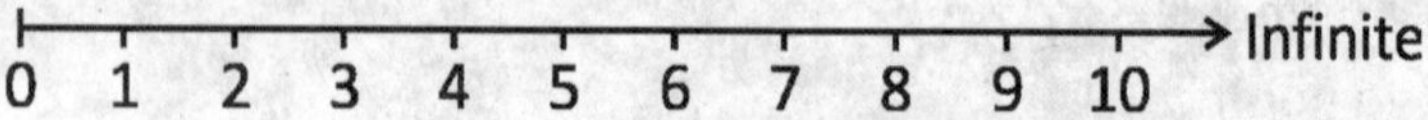

The arrow-head on the right side shows the whole numbers counting up to infinite.

Example:

Which of the following correctly describes the given set of numbers?

{0, 1, 2, 3, 4, 5}

(A) Set of natural numbers upto 5

(B) Set of whole numbers upto 5

(C) Set of all whole numbers below 10

(D) Set of natural numbers below 6

(E) None of these

Answer (B)

Explanation: Given set of numbers is the set of whole numbers which starts from 0 upto 5.

Even Numbers and Odd Numbers

Even Numbers

The numbers which are divisible by 2 are known as **even numbers**. For example, 2, 4, 6, 8, 10, 12, 24, ... etc, are even numbers.

Odd Numbers

The numbers which are not divisible by 2 are known as **odd numbers**. For example, 1, 3, 5, 7, 9, 11, 13, 15, ... etc, are odd numbers.

Remember that even numbers come in the table of 2 while odd numbers do not come in the table of 2. The last digit in an even number is 0, 2, 4, 6, or 8. The last digit in an odd number is 1, 3, 5, 7, or 9.

Example:

First 5 odd numbers are:

(A) 2, 4, 6, 8, 10 (B) 1, 2, 3, 4, 5, (C) 3, 5, 7, 9, 11 (D) 1, 3, 5, 7, 9

(E) None of these

Answer (D)

Explanation: Odd numbers are 1, 3, 5, 7, 9, 11, 13, 15, ... etc.

Example:

The number 3890 is:

(A) an odd number.

(B) an even number.

(C) either an even number and or an odd number.

(D) neither an even number nor an odd number.

(E) None of these

Answer (B)

Explanation: The last digit at the given number 3890 is 0. So it is an even number.

Prime Numbers and Composite Numbers

Prime Numbers

A prime number is a whole number which has only two factors which are 1 and the number itself. For example, 2, 3, 5, 7, 11, 13, 17, ... etc are prime numbers. The number 2 does not have the factors other than 1, therefore, 2 is a prime number.

Look at the following table of prime numbers between 1 and 100.

1	2	3	4	5	6	7	8	9	10
11	12	13	14	15	16	17	18	19	20
21	22	23	24	25	26	27	28	29	30
31	32	33	34	35	36	37	38	39	40
41	42	43	44	45	46	47	48	49	50
51	52	53	54	55	56	57	58	59	60
61	62	63	64	65	66	67	68	69	70
71	72	73	74	75	76	77	78	79	80
81	82	83	84	85	86	87	88	89	90
91	92	93	94	95	96	97	98	99	100

In the table given above, highlighted numbers are prime numbers in which 2 is only a number from group of even numbers which has only two factors (1 and 2), so 2 is the even prime number.

Composite Numbers

A composite number is one which has at least one factor other than 1 and the number itself.

Look at the following table of composite numbers between 1 and 100.

1	2	3	4	5	6	7	8	9	10
11	12	13	14	15	16	17	18	19	20
21	22	23	24	25	26	27	28	29	30
31	32	33	34	35	36	37	38	39	40
41	42	43	44	45	46	47	48	49	50
51	52	53	54	55	56	57	58	59	60
61	62	63	64	65	66	67	68	69	70
71	72	73	74	75	76	77	78	79	80
81	82	83	84	85	86	87	88	89	90
91	92	93	94	95	96	97	98	99	100

In the table given above, highlighted numbers are composite numbers. So we can say, all even numbers except 2 are composite numbers. Remember that the numbers 0 and 1 are neither prime nor composite numbers.

Example:

Prime numbers below 10 are:

(A) 1, 3, 5, 7 and 9.
(B) 2, 3, 5, 7 and 9.
(C) 2, 3, 5 and 7.
(D) 3, 5, 7 and 9.
(E) None of these

Answer (C)

Explanation: There are five prime numbers between 1 to 10 which are 2, 3, 5 and 7.

Example:

Composite numbers below 10 are:

(A) 2, 4, 6 and 8.
(B) 2, 4, 6, 8 and 9.
(C) 1, 4, 6, 8 and 9.
(D) 4, 6, 8 and 9.
(E) None of these

Answer (D)

Explanation: There are four composite numbers between 1 to 10 which are 4, 6, 8 and 9.

Twin Primes

Two prime numbers are known as twin-primes if there is only one composite number between them. For example, pairs of twin-primes between 1 and 20 are: (3, 5); (5, 7); (11, 13); and (17, 19).

Example:

There are four prime numbers between 1 and 10 and again four prime numbers between 10 and 20. How many prime numbers are there between 91 and 100?

(A) 1
(B) 2
(C) 3
(D) 4
(E) None of these

Answer (A)

Explanation: The numbers from 91 to 100 are 92, 93, 94, 95, 96, 97, 98, 99. The number 97 has only two factors 1 and 97 itself. Hence, 97 is the only prime number between 91 and 100.

Successor and Predecessor of a Number

Successor of a Number

Successor of a number is obtained by adding 1 to the number. The successor of 1 is 1 + 1 = 2, successor of 5 is 5 + 1 = 6. Therefore, the successor of a number N is N + 1.

Predecessor of a Number

Predecessor of a number is obtained by subtracting 1 from the number. The predecessor of 4 is 4 – 1 = 3, predecessor of 9 is 9 – 1 = 8. Therefore, the predecessor of a number N is N – 1.

Example:

Which one of the following numbers is the successor of the sum of given expression?

(5 + 6 + 7)

(A) 17
(B) 18
(C) 19
(D) 13
(E) None of these

Answer (C)

Explanation: Here, 5 + 6 + 7 = 18. So, the successor of 18 is 18 + 1 = 19

Example:

Which one of the following numbers is the predecessor of the sum of given expression?

(4 + 3 + 8)

(A) 13 (B) 15 (C) 16 (D) 14

(E) None of these

Answer (D)

Explanation: Here, 4 + 3 + 8 = 15. So, the predecessor of 15 = 15 – 1 = 14

Rounding Numbers

Rounding a number means making the number simpler but keeping its value close to what it was. After rounding a number nearest to 10, 100 or 1000, the result is less accurate, but easier to use. For example, the nearest of 18 is 20 and the nearest of 321 is 300.

Rules for rounding to the nearest 10

- If the ones figure is 0, 1, 2, 3 and 4 get rounded down.
- If the ones figure is 0, 5, 6, 7, 8 and 9 get rounded up.

For example, the nearest of 47 is 50 and the nearest of 44 is 40.

Rules for rounding to the nearest 100

- If the tens figure is 0, 1, 2, 3 or 4, it gets round down.
- If the tens figure is 5, 6, 7, 8 or 9, it gets round up.

For example, the nearest of 152 is 200 and the nearest of 342 is 300.

Rules for rounding to the nearest 1000

- If the hundreds figure is 1, 2, 3 or 4, it gets rounded down.
- If the hundreds figure is 5, 6, 7, 8 or 9, it gets rounded up.

For example, the nearest of 4136 is 4000 and the nearest of 8624 is 9000.

Example:

The salary of a worker in a company is ₹4538. How much salary does the worker get in round figure to nearest 10?

(A) ₹4530 (B) ₹4500 (C) ₹4540 (D) ₹4340

(E) None of these

Answer (C)

Explanation: ₹4538 = ₹4500 + ₹38 and the nearest 10 of 38 is 40.

Ascending and Descending Order

Ascending Order

Numbers in a group are said to be in ascending order when they are arranged from the smallest to the largest number. For example, the ascending order of the numbers: 45, 23, 34, 76, 87, 90 is 23 < 34 < 45 < 76 < 87 < 90

Example:

The capacities of five different boxes are 19 kg, 42 kg, 44 kg, 33 kg and 49 kg. Which one of the following arrangements is in ascending order of capacities?

(A) 49 kg < 44 kg < 42 kg < 33 kg < 19 kg

(B) 19 kg < 33 kg < 42 kg < 44 kg < 49 kg

(C) 42 kg < 33 kg < 44 kg < 19 kg < 49 kg

(D) 19 kg < 44 kg < 42 kg < 49 kg

(E) None of these

Answer (B)

Explanation: 19 kg is the smallest and 49 kg is the biggest capacity among all.

Descending Order

Numbers in a group are said to be in descending order when they are arranged from the largest to the smallest. For example, the descending order of the numbers: 56, 34, 46, 23, 55 is 56 > 55 > 46 > 34 > 23

Example:

There are 5 workers in a company and the salaries of the workers in rupees are ₹ 2234, ₹ 3452, ₹ 2235, ₹ 5600 and ₹ 7000. Which one of the following options is correct arrangement of the salaries of the workers in descending order?

(A) ₹ 7000 > ₹ 5600 > ₹ 3452 > ₹ 2235 > ₹ 2234

(B) ₹ 5600 > ₹ 7000 > ₹ 3452 > ₹ 2235 > ₹ 2234

(C) ₹ 2234 > ₹ 7000 > ₹ 5600 > ₹ 2235 > ₹ 3452

(D) ₹ 7000 > ₹ 3452 > ₹ 5600 > ₹ 2235 > ₹ 2234

(E) None of these

Answer (A)

Explanation: The descending order of the salaries of the workers is:

₹7000 > ₹5600 > ₹3452 > ₹2235 > ₹2234

Face Value and Place Value

We have already learnt about ones, tens and hundreds upto three places. Now, we will learn about the fourth place which is 'thousands' or 1000s. A number with thousands place will have four digits in it.

Face Value of a Digit

The face value of a digit in a number is the value of the digit itself. Therefore, the face value of a number does not change on changing its place. For example, in the number 4673, the face value of 6 is 6. If the digit 6 changes its place from hundreds to tens (4763), then the face value of 6 remains same as 6.

Place value of a Digit

The place value of a digit is the value of where the digit is in the number. The place value of a number changes according to the placement of digits in the number. The place value of 6 in the number 4673 is 600. On changing the place of 6 from 4673 to 4763, the place value of 6 changes from 600 to 60.

Example:

Difference between the face value and place value of 3 in the number 4312 is:

(A) 300 (B) 297

(C) 2997 (D) 27

(E) None of these

Answer (B)

Explanation: In the given number 4312, the place value of 3 is 300 and its face value is 3.

Therefore, the required difference = 300 – 3 = 297

Expanded Form of a Number

Expanded form means expansion of a number according to place value of the digits. For example, expanded form of 9314 is: 9000 + 300 + 10 + 4

Remember that the expanded form of 3007 is (3000 + 7) and is not (3000 + 00 + 0 + 7)

Example:

Which one of the following is the expanded form of 7206?

(A) 7000 + 20 + 6
(B) 700 + 200 + 6
(C) 7000 + 200 + 6
(D) 7000 + 200 + 60
(E) None of these

Answer (C)

Explanation: Expanded form of 7206 is 7000 + 200 + 6.

Writing Standard Numbers

We can change both expanded numerals and the number names to standard numerals. For example, 7000 + 300 + 10 + 6 = 7316 and 'two thousand five hundred seventy five' = 2575

Example:

How many hundreds are there in 7329?

(A) 3
(B) 30
(C) 2
(D) 7
(E) None of these

Answer (A)

Explanation: Here, 7329 = 7000 + 300 + 20 + 9 = 7000 + (3 × 100) + 20 + 9

Clearly, there are 3 hundreds in the number 7329.

Example:

Garima has ₹ 1349. Which of the following is the correct number name for 1349?

(A) One thousand four hundred thirty nine
(B) One thousand three hundred forty nine
(C) One thousand thirty four hundred
(D) One thousand four thirty nine
(E) None of these

Answer (B)

Explanation: Here, 1349 = 1000 + 300 + 40 + 9

So, 1349 = one thousand three hundred and forty nine

Place Value on the Abacus

We use the abacus to show, to read and to write a number properly. Look at this. 4324 is a 4-digit number that can be shown on the abacus as follow:

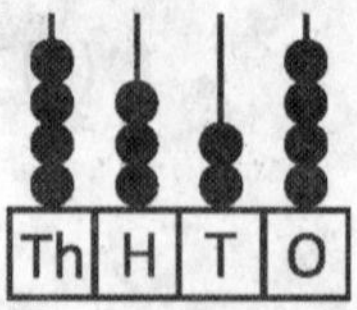

Example:
Which of the following has the place value of 3 as 300?

(A) 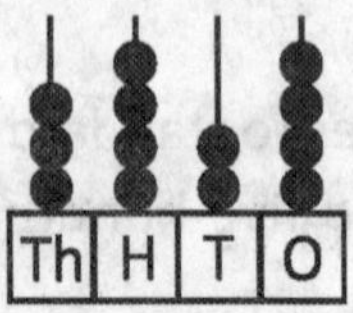

(B) 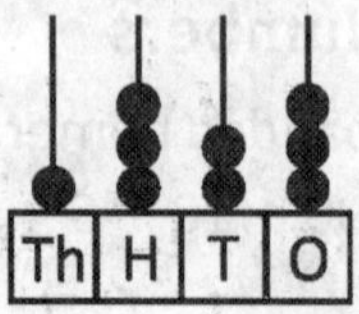

(C) 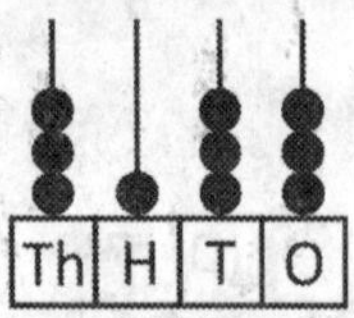

(D) 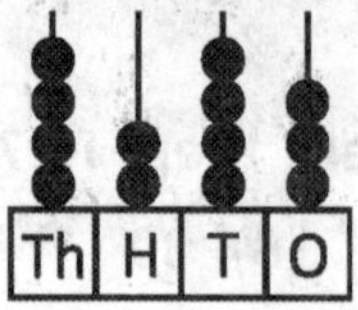

(E) None of these

Answer (B)

Explanation: On the abacus given in option (B), there are 3 beads on its hundreds place column. Thererfore, the place value of 3 as 300 is shown by the abacus given in option (B).

Example:
Which one of the following abacuses shows the number less than 4000?

(A) 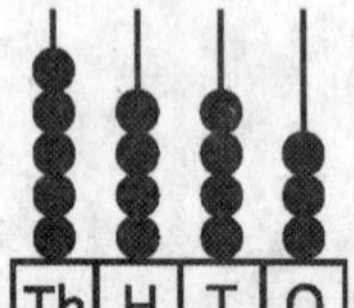

(B) 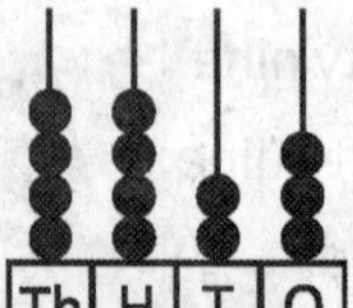

(C) 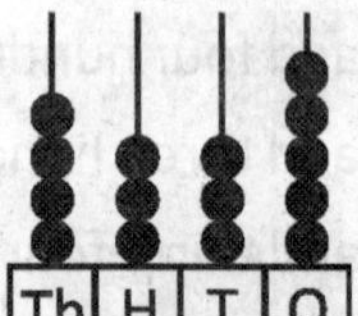

(D) 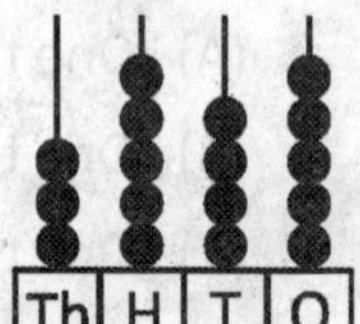

(E) None of these

Answer (D)

Explanation: On the abacus given in option (D), there are 3 beads on its thousands place column. Therefore, the place value less than 4000 is shown by the abacus given in option (D).

Number Facts

- We use 10 digits 0, 1, 2, 3, 4, 5, 6, 7, 8, 9 to form numbers.
- If we use 4 digits, without repeating the digits we form a 4-digit number, for example 3782.
- The smallest and the largest 3-digit numbers are 100 and 999.
- The smallest 4-digit number is 999 + 1 = 1000 (One thousand).
- The largest 4-digit number is 10000 – 1 = 9999 (Nine thousand nine hundred ninety nine).
- A comma is used to separate the thousands place. For example 4976 or 4,976.
- The greater the number of digits, the greater is the number. For example 7312 > 712.
- If two numbers have the same number of digits, the number with the bigger digit on the left side of numbers is greater. For example, 6219 > 5691.
- Remember that 10 ones = 1 ten; 10 tens = 1 hundred; and 10 hundreds = 1 thousand.
- Successor of the largest 4-digit number or, 9999 + 1 = 10000 is the smallest 5-digit number.
- Successor of the largest 3-digit number or, 999 + 1 = 1000 is the smallest 4-digit number.

Number Patterns

Pattern means repetition. We can create pattern with numbers too. A number pattern is a list of numbers that follows a certain rule, sequence or pattern. Look at the following number pattern:

1, 5, 9, 13, 17

Here, starting from 1, every alternate number is a part of this pattern. When we observe this number pattern, we find that 4 is added each time to get the next term of the pattern.

Example:

Find the next two numbers in the given number pattern.

3, 6, 12, 24 ___?___ , ___?___

(A) 48, 96 (B) 42, 84 (C) 36, 72 (D) 48, 72

(E) None of these

Answer (A)

Explanation: The given number pattern is obtained by multiplying 2 to each number to get the next number in the pattern. Therefore, the next two numbers in the pattern are 24 × 2 = 48 and 48 × 2 = 96

Problems Based on Numbers

Number based word problems are mathematical exercise based on numbers and to solve these problems, we extract the Math from English text. Look at the following examples based on numbers.

Example:

Rekha, Garima, Monika and Sumita are playing a number game. Each of them are writing their favorite number. Who wrote the greatest number?

Rekha	Garima	Monika	Sumita
↓	↓	↓	↓
7532	3725	7325	5723

(A) Sumita (B) Monika

(C) Rekha (D) Garima

(E) None of these

Answer (C)

Explanation: Here, Rekha wrote 7532 and Monika wrote 7325. Both numbers have 7 at thousands place but at hundreds place, 5 > 3. Therefore, 7532 is the greatest number of all four written numbers.

Example:

The chart given below shows the number of plants that were planted in a city in the first four months of a year.

Month	Number of Plants
January	7005
February	7913
March	6425
April	5928

Which one of the following statements is true?

(A) The number of plants that were planted in January is more than those planted in February.

(B) The number of plants that planted in March is more than those planted in April.

(C) The number of plants that planted in April is more than those planted in February.

(D) The number of plants that planted in February is less than in March.

(E) None of these

Answer (B)

Explanation: Here, 7913 > 7005 > 6425 > 5928, Or, 5928 < 6425 < 7005 < 7913. Clearly, the number of plants that planted in March is more than in April.

An Introduction to Roman Numerals

Numeral is a symbol or name used to represent a number. We use Hindu–Arabic numerals in which there are ten symbols 0, 1, 2, 3, 4, 5, 6, 7, 8 and 9. Ancient Romans used a special method of showing numbers. Roman numerals are represented by seven different letters: I, V, X, L, C, D and M, where I = 1, V = 5, X = 10, L = 50, C = 100, D = 500 and M = 1000. We use these seven letters to make thousands of different numbers. For example, we write 9 = IX, 13 = XIII, 56 = LVI and 115 = CXV, etc. We will study Roman numerals in details in the next class.

Summary

- The group of figures representing a number is called **numerals** for that number.
- Counting numbers are known as **natural numbers**. There are infinite natural numbers starting from 1. Therefore, natural numbers, N = {1, 2, 3, 4, 5, ...}
- Counting numbers including 0 are known as **whole numbers**.
  Therefore, whole numbers, W = {0, 1, 2, 3, 4, 5, ...}
- The numbers such as 2, 4, 6, 8, 10 12, ... are divisible by 2 are known as **even numbers**.
- The numbers such as 1, 3, 5, 7, 9, 11, ... are not divisible by 2 are known as **odd numbers**.
- **Successor** of a number is obtained by adding 1.

- **Predecessor** of a number is obtained by subtracting 1.
- Numbers in a group are said to be in **ascending order** when they are arranged from the smallest to the largest.
- Numbers in a group are said to be in **descending order** when they are arranged from the largest to the smallest.
- The **face value** of a digit in a number is the value of the digit itself.
- The **place value** of a digit is the value of where the digit is placed in the number.

Did You Know?

- Hindu–Arabic numerals which are the combination of 10 digits, is now used throughout the world.
- Tally bars are a unary numeral system which were used for counting.
- The number 1 is neither a prime number nor a composite number. It is called unique number.
- Aryabhata developed the place-value notation.
- Brahmagupta introduced the symbol for zero.

Solved Problems

1. I had ₹ 745. Which of the following is the correct number name for 745?

(A) Seven fourth five
(B) Seven hundred and forty five
(C) Seven hundred and five
(D) Seven four five
(E) None of these

Answer (B)

Explanation: Here, 745 = 700 + 40 + 5. Therefore, the number name for 745 is 'seven hundred and forty five'.

2. How many hundreds are there in 7308?

(A) Zero
(B) Three
(C) Eight
(D) Seven
(E) None of these.

Answer (B)

Explanation: Here, $7308 = 7 \times 1000 + 3 \times 100 + 8 \times 1$

3. The greatest 4-digit number that can be formed by using the digits 3, 2, 0, 8 without repeating the digits is:

(A) 8032
(B) 2038
(C) 8302
(D) 8320
(E) None of these

Answer (D)

Explanation: Here, $8 > 3 > 2 > 0$

Therefore, the required greatest 4-digit number = 8320

4. Which of the following sets of the numbers is in descending order?

(A) 3526, 3915, 3312, 3419
(B) 5581, 5518, 5185, 5815
(C) 2901, 2894, 2848, 2839
(D) 7356, 7536, 7635, 7736
(E) None of these

Answer (C)

Explanation: Set of numbers given in option (C) is: 2901, 2894, 2848, 2839

Where, 2901 > 2894 > 2848 > 2839, which is in descending order.

5. 8215 is same as:

(A) 8000 + 200 + 10 + 5 (B) 800 + 20 + 15

(C) 8000 + 210 + 50 (D) 800 + 200 + 10 +5

(E) None of these

Answer (A)

Explanation: 8215 in expanded form is (8000 + 200 + 10 + 5).

6. Which place value will determine the larger number among the given two numbers?

8347, 8437

(A) Ones place (B) Tens place

(C) Hundreds place (D) Thousands place

(E) None of these

Answer (C)

Explanation: In the given 4-digit numbers, if the left most digits are the same, we compare the next digit to the right and continue in this manner. Here, in (8)347 and (8)437, thousands place digits are same, therefore we compare their hundreds place digits. Hence, 8(4)37 > 8(3)47 as 4 > 3.

7. Aman wrote a 4-digit number on a cardboard as show below.

3		9	7

If it is formed from different digits, then which of the following digits could be placed in the gap to make it the smallest number out of the given options?

(A) 9 (B) 6

(C) 4 (D) 2

(E) None of these

Answer (D)

Explanation: If we put the digits given in all option one-by-one, we get,

3(9)97 > 3(6)97 > 3(4)97 > 3(2)97, Or, 3(2)97 < 3(4)97 < 3(6)97 < 3(9)97

Hence, the smallest number of all four numbers is 3297.

Therefore, the required digit is 2 to make it the smallest number out of the given options.

8. Which one of the following numbers will replace the question mark (?) in the number pattern given below?

17, 15, 13, ___?___ , 9, 7

(A) 10 (B) 11 (C) 12 (D) 8

(E) None of these

Answer (B)

Explanation: Here, the pattern is as follow:

17 – 2 = 15; 15 – 2 = 13; 13 – 2 = 11; 11 – 2 = 9; 9 – 2 = 7

9. Number name of the biggest 4-digit number that can be formed by using the digits 2, 7, 3, 4 without repeating the digits is:

(A) Seven thousand two hundred thirty four

(B) Seven thousand three hundred forty two

(C) Seven thousand four hundred thirty two

(D) Seven thousand two hundred forty three

(E) None of these

Answer (C)

Explanation: Here, numbers are: in option (A): 7234; in option (B): 7342;

In option (C): 7432; in option (D): 7243

We have, 7234 < 7243 < 7342 < 7432

Therefore, 'seven thousand four hundred thirty two' is the biggest number of all.

10. If we interchange the hundreds place digit and the ones place digit in each number given below, which one of the following numbers will be an odd number?

6835, 4378, 7438, 8473

(A) 6835 (B) 4378 (C) 7438 (D) 8473

(E) None of these

Answer (B)

Explanation: Hundreds place digit in 6835 is 8, in 4378 is 3, in 7438 is 4 and in 8473 is 4. Therefore, when digits change in 4378, the new number is 4873 which is an odd number.

Practice Exercise 1

1. **Sum of the even prime number and the smallest odd prime number is:**

(A) 5 (B) 6
(C) 7 (D) 4
(E) None of these

2. **Sum of place value and face value of 9 in the number 4987 is:**

(A) 900 (B) 929
(C) 990 (D) 99
(E) None of these

3. **Which one of the following numbers will replace the question mark (?) in the number pattern given below?**

10, 30, 20, 40, 30, 50, ___?___

(A) 40 (B) 30
(C) 60 (D) 70
(E) None of these

4. **The smallest 4-digit number that can be formed by using the digits 2, 5, 0, 7 without repeating the digits is:**

(A) 2075 (B) 2507 (C) 2750 (D) 2057
(E) None of these

5. **Which one of the given abacuses shows the number greater than 4000?**

(A) 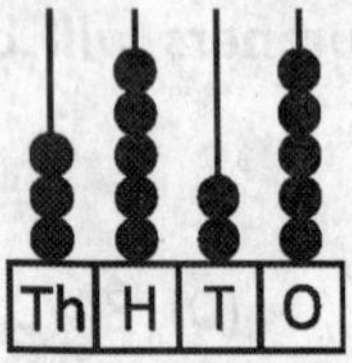

(B) 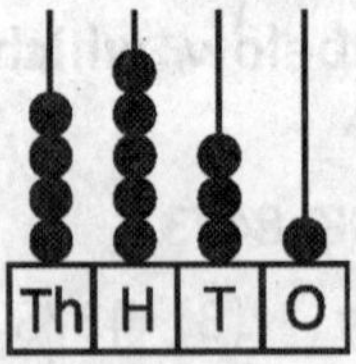

(C) 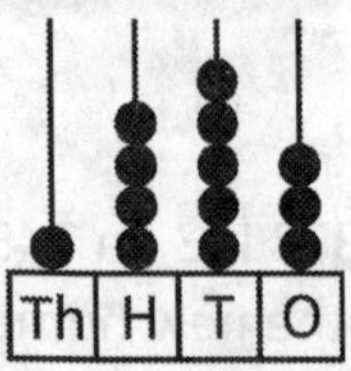

(D) 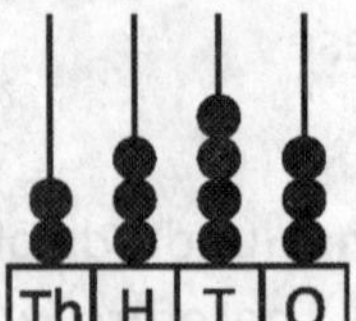

(E) None of these

6. **Which one of the following place values will determine the larger number among the given two numbers?**

8927 and **8972**

(A) Ones place
(B) Tens place
(C) Hundreds place
(D) Thousands place
(E) None of these

7. **The largest 4-digit even number is:**

(A) 9999
(B) 9996
(C) 9997
(D) 9998
(E) None of these

8. **How many 3-digit numbers can be formed by using the digits 7, 4, 1 only once in a number?**

(A) 3
(B) 6
(C) 12
(D) 8
(E) None of these

9. **What should be subtracted from 18 to get the predecessor of 14?**

(A) 3
(B) 4
(C) 5
(D) 6
(E) None of these

10. **Successor of the largest 4-digit number is:**

(A) the largest 4-digit number.
(B) the smallest 4-digit number.
(C) the largest 5-digit number.
(D) the smallest 5-digit number.
(E) None of these

Chapter 2

Addition and Subtraction

Learning Objectives

- Introduction
- Addition
- Subtraction
- Number Sentence
- Word Problems Based of Addition and Subtraction

Introduction

In our everyday life, we come across many activities when we need to apply the method of addition and subtraction. Addition and Subtraction are the basic arithmetic operations. The combination of two or more counted objects is represented by a single notion, is called addition. Subtraction means 'to take away'. It is the difference of two numbers or quantities. Subtraction is the inverse process of addition. In this chapter we will learn about the addition and subtraction of 4-digit numbers.

Addition

Addition is bringing two or more numbers (or things) together to make a new total. The numbers which are added to each other are called **addends** and the result is called **sum**. For example, in 456 + 567 = 1023, the numbers 456 and 567 are addends and the resulting number 1023 is their sum. The process of addition of the numbers always starts from ones place digit. Other names used for addition are: plus, increase, total and sum. The term used for addition is '**plus**' and the symbol for plus is (**+**)

Regrouping

As we know, every place in the number can hold only one digit out of the digits from 0 to 9 and when one more digit comes, it gets regrouped and moves to the next place where the value changes. Only nine ones can be in the ones place and the tenth one gets regrouped as one ten. Similarly, when the tenth ten or tenth hundred or tenth thousand comes, its gets regrouped as one hundred or one thousand or one ten thousand. This goes on with every place value.

- Regrouping ones as tens and ones

  23 ones = 2 tens + 3 ones

  95 ones = 9 tens + 50 ones

- Regrouping tens as hundreds and tens

  86 tens = 8 hundreds + 6 tens

  92 tens = 9 hundreds + 2 tens

- Regrouping hundreds as thousands and hundreds

  24 hundreds = 20 hundreds + 4 hundreds = 2 thousands + 4 hundreds

  57 hundreds = 50 hundreds + 7 hundreds

  = 5 thousands + 7 hundreds

Example:

How many thousands are there in 97 hundreds?

(A) 7 (B) 70

(C) 9 (D) 90

(E) None of these

Answer (C)

Explanation: Here, 97 hundreds = 90 hundreds + 7 hundreds

= 9 thousands + 7 hundreds

Addition of 4-digit Numbers without Carrying

Following steps are used for the addition of 4-digit numbers:

Step 1 : Arrange the numbers according to their proper place values.

Step 2 : Add the ones places first, then the tens places and at last the thousands places.

Example:

Add 4321 and 3254.

Solution: As we know, the process of addition of numbers always starts from ones place digits.

Now, addition is as follow:

Add Thousands
Add Hundreds
Add Tens
Add Ones

Th	H	T	O
4	3	2	1
+ 3	2	5	4
7	5	7	5

Therefore, 4321 + 3254 = 7575

Addition of 4-digit Numbers with Carrying

Following steps are used for the addition of 4-digit numbers:

Step 1 : Arrange the numbers according to their proper place values.

Step 2 : First add ones and if carry is generated then add the carry to addition of tens.

Step 3 : Then, add tens, hundreds and thousands and if carry is generated then add the carry to addition of hundreds and thousands, respectively.

Example:

Add 6257 and 1894.

Solution: Here, addition is as follow:

①	①	①		← Carry
Th	**H**	**T**	**O**	
6	2	5	7	
+ 1	8	9	4	
8	1	5	1	

Therefore, 6257 + 1894 = 8151

Properties of Addition

Some basic properties which involve addition are given below. Let us understand these properties.

Commutative Property of Addition

When two numbers added in any order give the same result.

For example, in 2 + 7 = 9, if we change the order of numbers and add them, we have 7 + 2 = 9. Here, answer is still 9.

Associative Property of Addition

When three or more numbers added in any order give the same result.

For example, (2 + 3) + 1 = 5 + 1 = 6; 2 + (3 + 1) = 2 + 4 = 6; (2 + 1) + 3 = 3 + 3 = 6. Here, answer is still 6 in all additions.

Additive Property of Zero

When zero is added to any number gives the number itself.

For example, 7 + 0 = 7. Here, the result is the number itself.

Also, when any number added to zero gives the number itself. For example, 0 + 7 = 7

Example:

Find the missing number (?) in the statement given below.

2598 + 3201 = __?__ + 2598

(A) 0 (B) 1

(C) 2598 (D) 3201

(E) None of these

Answer (D)

Explanation: According to the commutative property of addition,

2598 + 3201 = [3201] + 2598

Subtraction

Subtraction is the inverse process of addition. Subtraction is taking one number (or thing) away from another. It is a method by which we know the remaining after taken away some quantity from a certain quantity. Number which is subtracted is called

subtrahend and the number from which we subtract is called **minuend**. The number left after subtraction is called the **difference**.

For example, in the subtraction, 29 – 14 = 15, the number 14 is subtrahend and 29 is minuend. The result 15 is the difference of 29 and 14.

The process of subtraction of the numbers always starts from ones place digits. The term used for subtraction is minus and its symbol is (–).

Borrowing in Subtraction

While subtracting large numbers, if the top digit in a column is smaller than the bottom digit in that column. In this case, we need to borrow from the next column to the left. Remember that borrowing is a two step process:

(a) Subtraction of 1 from the top number in the column to the left, and

(b) Addition of 10 to the top number in the column.

Suppose we subtract 89 from 217 or, 217 – 89. Here, subtraction is as follow:

		10	
	1	~~0~~	17
	H	T	O
	~~2~~	~~1~~	7
–		8	9
	1	2	8

Since, 7 is less than 9, so we need to borrow from tens column and first we subtract 9 from 17. Now 1 replaced with 0 after borrowing from hundreds column, it become 10, and then 8 is subtracted from 10. The final step is simple, it is 1 – 0 = 1.

Subtraction of 4-digit Numbers without Borrowing

Following steps are used for the subtraction of 4-digit numbers:

Step 1 : Arrange the numbers according to their proper place values.

Step 2 : Subtract the ones places first, then tens places and at last, the thousands places.

Example:

Subtract 3254 from 9578.

Solution: As we know, the process of subtraction of numbers always starts from ones place digits. Now, subtraction is as follow:

Subtract Thousands
Subtract Hundreds
Subtract Tens
Subtract Ones

	Th	H	T	O
	9	5	7	8
−	3	2	5	4
	6	3	2	4

Therefore, 9578 – 3254 = 6324

Subtraction of 4-digit Numbers with Borrowing

Following steps are used for the subtraction of 4-digit numbers:

Step 1 : Arrange the numbers according to their proper place values.

Step 2 : First, subtract ones and if borrow is needed then borrow 1 ten from the tens place.

Step 3 : Then subtract tens, hundreds and thousands and if borrow is needed borrow 1 hundred and 1 thousand, respectively.

Example:

Subtract 4894 from 6251.

Solution: Here, subtraction is as follow:

	11	14	
5	~~1~~	~~4~~	11
Th	**H**	**T**	**O**
~~6~~	~~2~~	~~5~~	~~1~~
4	8	9	4
1	3	5	7

Therefore, 6251 – 4894 = 1357

Properties of Subtraction

Zero Property of Subtraction

When zero is subtracted from a number, the result is always the number itself. It means nothing really has been taken away. For example, 24 – 0 = 24. Any number subtracted from zero is not defined. For example, (0 – 24) is not defined.

Addition and Subtraction

Subtraction is the inverse process of addition. For example, 7 – 3 = 4, then 4 + 3 = 7

Example:

Which one of the following is *not* true?

(A) 271 + 0 = 271

(B) 271 – 0 = 271

(C) 0 + 271 = 271

(D) 0 – 271 = 271

(E) None of these

Answer (D)

Explanation: Here, 271 + 0 = 271 (Additive Property of Zero), 0 + 271 = 271 (Additive Property of Zero), 271 – 0 = 271 (Additive Property of Subtraction) but (0 – 271) is not defined.

Example:

What should be added to 27 to get 72?

Solution: As we know, subtraction is the inverse process of addition. Therefore, we first subtraction 27 from 72. Here, 72 – 27 = 45. So we have, 45 should be subtracted from 72 to get 27.

Verification: 72 – 27 = 45 and 45 + 27 = 72

Addition and Subtraction Together

Following steps are used for combining addition and subtraction:

Step 1 : First add and then subtract the numbers.

Step 2 : If some numbers enclosed within brackets, first solve the bracket's operation(s) and then solve it as given in step 1.

Example:

Solve: (45 – 23) + 39 – 4

Solution: Here, some numbers are enclosed within a bracket, so we solve the bracket first.

Therefore, (45 – 23) + 39 – 4 = 22 + 39 – 4 = 61 – 4 = 57

Number Sentence

A number sentence is a group of numbers that includes a mathematical operation: addition, subtraction, multiplication or division.

Example:

Which one of the following numbers will replace the question mark (?) in the number sentence given below?

137 – 49 = 24 + [?]

(A) 65 (B) 64 (C) 62 (D) 63

(E) None of these

Answer (B)

Explanation: Here, 137 – 49 = 88. Now, 24 + [?] = 88.

As we know, subtraction is the inverse process of addition.

Therefore, 88 – 24. So, we have, 24 + [64] = 88.

Or, the required missing number is 64.

Word Problems Based on Addition and Subtraction

The key words used in problems involving addition are: sum, total, in all, all together, altogether, etc. The key words used in problems involving subtraction are: take away, how many more, how many less, smaller than, greater than etc. Let us see the following examples based on addition and subtraction.

Example:

Ankita put 17 books on a bookshelf. Rahul put 73 more books on the bookshelf. How many books are there on the bookshelf altogether?

(A) 85 (B) 80 (C) 90 (D) 56

(E) None of these

Answer (C)

Explanation: Clearly, the number of books altogether means sum of the numbers of all books. Therefore,

Number of books put by Ankita	=	17
Number of books put by Rahul	=	+ 73
Total number of books	=	90

So, there are 90 books altogether on the bookshelf.

Example:

Garima has 172 red pins and 148 black pins. How many more red pins than black pins does she have?

(A) 36
(B) 42
(C) 28
(D) 24
(E) None of these

Answer (D)

Explanation: Clearly, the number of more pins means difference of the numbers of pins. Therefore,

Number of red pins	=	172
Number of black pins	=	– 148
		024

So, Garima has 24 more red pins than black pins.

Summary

- Addition is bringing two or more numbers (or things) together to make a new total.
- The numbers which are added to each other are called **addends** and the result is called **sum**.
- When two numbers added in any order give the same result.
- When two or more numbers added in any order give the same result.
- When zero is added to any number gives the number itself.

- Subtraction is taking one number (or thing) away from another.
- The number which is subtracted is called **subtrahend** and the number from which we subtract is called **minuend**. The number left after subtraction is called **difference**.
- When zero is subtracted from a number, the result is always the number itself.
- Addition and subtraction are inverse operations.
- A number sentence is a group of numbers that includes a mathematical operation, i.e. addition, subtraction, multiplication or division.

Did You Know ?

- The ability to add numbers in your head is used when you play, or watch sports and when you buy a couple of items at the shops.
- When a number is, first, added to the same number and then subtracted from the sum, the result is the number itself.
- It is assume that addition was first used by Chinese.

Solved Problems

1. If ■ + ▲ = 3215 and ■ + ▲ + ● = 5427, then the value of ● will be:

(A) 2392 (B) 2212 (C) 3462 (D) 4622

(E) None of these

Answer (B)

Explanation: Here, given that

■ + ▲ = 3215 and ■ + ▲ + ● = 5427

Or, 3215 + ● = 5427

As we know, subtraction is the inverse process of addition.

Therefore, difference of 5427 and 3215 is 5427 – 3215 = 2212

So, we have, 3215 + ● = 5427 or, 3215 + 2212 = 5427

Or, ● = 2212.

2. **Difference of the largest 4-digit number and the smallest 4-digit number is:**
(A) 9899
(B) 9989
(C) 8990
(D) 8999
(E) None of these

Answer (D)

Explanation: Here,

The largest 4-digit number	=	9999
The smallest 4-digit number	=	– 1000
		8999

So, the required difference = 9999 – 1000 = 8999

3. **Find the sum of missing two digits ? in the addition given below.**

	4	**0**	**3**	**2**
+	**2**	**4**	**?**	**5**
	?	**4**	**4**	**7**

(A) 6 (B) 7 (C) 5 (D) 9
(E) None of these

Answer (B)

Explanation: Here, addition is as follow:

	4	0	3	2
+	2	4	1	5
	6	4	4	7

Clearly, at the tens place, the one missing digit is 3 + 1 = 4

And, at the thousands place, the other missing digit = 4 + 2 = 6

So, the required sum = 1 + 6 = 7

4. Which one of the following numbers will replace the question mark [?] in the subtraction given below?

	6	9	4	5
–	2	?	1	3
	4	3	3	2

(A) 6 (B) 5 (C) 4 (D) 7
(E) None of these

Answer (A)

Explanation: Here, subtraction is as follow:

	6	9	4	5
–	2	6	1	3
	4	3	3	2

Clearly, at the hundreds place in 2[?]13, the missing digit is 9 – [6] = 3 or, 3 + [6] = 9. So, the required missing digit is 6.

5. Which one of the following numbers will replace the question mark [?] in the number sentence given below?

71 + 17 – [?] = 75

(A) 19 (B) 14 (C) 13 (D) 12
(E) None of these

Answer (C)

Explanation: Here, 71 + 17 – [?] = 75 or, 88 – [?] = 75

As we know, subtraction is the inverse process of addition.

Therefore, difference of 88 and 75 = 88 – 75 = 13

So we have, 88 – [13] = 75 or, 88 – 75 = [13]

Hence, the required missing digit is 13.

6. How many ones, tens, hundreds and thousands, respectively should be added to give the largest 4-digit even number?

(A) 8, 9, 9, 9 (B) 6, 9, 9, 9 (C) 8, 9, 9, 4 (D) 8, 9, 9, 8
(E) None of these

Answer (A)

Explanation: The largest 4-digit number = 9999

The largest 4-digit odd number = 9999.

The largest 4-digit even number = 9998. Now, in 9998,

Number of ones = 8

Number of tens = 9

Number of hundreds = 9

Number of thousands = 9

Therefore, the required digits are 8, 9, 9, 9.

7. Difference between 324 tens and an [Unknown Number] is 1462. Find the [Unknown Number]

(A) 2468 (B) 1778 (C) 1628 (D) 1968

(E) None of these

Answer (B)

Explanation: Here, 324 tens = 300 tens + 20 tens + 4 tens

= 30 hundreds + 2 hundreds + 4 tens

= 3 thousands + 2 hundreds + 4 tens

= 3000 + 200 + 40 = 3240

Now, 3240 – [Unknown Number] = 1462

As we know, subtraction is the inverse process of addition.

Therefore, 3240 – 1462 = 1778

Or, 3240 – [1778] = 1462. So we have, [Unknown Number] = 1778

8. Difference of 63 and 93 is added to their sum. The result will be:

(A) 176 (B) 183 (C) 196 (D) 186

(E) None of these

Answer (D)

Explanation: Here, Difference of 63 and 93 = 93 – 63 = 30

Sum of 63 and 93 = 63 + 93 = 156

Therefore, the required sum = 156 + 30 = 186

8. If ■ + ● = 64 and ▲ – ● = 14, then ■ + ▲ = ?

(A) 78 (B) 72 (C) 50 (D) 98

(E) None of these

Answer (A)

Explanation: Here, ■ + ● = 64 and ▲ – ● = 14

So, ■ + ● + ▲ – ● = 64 + 14 Or, ■ + ▲ + (● – ●) = 78

Or, ■ + ▲ + 0 = 78. Or, ■ + ▲ = 78

Because, a number ● is subtracted from the number ● gives 0 as result.

9. The cost difference of 1 pen and 1 pencil is ₹ 7. If the cost of 1 pencil is ₹ 3, then the cost of 1 pen will be:

(A) ₹ 5 (B) ₹ 10 (C) ₹ 9 (D) ₹ 11

(E) None of these

Answer (B)

Explanation: Here, the cost of 1 pencil = ₹ 3, and the cost difference = ₹ 7

Therefore, the cost of 1 pen = cost of 1 pencil + cost difference = ₹ (3 + 7) = ₹ 10

10. There are 2100 students in a school. If the number of girls is 977, then find the number of boys in the school.

(A) 1321 (B) 1223 (C) 1123 (D) 1243

(E) None of these

Answer (C)

Explanation: Here,

Number of total students	=	2100
Number of girls	=	– 977
Number of boys	=	1123

So, there are 1123 boys in the school.

Practice Exercise 2

1. If □ + △ + ○ = 7215 and □ + ○ = 2946, the value of △ is:

(A) 3849 (B) 4479 (C) 4269 (D) 5219

(E) None of these

2. Difference of the largest 4-digit even number and the largest 3-digit even number is:

(A) 9800 (B) 8000 (C) 9600 (D) 9000

(E) None of these

3. How many thousands are there in the sum of 1234, 4432 and 3314?

(A) 9 (B) 8 (C) 7 (D) 10

(E) None of these

4. Find the sum of missing digits in the subtraction given below.

	8	**7**	**?**	**5**
–	**7**	**?**	**3**	**4**
	1	**3**	**5**	**1**

(A) 12 (B) 11 (C) 13 (D) 14

(E) None of these

5. Which one of the following numbers will replace the question mark ? in the statement given below?

86 – ? + 13 = 27

(A) 69 (B) 68 (C) 53 (D) 76

(E) None of these

6. Sum of 29 and 92 is subtracted from 2992. The result will be:

(A) 2895 (B) 2761 (C) 2871 (D) 2891

(E) None of these

7. **In the given magic square, three numbers in each row, column and diagonal add up to the same total. Find the sum of all three missing numbers.**

?	7	6
9	5	?
4	?	8

(A) 5 (B) 6 (C) 7 (D) 8
(E) All of these

8. **There are 679 boys and 438 girls in a school. How many more boys than girls are there in the school?**

(A) 281 (B) 301 (C) 291 (D) 241
(E) None of these

9. **How many thousands are there in 89 hundreds?**

(A) 7 (B) 8 (C) 9 (D) 6
(E) None of these

10. **Number pattern given below is based on addition. Find the missing number in place of question mark (?).**

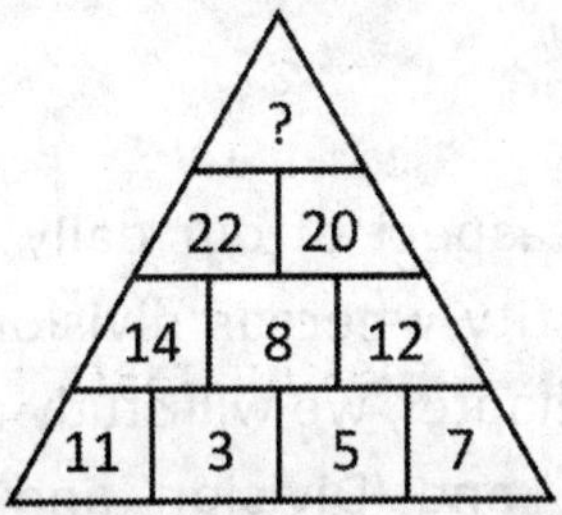

(A) 42 (B) 52
(C) 40 (D) 48
(E) None of these

Chapter 3

Multiplication and Division

Learning Objectives

- Introduction
- Multiplication
- Division
- Divisibility Rules and Division Facts
- Problems Based on Multiplication and Division

Introduction

Multiplication and division are used in almost every aspect of our daily lives. Multiplication is repeated addition of a specific quantity whereas division is a distributed of a quantity into some equal parts. In this chapter, we will study about two important arithmetic operations: 'Multiplication' and 'Division' and their properties.

Multiplication

Multiplication means repeated addition. It is a faster way of adding the same number. When thinking of multiplication as repeated addition, the multiplication of two whole numbers is equal to adding as many copies of one of them. For example, the product 5 × 4 is equal to the sum of four 5's, or, 5 + 5 + 5 + 5. When a quantity is added to itself number of times, we use operation of multiplication to find the resulting quantity. In a multiplication, the number which is multiplied is called **multiplicand**. The number by which the multiplicand is multiplied is called **multiplier**. The answer or the result of multiplication is called its **product**. The term used for multiplication is '**multiply by**' and the symbol for multiplication is (×).

Example:

If a box contains 10 balls, how many balls are there in 32 such boxes?

Solution:

Here, we have to add the number of balls contained in all 32 boxes.

Therefore, 10 + 10 + 10 . . . . . . upto 32 times = 10 × 32 = 320

So, there are 320 balls in 32 such boxes.

Example:

The value of which one of the following is same as the value of the statement given below?

(3 + 3 + 3 + 3 + 3 + 3)

(A) 3 × 3

(B) 3 × 6

(C) 3 × 9

(D) 3 + 6

(E) None of these

Answer (B)

Explanation: The sum of six 3's is equal to 3 × 6.

Multiplication Table

A multiplication table is a list that shows the results or products of multiplying certain numbers (such as 1 through 12) by each other.

Multiplication Tables (1–12)

X	1	2	3	4	5	6	7	8	9	10	11	12
1	1	2	3	4	5	6	7	8	9	10	11	12
2	2	4	6	8	10	12	14	16	18	20	22	24
3	3	6	9	12	15	18	21	24	27	30	33	36
4	4	8	12	16	20	24	28	32	36	40	44	48
5	5	10	15	20	25	30	35	40	45	50	55	60
6	6	12	18	24	30	36	42	48	54	60	66	72
7	7	14	21	28	35	42	49	56	63	70	77	84
8	8	16	24	32	40	48	56	64	72	80	88	96
9	9	18	27	36	45	54	63	72	81	90	99	108
10	10	20	30	40	50	60	70	80	90	100	110	120
11	11	22	33	44	55	66	77	88	99	110	121	132
12	12	24	36	48	60	72	84	96	108	120	132	144

In the given multiplication table above, shaded parts represent 6 × 7 = 42

Remember that when we multiply two or more numbers, it does not matter which is first or second, or last, the answer is always the same, so no need to memorize both '6 × 7' and '7 × 6', just memorize that a '7' and a '6' make 42 when multiplied.

Properties of Multiplication

Multiplication has the same properties as addition. Basic properties involving multiplication that will problems easier to solve are as follow:

Commutative Property of Multiplication

When two numbers multiplied in any order give the same result.

For example, 7 × 9 = 63 and also, 9 × 7 = 63

Associative Property of Multiplication

When three or more numbers multiplied in any order give the same result. For example, 2 × 3 × 4 = 24; 3 × 4 × 2 = 24; and 4 × 2 × 3 = 24

Example:

Find the product (7 × 9) × 3 and also the product (7 × 3) × 9.

Solution: Here, the required product is as follow:

(7 × 9) × 3 = 63 × 3 = 189	(7 × 3) × 9 = 21 × 9 = 189

Multiplication Property of Zero

When a number multiplied by zero or zero multiplied by a number will give only zero as the product. We conclude that multiplication of any number with zero reduced the number to zero.

For example 12 × 0 = 0, and (3 × 7) × 0 = 21 × 0 = 0

Multiplication Property of One

When any number multiplied by one or one multiplied by any number will give the number itself as product.

For example, 4612 × 1 = 4612 and 1 × 4612 = 4612

Example:

Which one of the following mathematical statements is *not* true?

(A) 4 × 40 = 40 × 4
(B) 0 × 40 = 400
(C) 1 × 40 = 40
(D) 1 × 4 × 0 × 40 = 0
(E) None of these

Answer (B)

Explanation: When a number is multiplied by zero or zero is multiplied by a number will give only zero as product.

Therefore, 0 × 40 = 0; not 40

Multiply a Number by 10, 100, 1000

- If we multiply a number by 10, the product will be the number followed by one zero. For example, 7 × 10 = 70, 12 × 10 = 120, 20 × 10 = 200
- If we multiply a number by 100, the product will be the number followed by two zeros. For example, 7 × 100 = 700, 12 × 100 = 1200, 20 × 100 = 2000
- If we multiply a number by 1000, the product will be the number followed by three zeros. For example, 7 × 1000 = 7000, 12 × 1000 = 12000, 20 × 1000 = 20000
- In order to multiply a number by 20, 30, 40, ..., 80, 90, we multiply the number by 2, 3, 4, ... 8, 9, respectively and insert a zero on the right of the product
- In order to multiply a number by 200, 300, 400, ... , 800, 900, we multiply the number by 2, 3, 4, ..., 8, 9, respectively and insert two zeros on the right of the product.

Example:

Find the product: 9 × 7 × 10

Solution: Here, 9 × 7 × 10 = (9 × 7) × 10 = 63 × 10 = 630

Multiplication of a 4-digit Number by a Single Digit Number

Following steps are used for the multiplication of a 4-digit number by a single digit number:

Step 1: Arrange the numbers in columns.

Step 2: First multiply ones and if carry is generated then add the carry to multiplication of tens.

Step 3: Then, multiply tens, hundreds and thousands and if carry is generated then add the carry to multiplication of hundreds and thousands, respectively.

Example:

Multiply 6257 by 8.

Solution: Here, multiplication is as follow:

	②	④	⑤	
	TH	H	T	O
	6	2	5	7
			×	8
5	0	0	5	6

Therefore, 6257 × 8 = 50056

Multiplication of a 4-digit Number by a 2-digit Number

Following steps are used for the multiplication of a 4-digit number by a 2-digit number:

Step 1: Arrange the numbers in columns.

Step 2: First, multiply by ones.

Step 3: While multiply by a digit at tens place write one zero (0) at the ones place and then multiply by tens.

Step 4: Finally, add the products.

Example:

Multiply 6215 by 13.

Solution: Here, multiplication is as follow:

	TH	H	T	O
	6	2	1	5
		×	1	3
1	8	6	4	5
6	2	1	5	0
8	0	7	9	5

Therefore, 6215 × 13 = 80795

Multiplication of a 3-digit Number by a 3-digit

Following steps are used for the multiplication of 3-digit number by a 3-digit number:

Step 1: Arrange the numbers in columns.

Step 2: First, multiply ones.

Step 3: While multiply by a digit at tens place write one zero (0) at the ones place and then multiply by tens.

Step 4: While multiply by a digit at hundreds place write two zeros (00) at the ones place and then multiply by hundreds.

Step 5: Finally, add the products.

Example:

Multiply 463 by 205.

Solution: Here, multiplication is as follow:

```
  |H|T|O|
   4 6 3
  ×1 2 7
 --------
   3 2 4 1
   9 2 6 0
 4 6 3 0 0
 ---------
 5 8 8 0 1
```

Therefore, 463 × 127 = 58801

Division

Division means repeated subtraction of the same number. It is splitting into equal parts or groups. It is the inverse process of multiplication. It determines the one value is how many times greater than the another value. In a division, the number to be divided is called the **dividend**. The number by which division is made is called the **divisor**. The number of groups we get is called the **quotient**. The leftover is called the **remainder**. In a division, we always have:

Dividend = (Divisor × Quotient) + Remainder

The term used for division is 'divided by' and the symbol for division is (÷).

Division as Repeated Subtraction

Division can be seen as repeated subtraction. Let us see the following example where 15 is divided by 5.

```
  15
 − 5
 ---
  10
 − 5
 ---
   5
 − 5
 ---
   0
```

Here, 5 is subtracted 3 times till we get 0. So, 15 – 5 – 5 – 5 = 0

Example:

What is the missing number?

[?] → [Multiply by 4] – [28] = 0

(A) 28 (B) 14 (C) 7 (D) 0

(E) None of these

Answer (C)

Explanation: Here, $\boxed{?} \times 4 - 28 = 0$. Or, $\boxed{?} \times 4 - 28 + 28 = 0 + 28$

Or, $\boxed{?} \times 4 = 28$. Or, $\boxed{7} \times 4 = 28$

So, the missing number is 7. Also, $28 \div 4 = 7$

Or, $\boxed{7} \times 4 - 28 = 28 - 28 = 0$

Division Using Number Line

We can use number line to divide. For example, If we divide 8 by 2, first we draw a number line that begins at 0 and ends at 8, as follows:

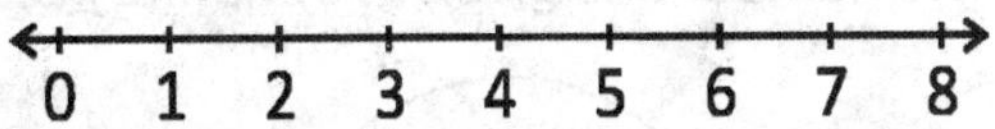

Now, to find the answer to 8 ÷ 2, just split this number line into four equal parts as shown in the following figure. This division occurs at 4, showing us that 8 ÷ 2 = 4

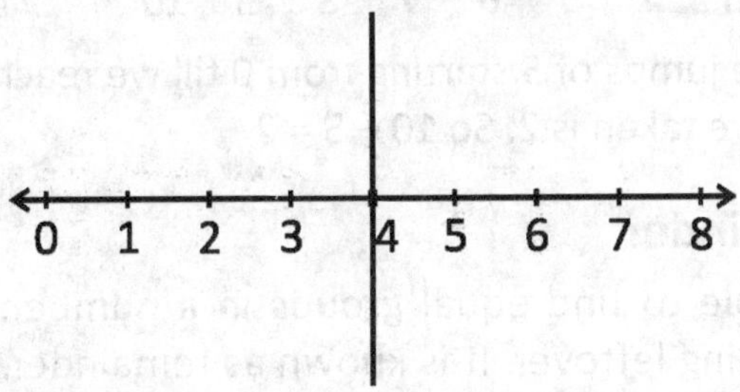

If we take jumps of 2 starting from 0 till we reach at 8, the number of jumps is 4.

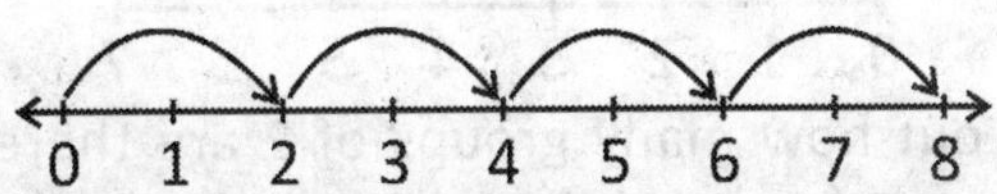

Or, the number of jumps = 8 ÷ 2 = 4. So, 8 ÷ 4 = 2 (groups)

Example:

Which one of the following number lines shows 10 ÷ 5 = 2?

(A)

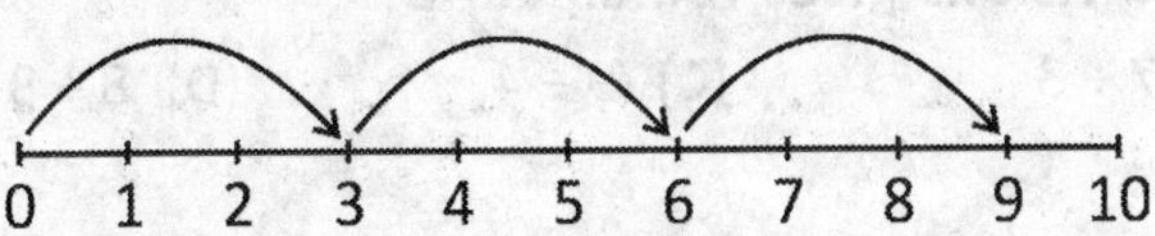

(B) 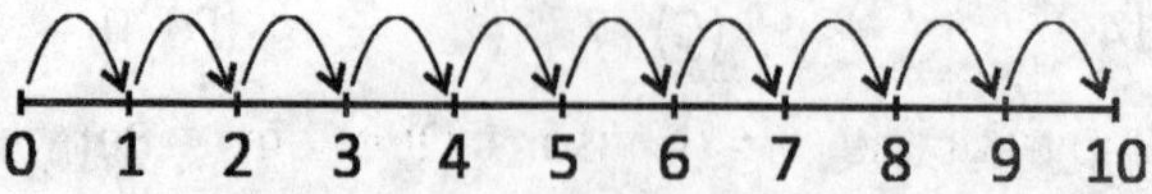

(C) 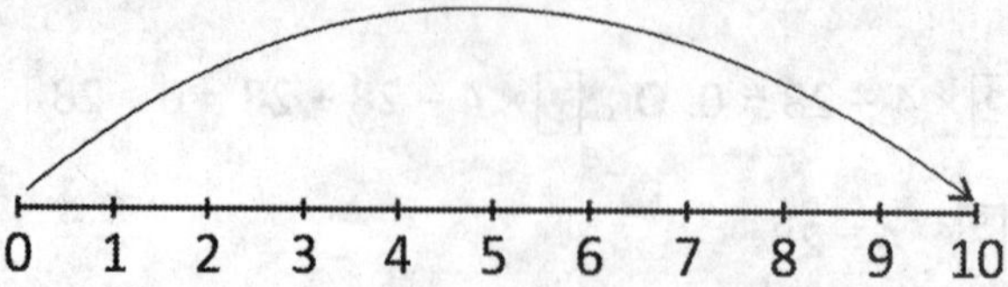

(D) 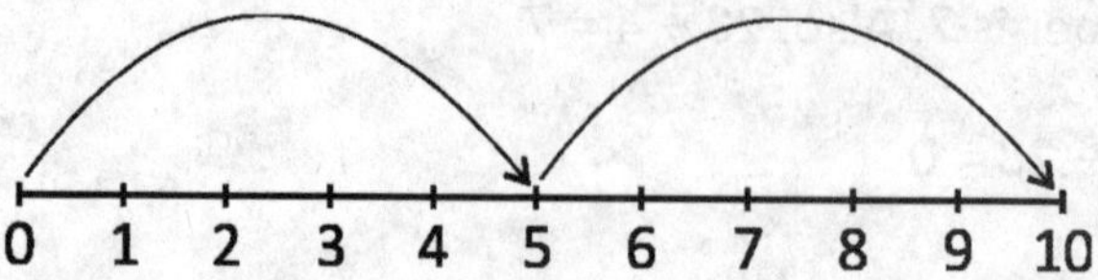

(E) None of these

Answer (D)

Explanation: The number line given in option (D) is:

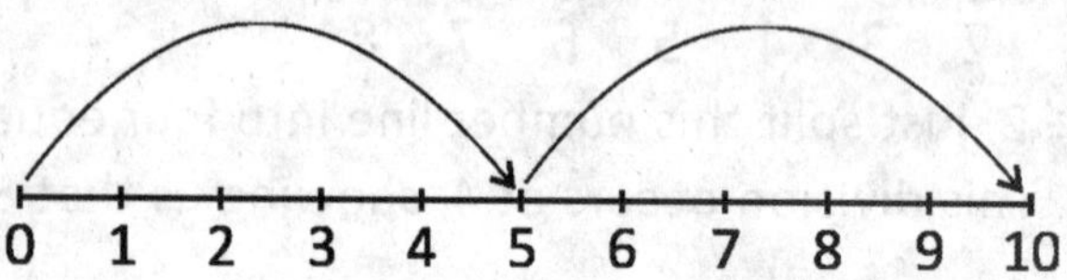

Here, we take jumps of 5 starting from 0 till we reach 10, and the number of jumps we have taken is 2. So 10 ÷ 5 = 2

Division and Remainder

it is not always possible to find equal groups in a number. Sometimes when we divide, there is something leftover. It is known as remainder. Look at 7 ÷ 2

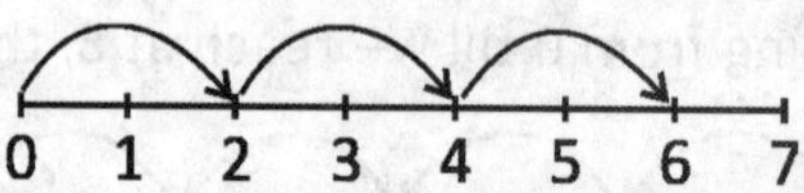

Here, we have to find out how many groups of 2 are there in 7. We can make 3 groups of 2, starting from 0 but 1 is left. So, 7 ÷ 2 = 3 and 1 is the remainder. This means 3 is quotient here and 1 is the remainder.

Example:

Which one of the following divisions gives remainder 2?

(A) 10 ÷ 3 (B) 7 ÷ 3 (C) 9 ÷ 4 (D) 8 ÷ 3

(E) None of these

Answer (D)

Explanation: As we know, Dividend = (Divisor × Quotient) + Remainder.

Now, divisions are as follow:

(A) 10 ÷ 3 = (3 × 3) + 1; (B) 7 ÷ 3 = (3 × 2) + 1

(C) 9 ÷ 4 = (4 × 2) + 1; (D) 8 ÷ 3 = (3 × 2) + 2

Therefore, in (8 ÷ 3), quotient is 2 and the remainder is 2.

Division of a 4-digit Number by a Single digit Number

Following steps are used for the division of a 4-digit number by a single digit number (Suppose 3142 ÷ 9):

Step 1: Arrange the numbers as follows.

```
9)3142
```

Step 2: Examine the first digit of the dividend (3). It is smaller than 9, so take the first two digits of the dividend (31) and determine how many 9's it contains. Here, 9 × 3 = 27 and 9 × 4 = 36. So, place the 3 in quotient and subtract 27 from 31.

```
     3
9) 3142
  -27
    4
```

Step 3: Now, put 4 to the right of the difference 4 to make it 44, and divide the 44 by 9 same as step 2.

```
     34
9) 3142
  -27↓
    44
   -36
     8
```

Step 4: Now, put 2 to the right of the difference 8 to make it 82 and divide the 82 by 9 same as step 3.

$$\begin{array}{r} 349 \\ 9\overline{)\,3142} \\ -27\downarrow \\ \hline 44 \\ -36\downarrow \\ \hline 82 \\ -81 \\ \hline 1 \\ \hline \end{array}$$

Here, when 9 × 9 = 81 is subtracted from 82, we have 1 is leftover which is remainder. In this division, the quotient is 349. So, (349 × 9) + 1 = 3142

Example:

Maximum how many sets of 5 can you get in 1234?

(A) 248 (B) 246 (C) 205 (D) 255

(E) None of these

Answer (B)

Explanation: Here, division is as follow:

$$\begin{array}{r} 246 \\ 5\overline{)\,1234} \\ -10\downarrow \\ \hline 23 \\ -20\downarrow \\ \hline 34 \\ -30 \\ \hline 4 \\ \hline \end{array}$$

We have, 246 is the quotient and 4 is the remainder.

Therefore, we can get 246 sets of 5 in 1234.

Division of a 4-digit Number by a 2-digit Number

Following steps are used for the division of a 4-digit number by a 2-digit number (Suppose 832 ÷ 13).

Step 1: Arrange the numbers as follows:

$13\overline{)832}$

Step 2: Examine the first digit of the dividend (8). It is smaller than 13. So take the first 2-digit number (83) and determine how many times 13's it contains. Here, 13 × 6 = 78 and 13 × 7 = 91. So, place the 6 in quotient and subtract 78 from 83.

```
      6
13) 832
   - 78
   ----
      5
```

Step 3: Now, put 2 to the right of the difference 5 to make it 52 and divide the 52 by 13 same as step 2.

```
     64
13) 832
   - 78↓
   ----
     52
   - 52
   ----
      0
```

Here, when 13 × 4 = 52 is subtracted from 52, we have 0 is leftover which is the remainder and in this division the quotient is 64. So, (64 × 13) + 0 = 832

Example:

The remainder and the quotient in the given division are:

(341 ÷ 12)

(A) 5 and 37 (B) 5 and 29

(C) 4 and 34 (D) 5 and 28

(E) None of these

Answer (D)

Explanation: Here, division is as follow:

```
     28
12) 341
  - 24
  -----
    101
   - 96
   ----
      5
```

Therefore, the remainder is 5 and the quotient is 28.

Properties of Division

Some properties involving division are given below:

Division Property of One

Any number divided by 1 will give the number itself as quotient. This property is known as the identity property of division. For example, 9 ÷ 1 = 9

Zero Property of Division

When zero is divided by any number will give zero as result. For example, 0 ÷ 7 = 0. Remember that any number divided by zero is not defined. For example, 7 ÷ 0 is not defined.

Equality Property of Division

If two numbers are equal and when both sides of the equation is divided by the same number. The resulting sides remain equal.

For example, 20 = 20 or, 20 ÷ 5 = 20 ÷ 5 or, 4 = 4

Example:

Which one of the following expressions is *incorrect* ?

(A) 18 × 0 = 0
(B) 0 ÷ 18 = 0
(C) 18 ÷ 1 = 1 ÷ 18
(D) 1 × 18 = 18 × 1
(E) None of these

Answer (C)

Explanation: In option (A), 18 × 0 = 0 (multiplication property of zero)

In option (B), 0 ÷ 18 = 0 (zero property of division)

In option (C), 18 ÷ 1 = 18 but 1 ÷ 18 is not equal to 18.

In option (D), 1 × 18 = 18 × 1 = 18 (multiplication property of one)

Divisibility Rules and Division Facts

Divisibility Rules

A divisibility test is a rule for determining whether one whole number is divisible by another without leaving remainder.

- A number is **divisible by 2** only if it is an even number, or , if it ends in 0, 2, 4, 6, or 8. For example, in the division (14 ÷ 2), 14 is divisible by 2 because, 14 ends in 4 which is an even number.
- If the sum of all digits of a number is divisible by 3, then the whole number is **divisible by 3**. For example, in the division (345 ÷ 3), sum of digits in 345 is 3 + 4 + 5 = 12, which is divisible by 3. Therefore 345 is also divisible by 3.
- A number is **divisible by 4** if the last two digits of the number is divisible by 4. For example, in the division (3012 ÷ 4), the last two digits make 12 which is divisible by 4. Therefore, 3012 is also divisible by 4.
- If the last digit of a number is 0, or 5, then the whole number is **divisible by 5**. For example, in the division (7395 ÷ 5), the last digit of 7395 is 5. Therefore, 7395 is divisible by 5.
- A number is **divisible by 6** if it is divisible by 2 and also it is divisible by 3. For example, in the division of (342 ÷ 6), the sum of the digits in 342 is 3 + 4 + 2 = 9, which is divisible by 3. So 342 is divisible by 3. Now last digit of 342 is 2 shows that it is an even number which is divisible by 2. Therefore 342 is also divisible by 6.
- A number is **divisible by 9** if the sum of the digits is divisible by 9. For example, in the division (846 ÷ 9), the sum of digits in 846 is 8 + 4 + 6 = 18 which is divisible by 9. Therefore, 846 is also divisible by 9.
- A number of **divisible by 10** if the last digit is 0. For example, in the division (9760 ÷ 10), the last digit of 9760 is 0. Therefore, the number 9760 is divisible by 10.

Example:

Which one of the following numbers is divisible by 5 and 6 both?

(A) 310 (B) 210 (C) 315 (D) 216

(E) None of these

Answer (B)

Explanation: The last digit of 210 is 0. Therefore, 210 is divisible by 2 and also divisible by 5. Now, the sum of digits of 210 is 2 + 1 + 0 = 3 Which is divisible by 3. Therefore, 210 is also divisible by 3. Since, 210 is divisible by both 2 and 3. Therefore, 210 is also divisible by 6. So, 210 is divisible by both 5 and 6.

Division Facts

Division is the result of 'fair sharing'. It is the opposite of multiplying. When we know a multiplication fact, we can find a division fact.

- Division should be continued till the remainder becomes either '0' or less than the divisor.
- Knowing multiplication tables well can make division easy.

  For example, it 6 × 7 = 42, then 42 ÷ 6 = 7 and 42 ÷ 7 = 6. This is the method of **reverse multiplication**.
- Any number divided by itself gives 1 as the quotient and 0 as the remainder. For example, 7 ÷ 7 = 1 and (1 × 7) + 0 = 7

Problems Based on Multiplication and Division

Multiplication is the expanded form of addition and division is the inverse of multiplication. Let us see the following examples based on multiplication and division.

Example:

There are 8 rows of seats in a theatre. Each row has the same number of seats. If there is a total of 472 seats, then how many seats are there in each row?

(A) 68 (B) 59 (C) 54 (D) 46

(E) None of these

Answer (B)

Explanation: Number of rows = 8

Total number of seats = 472

Number of seats in each row = 472 ÷ 8 = 59

Therefore, there are 59 seats in each row.

Example:

A school library has 15 racks of books and each rack holds 105 books. Find the total number of books in the school library.

(A) 1575 (B) 1665 (C) 1185 (D) 1395

(E) None of these

Answer (A)

Explanation: Number of racks = 15

Number of books on each rack = 105

Therefore, total number of books = 105 × 15 = 1575

$$\begin{array}{r} 105 \\ \times\ 15 \\ \hline 525 \\ 1050 \\ \hline 1575 \\ \hline \end{array}$$

So, there are 1575 books in the school library.

Example:

There were 324 chocolates packed equally in 9 boxes. How many chocolates were packed in each box?

(A) 28 (B) 24 (C) 36 (D) 32

(E) None of these

Answer (C)

Explanation: Total number of chocolates = 324

Number of box = 9

$$\begin{array}{r} 36 \\ 9\overline{)\,324} \\ -27 \\ \hline 54 \\ -54 \\ \hline 0 \\ \hline \end{array}$$

Therefore, the required number of chocolates in each box = 324 ÷ 9 = 36

Example:

There are 8 AC bogies and 12 sleeper bogies in a train. 72 berths are available for passengers in each bogie. How many passengers can travel in the train if each passenger occupies one berth?

(A) 1488 (B) 1440

(C) 1428 (D) 1460

(E) None of these

Answer (B)

Explanation: Number of AC bogies = 8

Number of sleeper bogies = 12

Total number of bogies = 12 + 8 = 20

Number of berth in each bogies = 72

Therefore, the total number of berths in the train = 72 × 20 = 1440

So we have, 1440 passengers can travel in the train if each passenger occupies one berth.

Summary

- **Multiplication** means repeated addition. It is a faster way of adding the same digits.
- In a multiplication, the number which is multiplied is called **multiplicand**. The number by which the multiplicand is multiplied is called **multiplier**. The answer or result of multiplication is called its **product**.
- When three or more numbers multiplied in any order give the same result.
- When number multiplied by zero or zero multiplied by any number will give only zero as the product.
- When any number multiplied by one or one multiplied by any number will give the number itself.
- If we multiply a number by 10, 100 and 1000, the product will be the number followed by one zero, two zeros and three zeros, respectively.
- In order to multiply a number by 20, 30, 40, ... 80, 90, we multiply the number by 2, 3, 4, ... 8, 9, respectively and insert a zero on the right of the product.
- Division is repeated subtraction of the same number. It is splitting into equal parts or groups.

- In a division, the number to be divided is called the **dividend**, by which division is made is called the **divisor**, the number of parts or groups we get is called the **quotient** and the leftover is called the **remainder**.
- In a division, we always have: **Dividend = (Divisor × Quotient) + Remainder**

Did You Know?

- The word 'multiply' was used in Mathematics sense which comes from the Latin word 'multi' meaning 'many' and 'plicare' meaning 'folds' giving 'multiplicand' — 'having many folds', which means 'many times greater in number'.
- The word 'divide' was used in Mathematics which comes from the Latin word 'divider' meaning 'to force apart' or 'distribute'.
- The symbol '×' for multiplication has been in use since 1931. It was chosen for religious reasons to represent the cross.
- The division symbol '÷' is known as the "Obelus" which was first used to signify division in the year 1659.

Solved Problems

1. How many times 12 should be subtracted from 72 to get 0?

(A) 4 (B) 5

(C) 7 (D) 6

(E) None of these

Answer (D)

Explanation: As we know, division is the repeated subtraction.

Now, 72 ÷ 12 = 6. Therefore, 6 times 12 should be subtracted from 72 to get 0.

Verification: 72 – 12 – 12 – 12 – 12 – 12 – 12

= 72 – (6 × 12) = 72 – 72 = 0

2. What is the missing number in the given box?

? → Divided by 7 → Plus 7 = **11**

(A) 24 (B) 28 (C) 35 (D) 21

(E) None of these

Answer (B)

Explanation: As we know, subtraction is the inverse process of addition and division is the inverse process of multiplication.

Therefore, $(11 - 7) \times 7 = 4 \times 7 = 28$

Verification: $(28 \div 7) + 7 = 4 + 7 = 11$

3. If 92 × 11 × 23 = 23276, then (23 × 92) × 11 will be equal to:

(A) 23672 (B) 23627 (C) 23276 (D) 32477

(E) None of these

Answer (C)

Explanation: As we know, when three or more numbers multiplied in any order give the same result.

Therefore, $92 \times 11 \times 23 = (23 \times 92) \times 11$

Hence, $(23 \times 92) \times 11 = 23276$

4. Which one of the following mathematical statements is *incorrect*?

(A) $0 \div 564 = 0$ (B) $564 \times 1 = 564$

(C) $564 \times 6 = 6 \times 564$ (D) $564 \div 564 = 564$

(E) None of these

Answer (D)

Explanation: Here, $0 \div 564 = 0$ is true. $564 \times 1 = 564$ is true.

$564 \times 6 = 3384$ and also $6 \times 564 = 3384$, so it is also true.

Now, $564 \div 564 = 1$, because a number divided by itself gives 1.

5. If we divide the smallest 4-digit number by the smallest 2-digit number, the quotient will be:

(A) 100 B) 1000 (C) 10 (D) 990

(E) None of these

Answer (A)

Explanation: The smallest 4-digit number = 1000

The smallest 2-digit number = 10

Therefore, the required quotient = 1000 ÷ 10 = 100

6. The value of ◯ is 7 times as much as the value of □. what is the value of □ + ◯, if □ + 16 is 29?

(A) 104 (B) 91

(C) 78 (D) 84

(E) None of these

Answer (A)

Explanation: Given that, □ + 16 = 29

So, □ + 16 – 16 = 29 – 16, or, □ = 13

Now, the value of ◯ is 7 times as much as the value of □

Therefore, the value of ◯ = 13 × 7 = 91

Hence, □ + ◯ = 91 + 13 = 104

7. Find the missing digit in the given multiplication

```
  4[?]1 6
      × 8
---------
3 6 1 2 8
---------
```

(A) 3 (B) 7

(C) 5 (D) 6

(E) None of these

Answer (C)

Explanation: As we know, division is the inverse process of multiplication.

Here, given that 4[?]16 × 8 = 36128

Therefore, 36128 ÷ 8 = 4[?]16, or, 4[5]16 = 4[?]16

So, the required missing digit [?] = 5

8. There are 30 days in the month of September. How many hours are there in the month of September?

(A) 540 hours (B) 720 hours

(C) 680 hours (D) 744 hours

(E) None of these

Answer (B)

Explanation: As we know, there are 24 hours in a day.

Here, the number of days in the month of September = 30

So, the required number of hours = (30 × 24) hours

$$\begin{array}{r} 30 \\ \times 24 \\ \hline 120 \\ 600 \\ \hline 720 \\ \hline \end{array}$$

So, there are 720 hours in the month of September.

9. The price of a pen is ₹ 18. Find the price of 18 such pens.

(A) ₹ 324 (B) ₹ 234

(C) ₹ 384 (D) ₹ 296

(E) None of these

Answer (A)

Explanation: Here, given that the price of a pen = ₹ 18

So, the price of 18 such pens = ₹ (18 × 18)

$$\begin{array}{r} 18 \\ \times 18 \\ \hline 144 \\ 180 \\ \hline 324 \\ \hline \end{array}$$

Therefore, the price of 18 such pens = ₹ 324

10. Which one of the following sets shows 5 × 3?

(A) 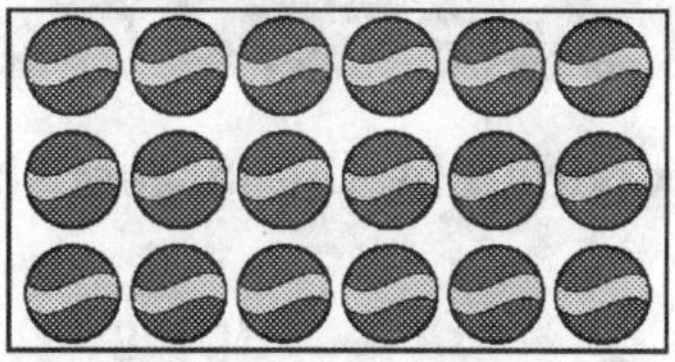

(B) 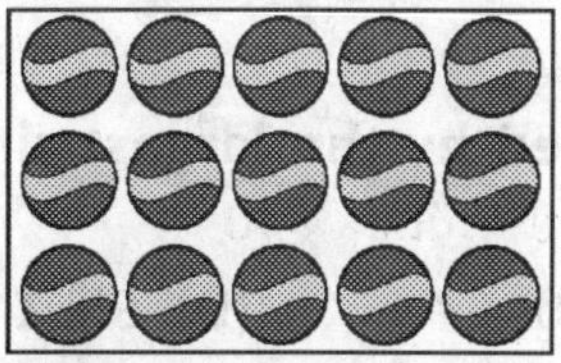

(C) 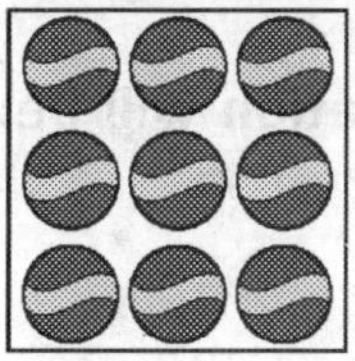

(D) 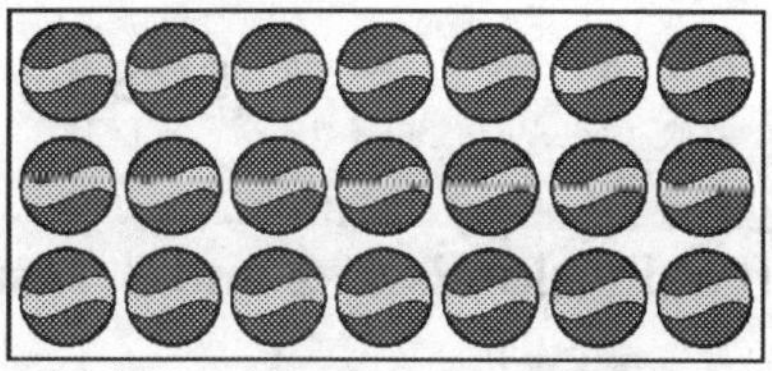

(E) None of these

Answer (B)

Explanation: Here, 5 × 3 = 15

Therefore, the number of balls given in option (B) is correct.

Practice Exercise 3

1. **When the largest 4-digit even number is divided by the largest single digit number, the remainder will be:**
(A) 9 (B) 0 (C) 1 (D) 8
(E) None of these

2. **When the largest 3-digit number is multiplied by the largest single digit number, the product will be:**
(A) 8991 (B) 891 (C) 990 (D) 9801
(E) None of these

3. **The sum of two missing digits in the given multiplication will be:**

$$\begin{array}{r} 2\boxed{?}4\boxed{?} \\ \times 7 \\ \hline 14301 \\ \hline \end{array}$$

(A) 4 (B) 3 (C) 5 (D) 8
(E) None of these

4. **The quotient, remainder and divisor in a division is 1, 2 and 3, respectively. Find the dividend.**
(A) 8 (B) 6 (C) 9 (D) 7
(E) None of these

5. **Product of the third multiple of 3 and 33 is:**
(A) 297 (B) 99 (C) 198 D) 1089
(E) None of these

6. **Product of 12 and 4 is divided by their sum. The quotient will be:**
(A) 8 (B) 2 (C) 4 (D) 3
(E) None of these

7. **There are eight coins in a stock. How many coins are there in all?**

(A) 64 (B) 56 (C) 72 (D) 48
(E) None of these

8. **I have bought the given badminton shuttles. Each shuttle costs ₹ 11. How much did the shuttles cost altogether?**

(A) ₹ 288 (B) ₹ 218 (C) ₹ 198 (D) ₹ 178
(E) None of these

9. **The product of 47 tens and 3 hundreds is:**

(A) 123000 (B) 423000
(C) 271000 (D) 141000
(E) None of these

10. **The number pattern given below is based on multiplication. Which one of the following numbers will replace the question mark (?) in the pattern?**

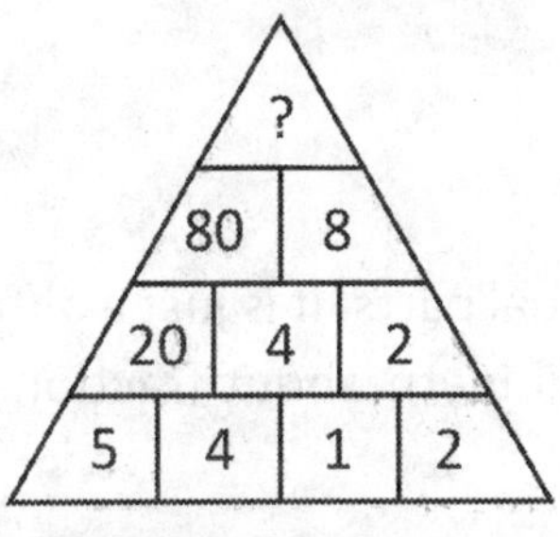

(A) 680 (B) 640
(C) 960 (D) 320
(E) None of these

Chapter 4

Fractions

Learning Objectives

- Introduction
- Fractions
- Types of Fractions
- Operations with Fractions
- Word Problems Based on Fractions

Introduction

A fraction represents a part of whole or any number of equal parts. It is just a different way of showing the same value. In this chapter, we will learn about fractions and their types and operations.

Fractions

A fraction is a part of whole. There are two numbers to every fraction, which are called **term**. A line separates the two terms. Number above the line is called **numerator** and the number below the line is called **denominator**. Denominator of a fraction tells us how many parts the whole is divided into and the numerator tells us how many parts are taken out the whole. For example, in the fraction $\frac{2}{5}$, 5 is denominator. So, the whole unit or one whole has been cut into 5 equal parts.

2 is the numerator. Now, 2 parts out of 5 parts is being talked about or 1 part is going to be shaded or taken out. Here, the number $\frac{2}{5}$ is known as **fractional number** and its symbol $\frac{2}{5}$ is called a **fraction**.

Example:

What fraction is one day of a week?

(A) $\frac{1}{24}$

(B) $\frac{1}{10}$

(C) $\frac{1}{7}$

(D) $\frac{1}{4}$

(E) None of these

Answer (C)

Explanation: There are 7 days in a week.

Therefore, 1 day out of 1 week or 1 part out of 7 parts is $\frac{1}{7}$.

Understanding Fractions

Fractions are formed when we have a whole that is divided into so many equal parts. The shaded portion or parts of a figure can also represented by a fraction as shown in the given table.

Shaded part	Fraction	Denominator	Numerator	Fractional Number	Figure
1 part out of 4 equal parts	$\frac{1}{4}$	4	1	One-fourth	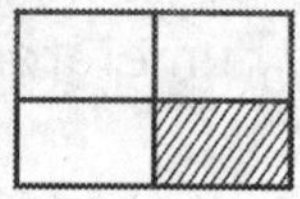
2 parts out of 4 equal parts	$\frac{2}{4}$	4	2	Two-fourth	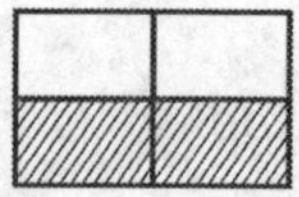
1 part out of 2 equal parts	$\frac{1}{2}$	2	1	One-half	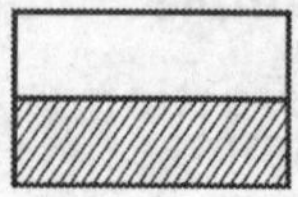
3 parts out of 4 equal parts	$\frac{3}{4}$	4	3	Three-fourth	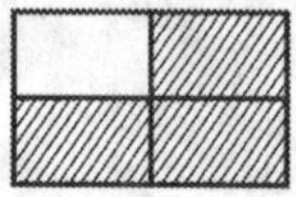
1 part out of 3 equal parts	$\frac{1}{3}$	3	1	One-third	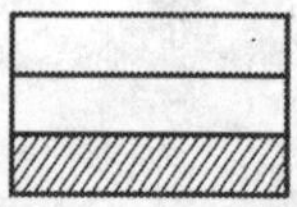

Example:

Which of the following shows 4 equal parts of whole?

(A) 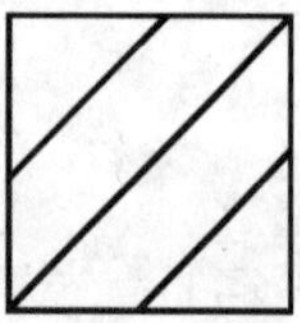

(B) 

(C) 

(D) 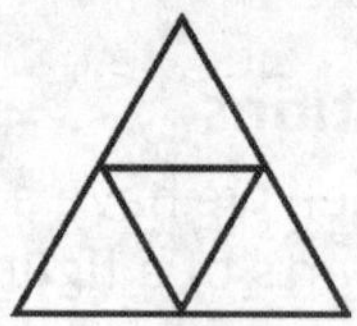

(E) None of these

Answer (D)

Explanation: Figure given in option (D) has four equal parts. Figures given in other options do not have equal parts.

Fraction Represented on the Number Line

We can represent a fraction on a number line. In order to represent $\frac{3}{4}$ on a number line, draw a line and mark a point A to represent 1 and a point P to represent O. Now, divide the gap between P and A into four equal parts. Let X, Y and Z by the points of division.

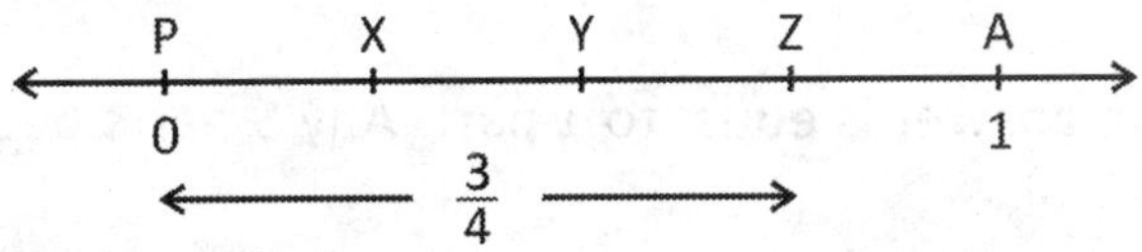

In the figure given above, the line PZ represents the fraction $\frac{3}{4}$.

Example:

On the number line given below, PQ is a line. Write the fraction represented by AB.

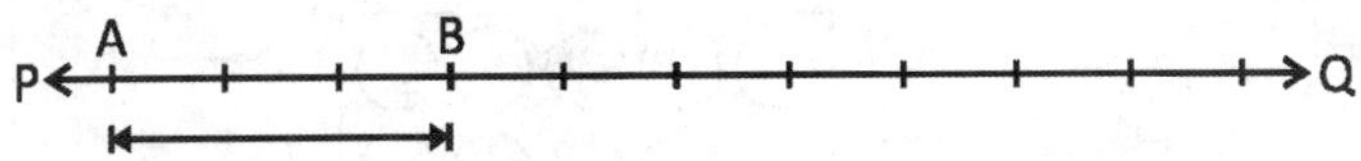

(A) $\frac{3}{10}$ (B) $\frac{2}{5}$

(C) $\frac{1}{10}$ D) $\frac{7}{10}$

(E) None of these

Answer (A)

Explanation: There are ten divisions on the given number line. AB represents 3 divisions. Therefore, the fraction represented by AB = $\frac{3}{10}$

Finding Fraction of a Group

Group means a number of people or things which are put together or consider as a whole. Look at the groups or collection of 15 circles shown below.

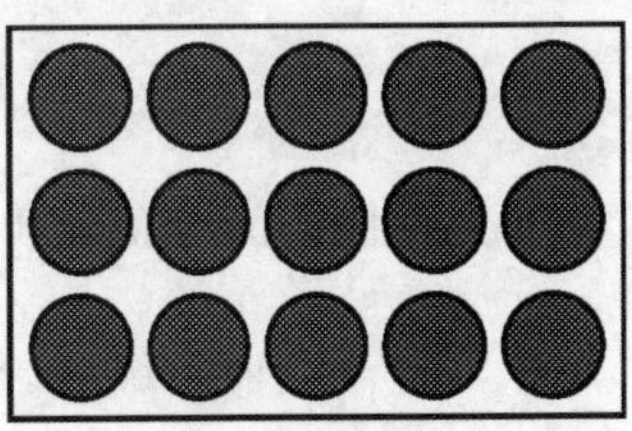
One whole

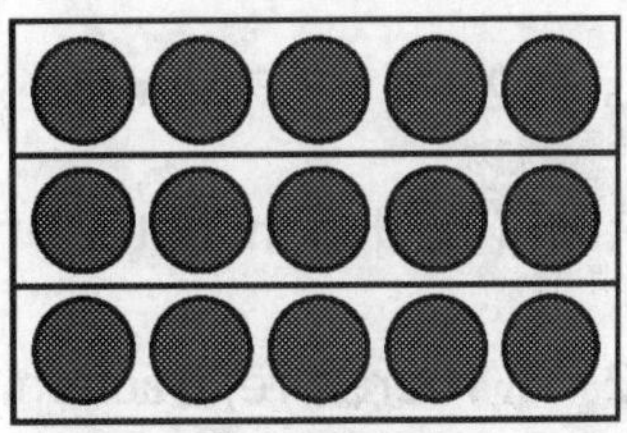
One-third

We can find $\frac{1}{3}$ of the group by dividing the whole by 3. In the picture given above, there are 15 circles.

15 ÷ 3 = 5. So, one part is 5, and 5 can become one part of 15. Therefore, to find $\frac{1}{3}$, divide 15 by 3 and the answer is equal to 1 part. Any 5 parts become $\frac{1}{3}$ of 15.

Example:

In which of the following figures, the fraction represented by shaded circles is equal to $\frac{1}{5}$?

(A) 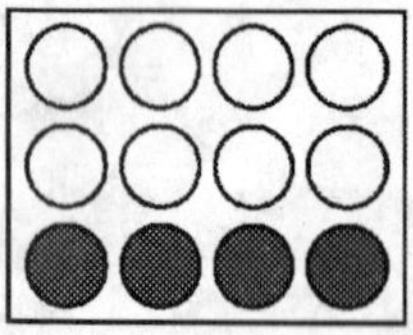

(B) 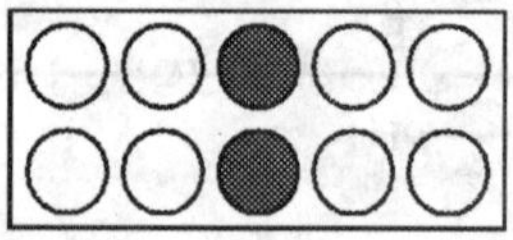

(C) 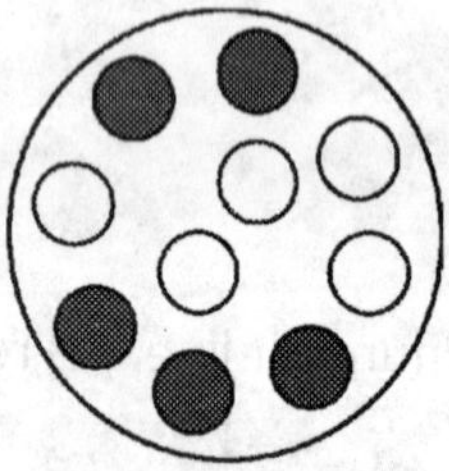

D) 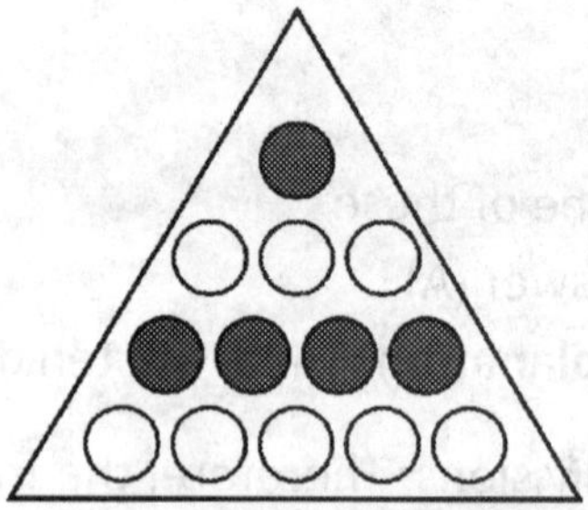

(E) None of these

Answer (B)

Explanation: In option (A), denominator of the fraction represented by shaded circles = 12 ÷ 4 = 3. Therefore, fraction = $\frac{1}{3}$

In option (B), denominator of the fraction represented by shaded circles = 10 ÷ 2 = 5. Therefore, fraction = $\frac{1}{5}$

In option (C), denominator of the fraction represented by shaded circles $= 10 \div 5 = 2$. Therefore, fraction $= \frac{1}{2}$ In option (D), denominator of the fraction represented by shaded circles $= 15 \div 5 = 3$. Therefore, fraction $= \frac{1}{3}$

Types of Fractions

There are several types of fractions. Let us study the fractions and their types.

Unit Fraction

A fraction, whose numerator is 1, is called a unit fraction. For example, $\frac{1}{5}, \frac{1}{3}, \frac{1}{9}, \frac{1}{10}$ are unit fractions. Here, the denominators of all fractions are different but numerators are 1.

Example:

In which of the following figures, the fraction represented by shaded parts is a unit fraction?

(A) 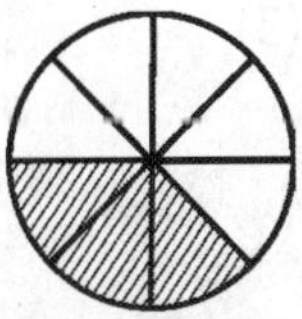

(B) 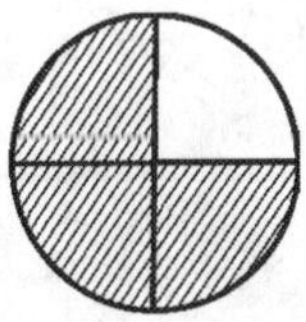

(C) 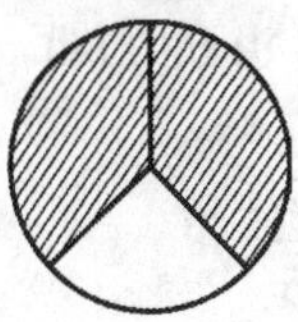

(D) 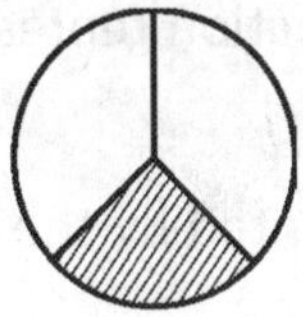

(E) None of these

Answer (D)

Explanation: Fraction represented by shaded parts in option (A) $= \frac{3}{8}$

Fraction represented by shaded parts in option (B) $= \frac{3}{4}$

Fraction represented by shaded parts in option (C) $= \frac{2}{3}$

Fraction represented by shaded parts in option (D) $= \frac{1}{3}$

Therefore, the fraction represented by the shaded parts in option (D) is a unit fraction.

Like and Unlike Fractions

Fractions in which the denominators are same, are called the **like fractions** and the fractions in which denominators are different, are called **unlike fractions**. For example, $\frac{2}{3}, \frac{1}{3}, \frac{4}{3}$ are like fractions and $\frac{2}{5}, \frac{7}{4}, \frac{3}{8}$ are unlike fractions.

Example:

In which of the following figures, the fractions represented by the shaded parts are like fractions?

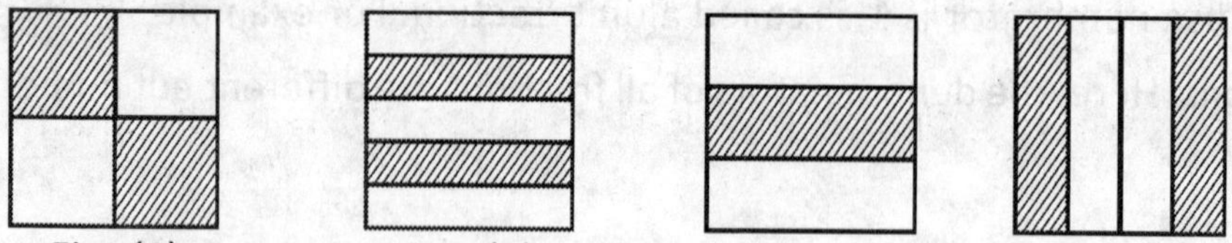

Fig. (1) Fig. (2) Fig. (3) Fig. (4)

(A) Fig. (2) and fig. (3)
(B) Fig. (1) and fig. (4)
(C) Fig. (1) and fig. (3)
(D) Fig. (2) and fig. (3)
(E) None of these

Answer (B)

Explanation: Fraction represented by the shaded parts in Fig. (1) = $\frac{2}{4}$

Fraction represented by the shaded parts in Fig. (2) = $\frac{2}{5}$

Fraction represented by the shaded parts in Fig. (3) = $\frac{1}{3}$

Fraction represented by the shaded parts in Fig. (4) = $\frac{2}{4}$

Thus, in Fig. (1) and Fig. (4), the fractions represented by shaded parts are like fractions.

Equivalent Fractions

Fractions which have the same value, though they may look different are called equivalent fractions.

Here, a rectangular box is dividing into three equal parts and one part is shaded. So it is $\frac{1}{3}$ of whole. Now, look at this.

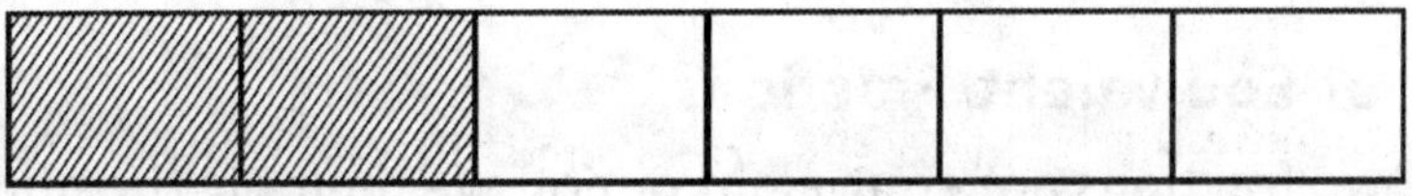

Here, a rectangular box of the same size is divided into six equal parts and its two parts are shaded. So it is $\frac{2}{6}$. Clearly, the given two boxes represent different fractions but the same size quantity. These are called equivalent fractions $\left(\frac{1}{3} \text{ and } \frac{2}{6}\right)$

- To find the equivalent fractions with the terms bigger than the given fraction, Simply multiply the numerator and denominator of the fractlon by a common number. For example, an equivalent fraction of $\frac{1}{3}$ is $\frac{1 \times 2}{3 \times 2} = \frac{2}{6}$
- To find the equivalent fractions with the terms smaller than the given fraction, simply divide the numerator and denominator of the fraction by a common number. For example, $\frac{2}{6} = \frac{2 \div 2}{6 \div 2} = \frac{1}{3}$

Example:

Which one of the following sets is a set of equivalent fractions?

(A) $\frac{3}{4}, \frac{4}{6}, \frac{5}{2}, \frac{8}{9}$

(B) $\frac{3}{4}, \frac{6}{8}, \frac{9}{12}, \frac{12}{16}$

(C) $\frac{1}{3}, \frac{3}{4}, \frac{2}{6}, \frac{6}{8}$

(D) $\frac{2}{8}, \frac{3}{9}, \frac{8}{16}, \frac{4}{12}$

(E) None of these

Answer (B)

Explanation: Here, the set of fractions given in option (B) is the set of equivalent fractions, which are $\frac{3}{4}, \frac{6}{8}, \frac{9}{12}, \frac{12}{16}$ because,

$$\frac{3}{4} = \frac{3}{4}, \frac{6}{8} = \frac{6 \div 2}{8 \div 2} = \frac{3}{4}, \frac{9}{12} = \frac{9 \div 3}{12 \div 3} = \frac{3}{4}, \frac{12}{16} = \frac{12 \div 4}{16 \div 4} = \frac{3}{4}$$

Verification of Equivalent Fractions

To verity that two fractions are equivalent or not, we multiply the numerator of one fraction by the denominator of other fraction. Similarly, we multiply the denominator of one fraction by the numerator of other fraction. If the products so obtained are same, the fractions are equivalent.

Example:

Are the fractions $\frac{2}{3}$ and $\frac{10}{15}$ equivalent?

Solution: Here, $\frac{2}{3} = \frac{10}{15}$ Or, $2 \times 15 = 3 \times 10$ Or, $30 = 30$

Therefore, the fractions $\frac{2}{3}$ and $\frac{10}{15}$ are equivalent.

Bigger and Smaller Fractions

Look at the fraction represented by shaded parts of whole:

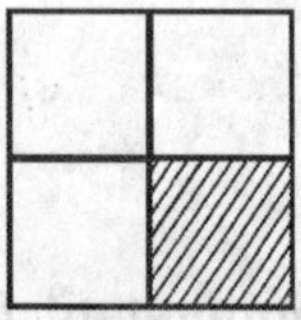

$\frac{1}{4}$

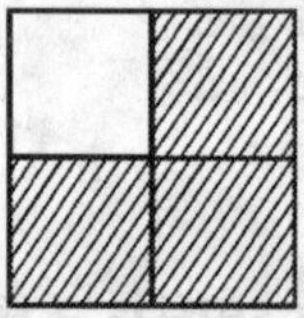

$\frac{3}{4}$

If we compare these two fractions, we conclude that $\frac{1}{4} < \frac{3}{4}$ or $\frac{3}{4} > \frac{1}{4}$

Remember that:

1. If the denominators of the fractions are same, then the fraction with the larger numerator is bigger.

2. If the numerators of the fractions are same, then the fraction with the smaller denominator is the bigger fraction.

Example:

Which one of the following sets of figures shows $\frac{3}{4} > \frac{2}{4}$ with respect to the fraction represented by shaded parts?

(A) 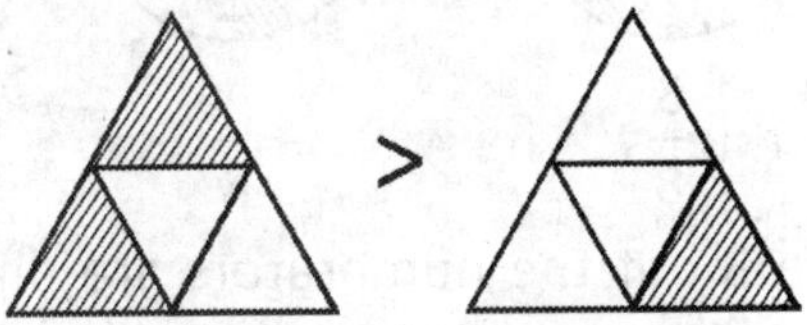

(B) 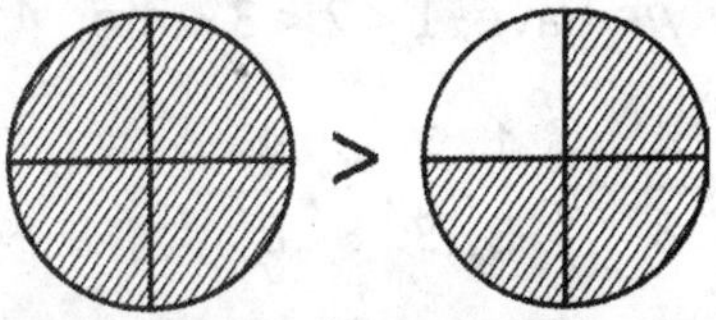

(C) 

(D) 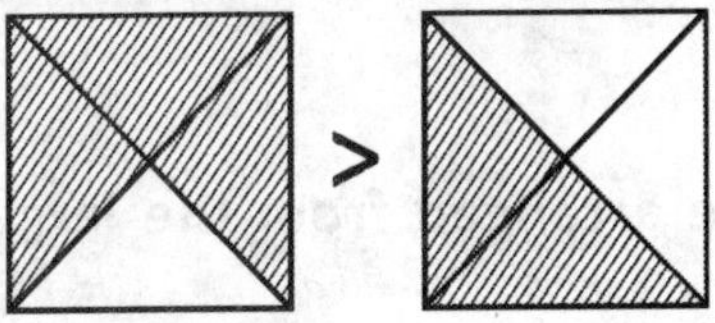

(E) None of these

Answer (D)

Explanation: In option (A), for the fractions represented by shaded parts, $\frac{2}{4} > \frac{1}{4}$

In option (B), for the fractions represented by shaded parts, $\frac{4}{4} > \frac{3}{4}$

In option (C), for the fractions represented by shaded parts, $\frac{4}{4} > \frac{2}{4}$

In option (D), for the fractions represented by shaded parts, $\frac{3}{4} > \frac{2}{4}$

Ascending and Descending Order of Fractions

As we know, when the denominators of the fractions are the same, then the bigger fractions has the larger numerator and if the numerator are same, the bigger fraction has the smaller denominator.

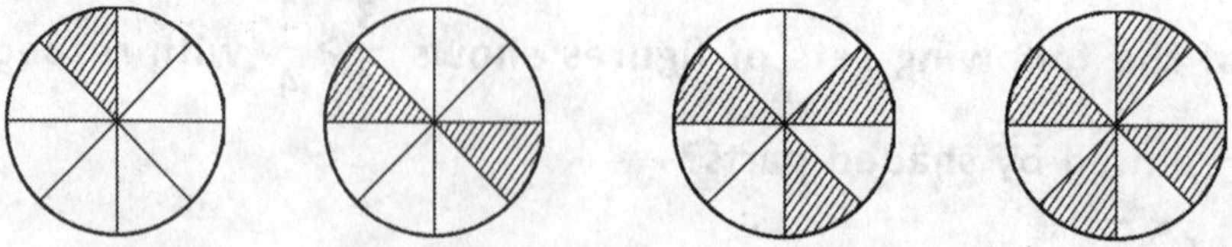

$\frac{1}{8}$ $\frac{2}{8}$ $\frac{3}{8}$ $\frac{4}{8}$

Here, denominators of all four fractions are 8 but the numerators are different. By comparing the numerators of all form fractions, we have, $1 < 2 < 3 < 4$ or, $4 > 3 > 2 > 1$

Therefore, in ascending order, it is $\frac{1}{8} < \frac{2}{8} < \frac{3}{8} < \frac{4}{8}$ or, $\frac{1}{8}, \frac{2}{8}, \frac{3}{8}, \frac{4}{8}$

In descending order, it is $\frac{4}{8} > \frac{3}{8} > \frac{2}{8} > \frac{1}{8}$ or, $\frac{4}{8}, \frac{3}{8}, \frac{2}{8}, \frac{1}{8}$

Example:

Which of the following sets of fractions are arranged from the largest to the smallest?

(A) $\frac{1}{4}, \frac{2}{4}, \frac{3}{4}, \frac{6}{4}, \frac{10}{4}$ (B) $\frac{18}{9}, \frac{16}{9}, \frac{11}{9}, \frac{4}{9}, \frac{1}{9}$

(C) $\frac{8}{3}, \frac{10}{3}, \frac{6}{3}, \frac{11}{3}, \frac{13}{3}$ (D) $\frac{12}{6}, \frac{8}{6}, \frac{9}{6}, \frac{3}{6}, \frac{4}{6}$

(E) None of these

Answer (B)

Explanation: As we know, if the denominators of the fractions are same, then the bigger fraction has the larger numerator. Here, in option (B),

$18 > 16 > 11 > 4 > 1$. Therefore, $\frac{18}{9} > \frac{16}{9} > \frac{11}{9} > \frac{4}{9} > \frac{1}{9}$

Or, in descending order, it is: $\frac{18}{9}, \frac{16}{9}, \frac{11}{9}, \frac{4}{9}, \frac{1}{9}$

Properties of Fraction

- A fraction is unity when its numerator and denominator are equal.

  For example, $\frac{3}{3} = 1$

- A fraction is equal to zero when its numerator alone is zero.

  For example, $\frac{0}{3} = 0$

- A fraction is meaningless if its denominator is zero.

  For example, $\frac{3}{0}$ is not defined.

- The value of a fraction does not change on multiplying or dividing the numerator and denominator by the same number.

  For example, $\frac{2}{3} = \frac{2\times5}{3\times5} = \frac{10}{15}$ and $\frac{10\div5}{15\div5} = \frac{2}{3}$

Example:

Convert $\frac{4}{5}$ and $\frac{3}{2}$ into like fractions.

Solution: Here, $\frac{4}{5}$ and $\frac{3}{2}$ are unlike fractions where denominators are 5 and 2.

Now, $\frac{4}{5} = \frac{4\times2}{5\times2} = \frac{8}{10}$ and, $\frac{3}{2} = \frac{3\times5}{2\times5} = \frac{15}{10}$

We have, $\frac{8}{10}$ and $\frac{15}{10}$ are equivalent fractions.

Operations with Fractions

Addition of Like Fractions

Suppose two fractions are $\frac{1}{5}$ and $\frac{3}{5}$ and we have to add them.

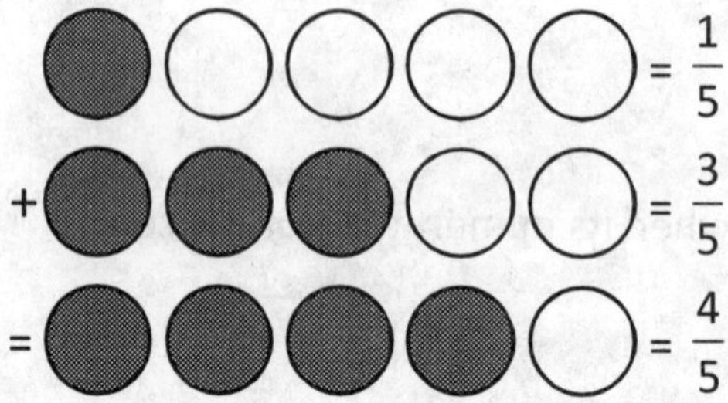

So, we have, $\frac{1}{5}+\frac{3}{5}=\frac{1+3}{5}=\frac{4}{5}$

Therefore, the sum of like fractions = $\frac{\text{Sum of Numerators}}{\text{Common Denominator}}$

Example:

When the fraction represented by the shaded parts in Figure (B) is added to the fraction represented by the shaded parts in Figure (A), the result is:

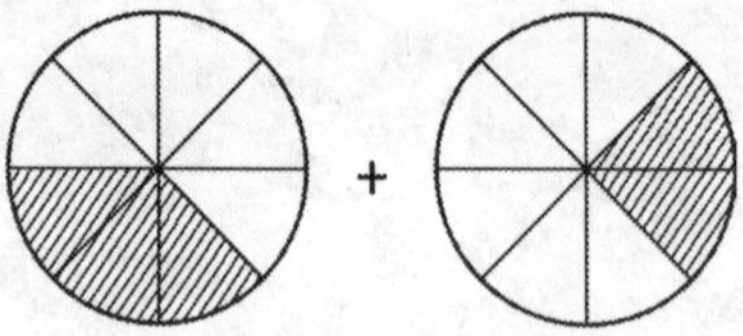

Figure (A) Figure (B)

(A) $\frac{7}{8}$ (B) $\frac{5}{8}$ (C) $\frac{3}{8}$ (D) $\frac{1}{8}$

(E) None of these

Answer (B)

Explanation: Here, 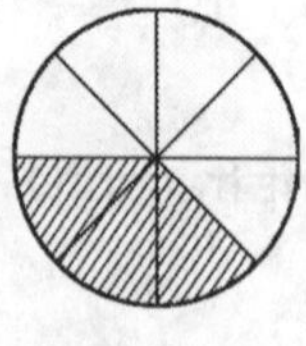 $=\frac{3}{8}$ and 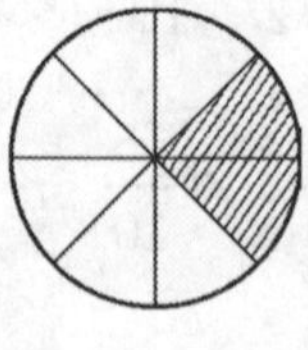 $=\frac{2}{8}$

Therefore, $\frac{3}{8}+\frac{2}{8}=\frac{3+2}{8}=\frac{5}{8}$

Subtraction of Like Fractions

Suppose two fractions are $\frac{3}{4}$ and $\frac{1}{4}$ and we have to find the difference.

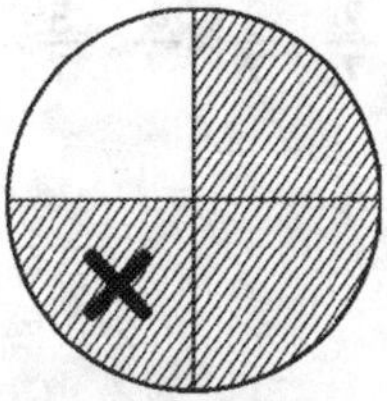

Here, each shaded part out of four parts of the circle represents $\frac{1}{4}$. If we cancle 1 out of these 3 shaded parts, we are left with 2 shaded parts. So, $\frac{3}{4}-\frac{1}{4}=\frac{3-1}{4}=\frac{2}{4}$

Therefore, the difference of like fractions = $\frac{\text{Difference of Numerators}}{\text{Common Denominator}}$

Example:

When the fraction represented by the shaded parts in Figure (B) is subtracted from the fraction represented by the shaded parts in Figure (A), the result is:

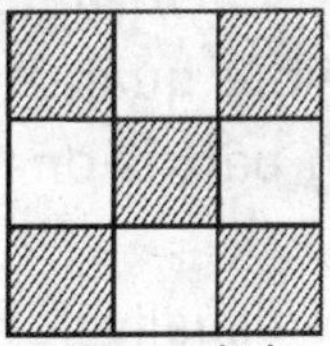

Figure (A)

−

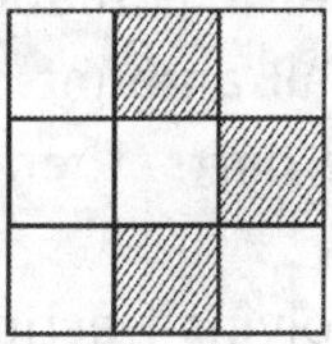

Figure (B)

(A) $\frac{2}{9}$ (B) $\frac{5}{9}$ (C) $\frac{7}{9}$ (D) $\frac{1}{9}$

(E) None of these

Answer (A)

Explanation: Here,

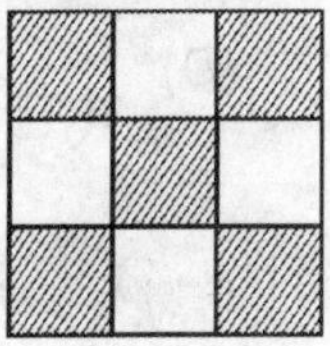

$=\frac{5}{9}$ and

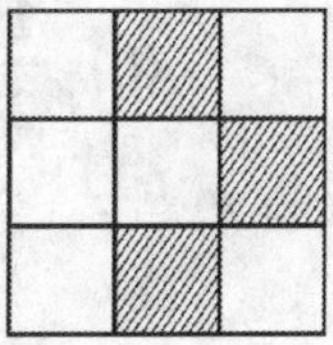

$=\frac{3}{9}$

Therefore, the required difference = $\frac{5}{9}-\frac{3}{9}=\frac{5-3}{9}=\frac{2}{9}$

Addition and Subtraction of Fractions on the Number Line

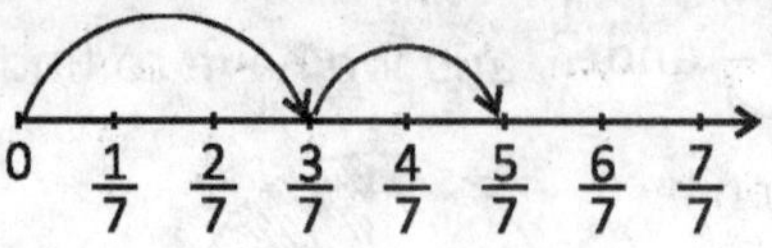

Addition: $\frac{3}{7}+\frac{2}{7}=\frac{3+2}{7}=\frac{5}{7}$

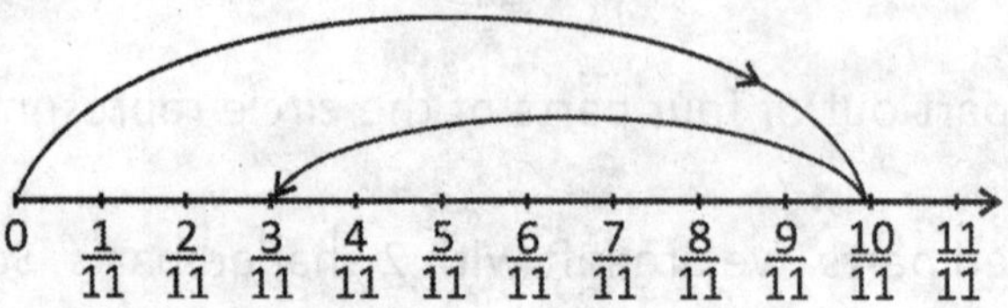

Subtraction: $\frac{10}{11}-\frac{7}{11}=\frac{10-7}{11}=\frac{3}{11}$

Word Problems Based on Fraction

A fraction is defined as a portion of the whole. It is made up of two numbers: Numerator and Denominator. Fraction is a small amount of whole quantity. For example, if a piece of wire is divided into three parts, then each part is one-third part or $\frac{1}{3}$ part of whole. The word problems involving fraction are usually based on real-life. Let us look at the following problems based on fraction.

Example:

Amit ate two-sixth of a pie and Rahul ate one-sixth of the pie. What fraction of the pie did they eat together?

(A) $\frac{1}{3}$ (B) $\frac{2}{5}$ (C) $\frac{1}{2}$ (D) $\frac{1}{4}$

(E) None of these

Answer (C)

Explanation: Fraction of pie eaten by Amit = $\frac{2}{6}$

Fraction of pie eaten by Rahul = $\frac{1}{6}$

Sum of fractions = $\frac{2}{6}+\frac{1}{6}=\frac{2+1}{6}=\frac{3}{6}=\frac{3\div 3}{6\div 3}=\frac{1}{2}$

Therefore, the required fraction = $\frac{1}{2}$

Example:

What fraction of fruits in the given tray are mangoes?

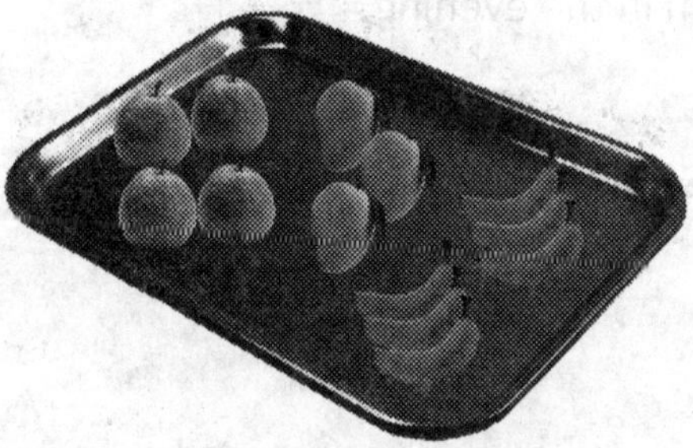

(A) $\frac{3}{13}$ (B) $\frac{4}{13}$

(C) $\frac{6}{13}$ (D) $\frac{3}{10}$

(E) None of these

Answer (A)

Explanation: Number of bananas = 6

Number of guavas = 4

Number of mangoes = 3

Total number of fruits = 6 + 4 + 3 = 13

Therefore, the required fraction of fruits = $\frac{\text{Number of mangoes}}{\text{Total number of fruits}}=\frac{3}{13}$

Example:

Meriam read $\frac{5}{9}$ of her book in the morning and $\frac{2}{9}$ in the evening. How much did she read her book now?

(A) 1 (B) $\frac{1}{9}$ (C) $\frac{4}{9}$ (D) $\frac{7}{9}$

(E) None of these

Answer (D)

Explanation: Fraction of the book read by Meriam in the morning = $\frac{5}{9}$

Fraction of the book read by Meriam in the evening = $\frac{2}{9}$

So, total fraction of the book read by Meriam = $\frac{5}{9}+\frac{2}{9} = \frac{5+2}{9} = \frac{7}{9}$

Summary

- A fraction is a part of whole or any number of equal parts. There are two numbers to every fraction, which are called **term**. A line separates the two terms. Number above the line is called **numerator** and the number below the line is called **denominator.**
- A fraction, whose numerator is 1 is called a **unit fraction**.
- Fractions, in which the denominators are same, are called the **like fractions**. Fractions, in which denominators are different, are called the **unlike fractions**.
- Fractions which have the same value, though they may look different are called **equivalent fractions**.

❖ Addition of the like fractions = $\frac{\text{Sum of numerators}}{\text{Common denominator}}$

❖ Subtraction of like fractions = $\frac{\text{Difference of denominators}}{\text{Common denominator}}$

Did You Know?

❖ The word fraction is derived from the Latin word 'fractus' which means 'to break'.

❖ Egyptians were one of the first group to study fractions and they wrote all their fractions using unit fractions.

❖ Fractions were written only in words in ancient Rome.

❖ In India, fractions were written as same as today but there was no division line between numerator and denominator.

Solved Problems

1. When the fraction represented by the shaded parts in Figure (B) is added to the fraction represented by the shaded parts in Figure (A), the result is:

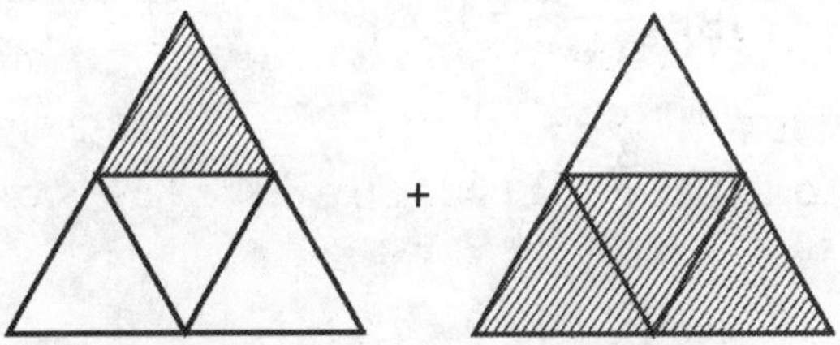

Figure (A) Figure (B)

(A) 2 (B) 1

(C) 3 (D) 4

(E) None of these

Answer (B)

Explanation: Sum of fractions represented by shaded parts = $\frac{1}{4}+\frac{3}{4}$

$$=\frac{1+3}{4}=\frac{4}{4}=\frac{4\div 4}{4\div 4}=\frac{1}{1}=1$$

2. What fraction of the whole part of given circle is shaded?

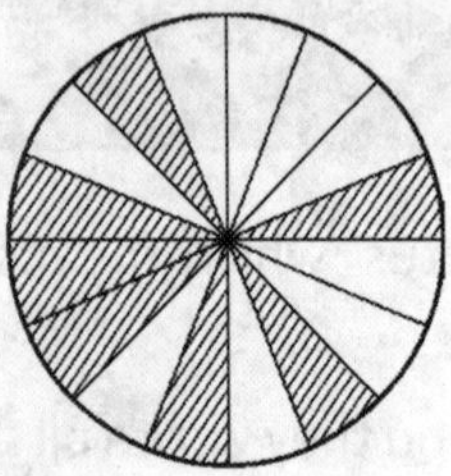

(A) $\frac{3}{8}$ (B) $\frac{7}{8}$ (C) $\frac{7}{16}$ (D) $\frac{9}{16}$

(E) None of these

Answer (C)

Explanation: Number of total parts of the circle = 16

Number of shaded parts = 7. Therefore, the required fraction = $\frac{7}{16}$

3. Which one of the following is *incorrect* expression?

(A) $\frac{3}{3}+\frac{0}{3}=1$ (B) $\frac{3}{3}-\frac{0}{3}=1$

(C) $\frac{3}{3}+\frac{3}{0}=1$ (D) $\frac{3}{3}+0=1$

(E) None of these

Answer (C)

Explanation: Here, $\frac{3}{3}=\frac{3\div 3}{3\div 3}=\frac{1}{1}=1$ and $\frac{0}{3}=0$.

But $\frac{3}{0}$ is not defined. Therefore, $\left(\frac{3}{3}+\frac{3}{0}\right)$ is not defined.

Hence, the expression $\frac{3}{3}+\frac{3}{0}=1$ given in option (C) is incorrect.

4. The sum of missing numerator and denominator in the fractions given below is:

$$\frac{\boxed{?}}{8}=\frac{1}{2}=\frac{3}{\boxed{?}}$$

(A) 12 (B) 10 (C) 8 (D) 11
(E) None of these

Answer (B)

Explanation: Here, $\frac{1}{2}=\frac{1\times4}{2\times4}=\frac{4}{8}$ and $\frac{1}{2}=\frac{1\times3}{2\times3}=\frac{3}{6}$

Therefore, $\frac{\boxed{4}}{8}=\frac{\boxed{1}}{2}$ and $\frac{1}{\boxed{2}}=\frac{3}{\boxed{6}}$

So, the required sum = 4 + 6 = 10

5. Half of the number is 80, then three-fourth of the same number will be:

(A) 100 (B) 140
(C) 120 (D) 160
(E) None of these

Answer (C)

Explanation: Half of the number = 80

Number = 80 × 2 = 160

Three-fourth of 160 = $\frac{3}{4}\times 160 = 120$

6. Which one of the following fractions is correctly matched for the fraction represented by shaded parts ?

(A) 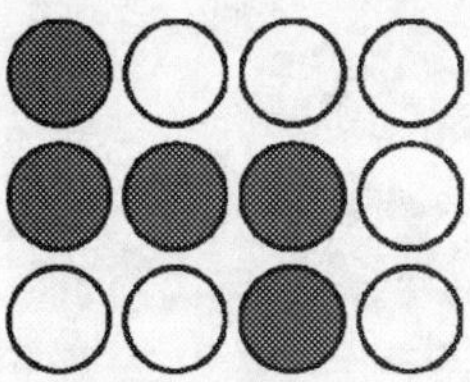 $=\frac{5}{7}$ (B) 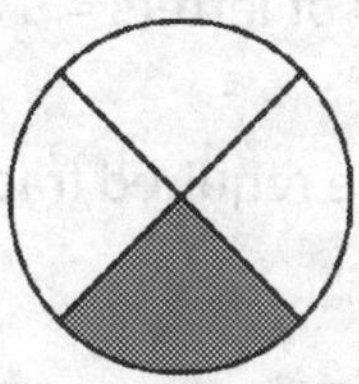 $=\frac{1}{3}$

(C) 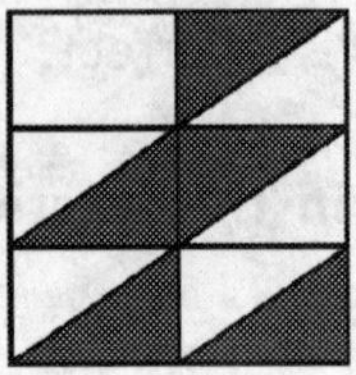 $= \frac{5}{12}$ (D) 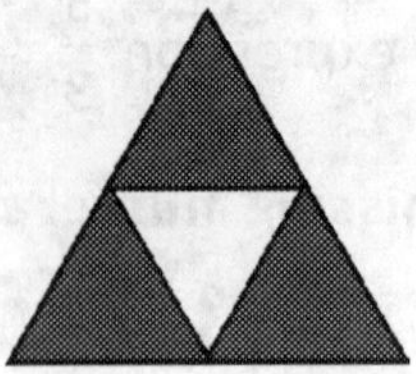 $= \frac{1}{4}$

(E) None of these

Answer (C)

Explanation: Fraction represented by shaded parts in option (A) = $\frac{5}{12}$

Fraction represented by shaded parts in option (B) = $\frac{1}{4}$

Fraction represented by shaded parts in option (C) = $\frac{5}{12}$

Fraction represented by shaded parts in option (D) = $\frac{3}{4}$

Therefore, the fraction represented by shaded parts in option (C) is correct.

7. In the word 'FRACTIONS', what fraction of letters are vowels?

(A) $\frac{2}{3}$ (B) $\frac{4}{9}$ (C) $\frac{1}{3}$ (D) $\frac{2}{9}$

(E) None of these

Answer (C)

Explanation: Given word is 'FRACTIONS'.

Vowels are: A, I, O. Number of vowels = 3

Total number of letters = 9

Therefore, the required fraction $= \frac{3}{9} = \frac{3 \div 3}{9 \div 3} = \frac{1}{3}$

8. Which one of the following sets of figures shows $\frac{2}{5} < \frac{4}{5}$ with respect to the fraction represented by shaded parts?

(A) 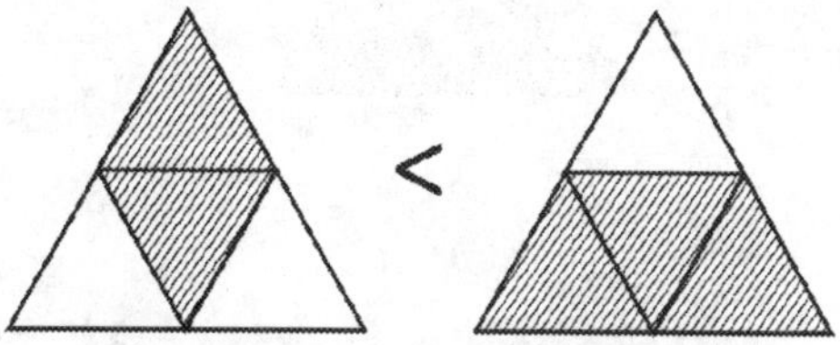

(B) 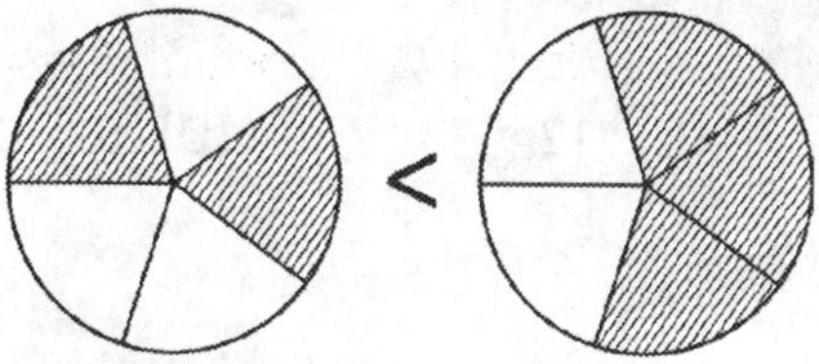

(C) 

(D) 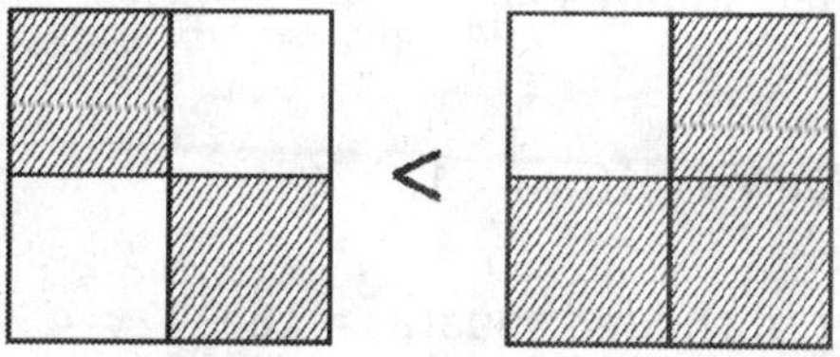

(E) None of these

Answer (C)

Explanation: In option (A), fractions represented by shaded parts is: $\frac{2}{4} < \frac{3}{4}$

In option (B), fraction represented by shaded parts is: $\frac{2}{5} < \frac{3}{5}$

In option (C), fraction represented by shaded parts is: $\frac{2}{5} < \frac{4}{5}$

In option (D), fraction represented by shaded parts is: $\frac{2}{4} < \frac{3}{4}$

Therefore, the fractions represented by the shaded parts in figure set given in option (C) shows $\frac{2}{5} < \frac{4}{5}$

9. For one square □, how many squares must be shaded so that $\frac{3}{4}$ of the given figure is *unshaded*?

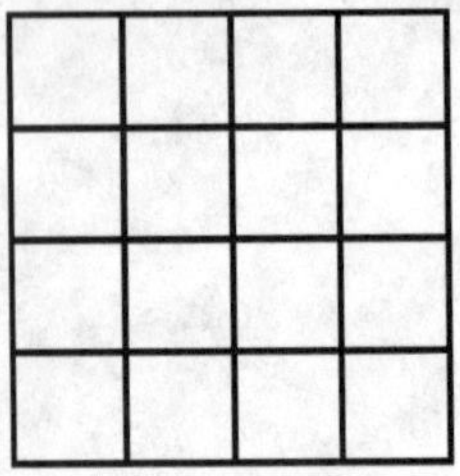

(A) 4 (B) 8 (C) 12 (D) 6

(E) None of these

Answer (A)

Explanation: Total number of squares = 16

Fraction represented by unshaded squares = $\frac{3}{4}$

So, the number of unshaded squares = $16 \times \frac{3}{4} = 12$

Therefore, the required number of shaded squares = 16 – 12 = 4

10. Rahul plays carom $\frac{2}{3}$ of an hour daily. How many minutes does Rahul play in a week?

(A) 160 minutes (B) 245 minutes

(C) 240 minutes (D) 280 minutes

(E) None of these

Answer (D)

Explanation: One hour = 60 minutes

$\frac{2}{3}$ of an hour = $\frac{2}{3}$ of 60 minutes = $\frac{2}{3} \times 60$ minutes = 40 minutes

Therefore, Rahul plays carom 40 minutes daily or (40 × 7) minutes = 280 minutes in a week.

Practice Exercise 4

1. In the figure given below, find the fraction represented by shaded parts of the whole figure.

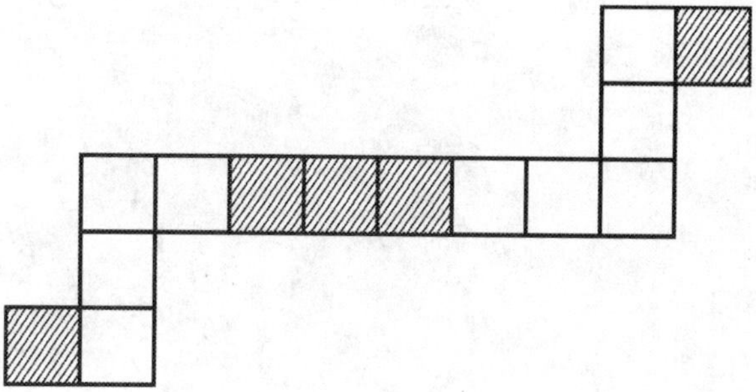

(A) $\frac{5}{13}$ (B) $\frac{6}{17}$ (C) $\frac{7}{14}$ (D) $\frac{5}{14}$

(E) None of these

2. Identify the $\frac{3}{5}$ part of 100.

(A) 50 (B) 80 (C) 60 (D) 40

(E) None of these

3. Identify the unpainted part of a wall if $\frac{5}{8}$th part of the wall is painted.

(A) $\frac{8-5}{8}$ (B) $\frac{5+8}{8}$ (C) $\frac{5-3}{8}$ (D) $\frac{5-1}{8}$

(E) None of these

4. When fraction represented by shaded parts in Figure (B) is subtracted from the fraction represented by shaded parts in Figure (A), the result is:

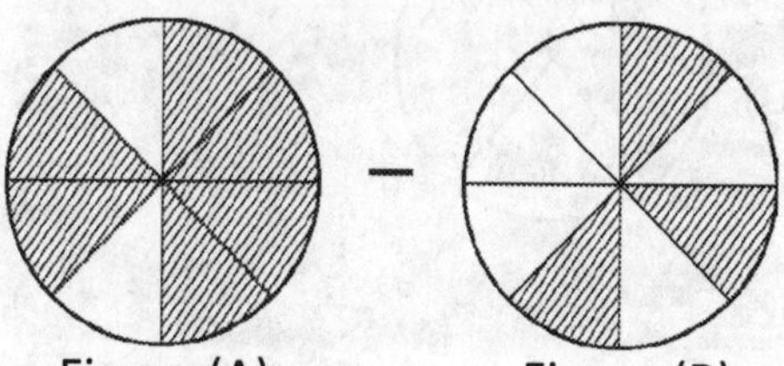

Figure (A) Figure (B)

(A) $\frac{5}{8}$ (B) $\frac{3}{8}$ (C) $\frac{1}{8}$ (D) $\frac{7}{8}$

(E) None of these

5. For one square 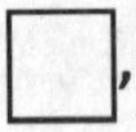 **, how many squares must be shaded so that $\frac{3}{8}$ of the given figure is *unshaded* ?**

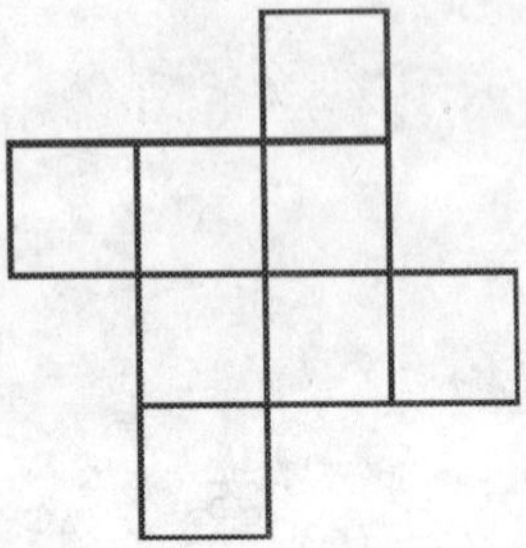

(A) 1 (B) 3

(C) 5 (D) 7

(E) None of these

6. In which one of the following figures, the fraction represented by shaded parts is $\frac{1}{4}$?

(A) 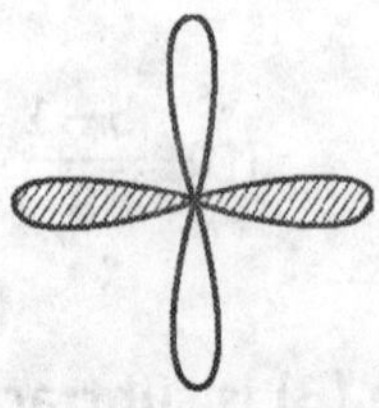

(B) 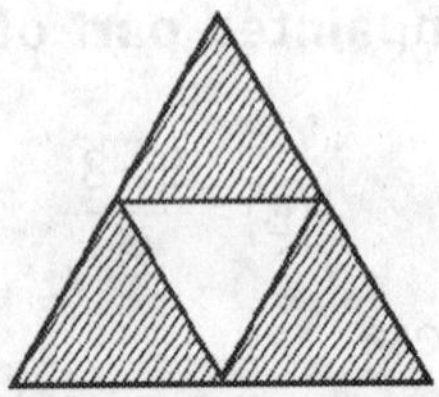

(C) 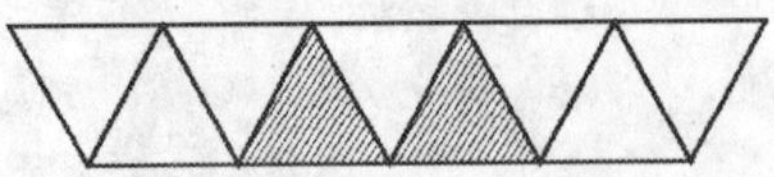

(D) 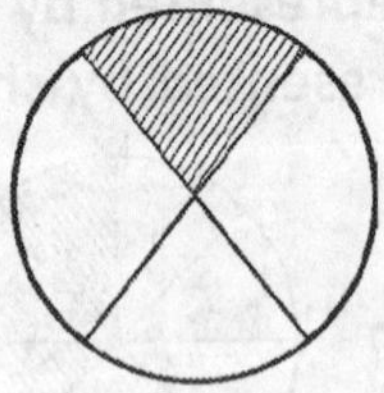

(E) None of these

7. Arrange the given fractions in ascending order and choose the correct option.

$\frac{3}{5}, \frac{2}{3}, \frac{1}{2}$

(A) $\frac{1}{2}, \frac{3}{5}, \frac{2}{3}$ (B) $\frac{2}{3}, \frac{3}{5}, \frac{1}{2}$ (C) $\frac{3}{5}, \frac{2}{3}, \frac{1}{2}$ (D) $\frac{3}{5}, \frac{1}{2}, \frac{2}{3}$

(E) None of these

8. The sum of missing numerator and denominator in the fractions given below is:

$\frac{\boxed{?}}{49} = \frac{3}{7} = \frac{24}{\boxed{?}}$

(A) 82 (B) 77 (C) 61 (D) 53

(E) None of these

9. Half of a number is 10, then the one-fourth of the same number will be:

(A) 2 (B) 8 (C) 6 (D) 4

(E) None of these

10. Codi read $\frac{3}{4}$ of his book in the class and $\frac{1}{4}$ of the book at home. What portion of the book he has read?

(A) Half of the book (B) Quarter of the book

(C) Whole of the book (D) Three-fourth of the book

(E) None of these

Chapter 5

Time and Calendar

Learning Objectives

- Introduction
- Time
- Calendar
- Problems Based on Time and Calendar

Introduction

'Time' is the ongoing sequence of events taking place. Time indicates past, present and future. Calendar is a chart or series of pages showing the days, weeks and months of a particular year. In this chapter, we will learn about 'Time and Calendar'.

Time and Clock

Time is important to plan our day. Time is the ongoing sequence of events. We use time to order events in the past, present and future. Time is passing non-stop. We use a clock or watch to measure time. Time is measured in seconds, minutes, hours, days, weeks, months and years with the help of clocks and calendars.

Parts of a Clock

We measure time with the help of a clock. A clock has three hands. The short hand is the **hour hand**, the long hand is the **minute hand** and the longest hand which length is bigger than minute hand is the **second hand**. The face of watch or clock is called its **dial**, which is divided into twelve big divisions from 1 to 12. The gaps among the numbers are divided into five small divisions that indicate minutes. Therefore, one small division between 1 and 12 which indicates 60 minutes. Minutes of a clock is calculated by the rotation of minute hand. Hour is calculated by rotation of the hour hand.

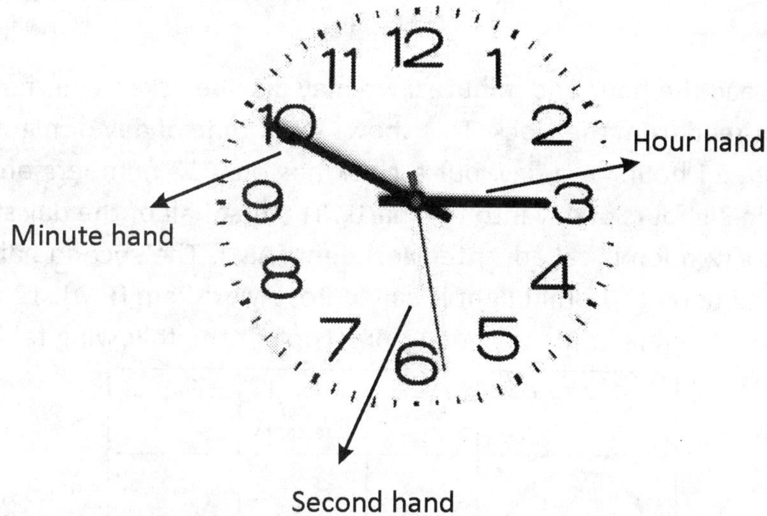

Quarter Past and Quarter To

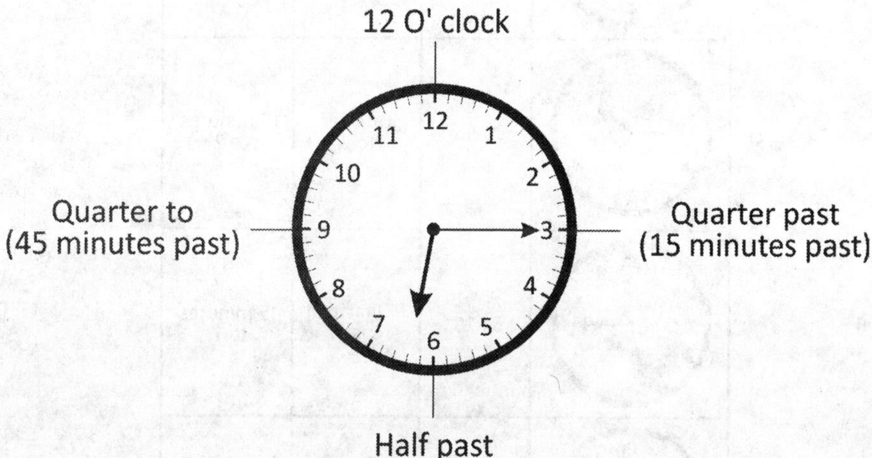

If we divide a clock into four parts, each part will be a quarter. When the minute hand of a clock has reached the number 3, it shows the first quarter is over and it is called **quarter past**. When the minute hand reaches 9, it shows that it has completed

3 quarters. As one quarter is left for the next hour, it means quarter to. We have two words here, 'past' and 'to'. Here, 'past' means the hour that the clock has crossed and 'to' means the hour it is going to complete. Now, when the minutes hand is at 6, it is 30 minutes past or half past the hour and when the minutes hand is at 9, it is 45 minutes past or 15 minutes is left for the next hour.

AM and PM

Once we can read the hour and minutes, we may also be asked whether it is AM or PM. This is not read from the clock. This shows what time of day or night it is. As we know there are 24 hours in a day, but a clock has only 12 numbers on its face (or dial). We divide 24 hours of day into two parts. The first half of the day starting from 12 midnight to 12 noon is called **Ante Meridiem (AM)**. The second half of the day starting from 12 noon to 12 midnight is called **Post Meridiem (PM)**. 12 noon means not 12 am and 12 midnight means not 12 pm. Look at the following table.

Clock Time	Time in Digit	Quarter past/ Quarter to	Minutes to
	9 : 30	Half past 9	30 minutes to 10
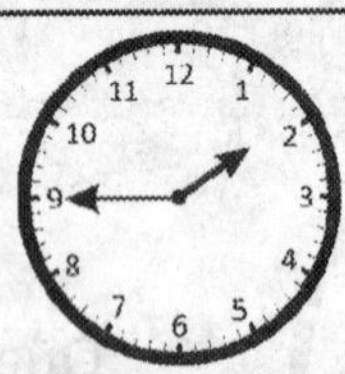	1 : 45	Quarter to 2	15 minutes to 2
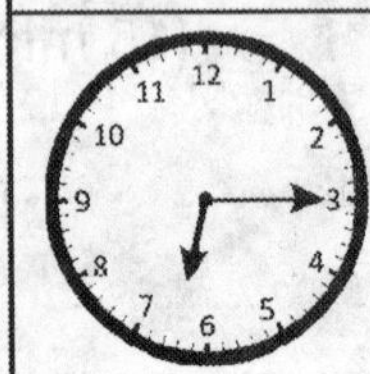	6 : 15	Quarter past 6	45 minutes to 7
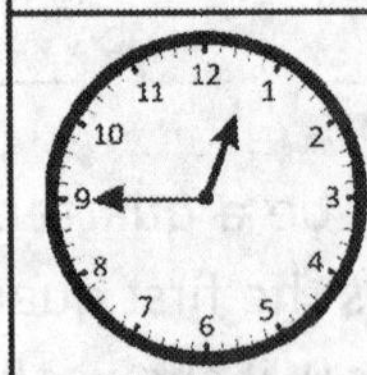	12 : 45	Quarter to 1	15 minutes to 1

Here time shown by each clock convey the same meaning.

Example:

Which one of the following clocks shows the time 15 minutes to 6?

(A) 

(B) 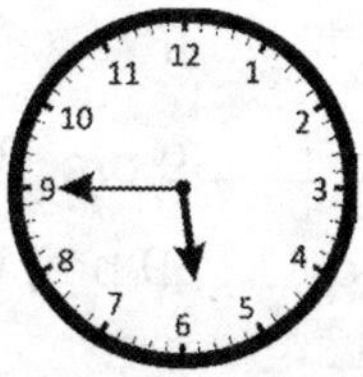

(C) 

(D) 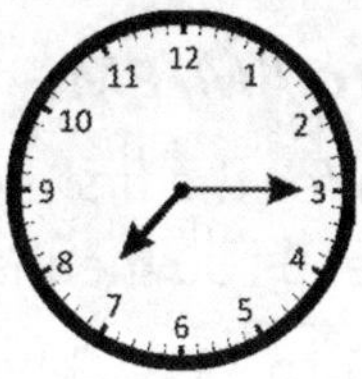

(E) None of these

Answer (B)

Explanation: Time shown by the clock given in option (B) is 5 : 45 which is Quarter to 6 or 15 minutes to 6.

24-Hour Clock

A 24-hour clock displays the time as the hour passed since midnight. This clock is used without 'AM' or 'PM'. In 24-hour clock, the day runs from midnight to midnight and it is divided into 24 hours. The 24-hour clock starts at midnight (00 : 00) and it indicates the hours passed from 0 to 23. The 24-hour time format is also sometimes known as military time. Normally time is shown as **Hours : Minutes** in the 24-hour clock. There are 24 hour in a day and 60 minutes in each hour. For example, 14 : 52 hours means 14 hours 52 minutes.

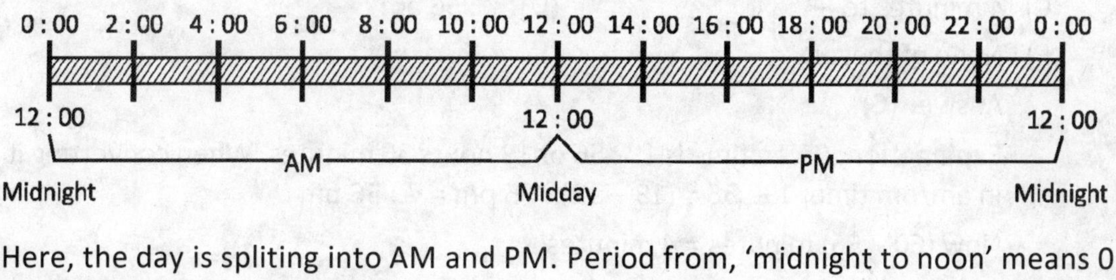

Here, the day is spliting into AM and PM. Period from, 'midnight to noon' means 0 : 00 to 11 : 59 and 'noon to midnight' means 12 : 00 to 25 : 59.

Converting AM/PM to 24 Hour Clock

1. We add 12 hours to any hour after noon and subtract 12 hours for the first hour of the day. For the first hour of the day or from 12 midnight to 12 : 59 am, we subtract 12 hours. For example, 12 midnight means 0 : 00 and 12 : 41 means 0 : 41.
2. From 1 : 00 am to 12 : 59 pm, there is no change.
3. From 1 : 00 pm to 11 : 59 pm, we add 12 hours. For example, 7 : 45 pm means (7 + 12) : 45 = 19 : 45.

Converting 24 Hours to AM/PM

1. We add 12 hours for the first hour of the day or from 0 : 00 to 0 : 59 to make it 'am'. For example, 0 : 30 means (0 + 12) : 30 am or 12 : 30 am.
2. Time from 1 : 00 to 11 : 59, we just make it 'am'. For example, 9 : 30 means 9 : 30 am.
3. Time from 12 : 00 to 12 : 59, we first make it 'pm'. For example, 12 : 45 means 12 : 45 pm.
4. Time from 13 : 00 to 23 : 59, we subtract 12 hours from it to make it pm. For example, 17 : 35 means (17–12) : 35 pm or, 5 : 35 pm.

Example:

Time shown by the clock given below is same as:

(A) 9 : 56 pm

(B) Quarter past 7

(C) 4 minutes to 8

(D) 7 : 56 am

(E) None of these

Answer (C)

Explanation: Given time is 19 : 56 or 19 hours 56 minutes. When converting it in am/pm time, 19 : 56 = (19 – 12) : 56 pm = 7 : 56 pm

Now (60 – 56) minutes = 4 minutes

Therefore, 7 : 56 pm means 4 minutes to 8.

Conversion of Time

One minute is equal to 60 seconds and one hour is equal to 60 minutes, therefore, one unit can be converted into another. For example, 110 minutes can be converted into hour as: 110 = 60 minutes + 50 minutes = 1 hour 50 minutes. Look at the following time-conversion table.

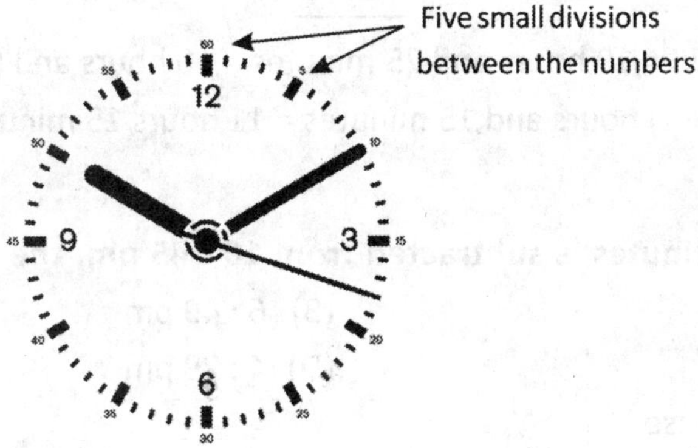

Adding and Subtracting Time

While adding or subtracting time, we add or subtract the hours and minutes separately. If the minutes end up 60 or more than 0 or less than 0, we need to do same adjustment in the minutes. Following are the steps for the addition and subtraction of times.

Step 1 : Add or Subtract the hours.

Step 2 : Add or Subtract the minutes.

Step 3 : **For addition**: If sum of minutes is 60 or more, subtract 60 from the minutes and add 1 hour to given hours.

For Subtraction: While subtracting minutes, take borrow from hours if needed. Remember that 1 hour = 60 minutes.

Example:

When 7 hours 50 minutes is added to 3 : 25 am, the new time is:

(A) 10 : 55 am (B) 10 : 45 am

(C) 11 : 15 am (D) 11 : 45 am

(E) None of these

Answer (C)

Explanation: Here, addition of hours and minutes is as follow:

$$\begin{array}{r} \boxed{H : M} \\ 3 : 25 \\ +\,7 : 50 \\ \hline 10 : 75 \\ \hline \end{array}$$

Now, 10 : 75 = 10 hours and 75 minutes = 10 hours and (60 + 15) minutes

= (10 + 1) hours and 15 minutes = 11 hours 15 minutes = 11 : 15 am

Example:

When 3 hours 56 minutes is subtracted from 10 : 45 pm, the new time is:

(A) 6 : 39 pm

(B) 6 : 49 pm

(C) 5: 39 pm

(D) 4 : 29 pm

(E) None of these

Answer (B)

Explanation: Here, subtraction hours and minutes is as follow:

$$\begin{array}{r} \text{(9)} \quad \text{(105)} \\ \boxed{H : M} \\ \cancel{10} : \cancel{45} \\ -\;\; 3 : 56 \\ \hline 6 : 49 \\ \hline \end{array}$$

So we have, the new time is 6 : 49 pm

Calendar

Birthdays, anniversaries, appointments and holidays, etc, all these have one thing in common, it is a day. Without the calendar, people everywhere would forget birthdays, anniversaries, miss appointments and never known what day. It is difficult to remember dates, so for that calendar comes to our rescue. Calendar helps us to know the days and months of a year. Calendar is a tool to tell time also.

2016

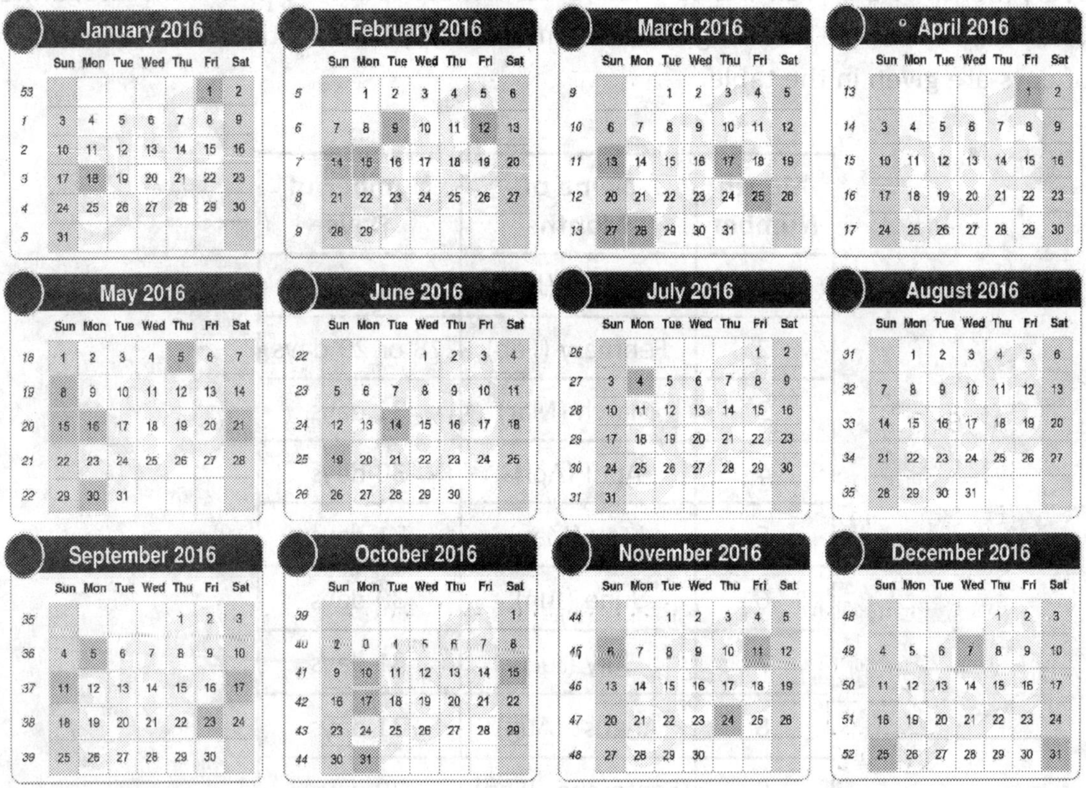

Days and Dates on Calendar

Calendar is a chart or series of pages showing the days, weeks and months of a particular year.

Sun	Mon	Tue	Wed	Thu	Fri	Sat
		1	2	3	4	5
6	7	8	9	10	11	12
13	14	15	16	17	18	19
20	21	22	23	24	25	26
27	28	29	30	31		

The name of days and months are arranged in a proper way. The name of days and months are shown on the calendar. The names of days are arranged in upper row for every month of the year. The calendar used in most countries now is the Gregarine Calendar. Look at the following table. The months of year, its Latin name and number of days are given in the table.

Month Number	Name of Months	Number of Days
1	January (Jan)	31 days
2	February (Feb)	28 or 29 days
3	March (Mar)	31 days
4	April (Apr)	30 days
5	May (May)	31 days
6	June (Jun)	30 days
7	July (Jul)	31 days
8	August (Aug)	31 days
9	September (Sep)	30 days
10	October (Oct)	31 days
11	November (Nov)	30 days
12	December (Dec)	31 days

Writing a Date

Sometimes, a date is written in long form. For example, **Sunday, August 17, 2016**. Clearly, there are commas after the day of the week and the day of the month, but there is no comma after the month. We can write a date in numerical form also. For example 17/8/2016 or 8/17/2016. Here, it is **date/month/year** or **month/date/year**. In some countries, it is **year/month/date**.

To write a date, steps are as follow:

Step 1 : First, write down the number of days of month.

Step 2 : Put a dot (.) or a slash (/) after the number of days.

Step 3 : Write down the number or name of the month after date.

Step 4 : Again put one more dot (.) or slash (/) after the number of month name.

Step 5 : Now, write down the year in number.

Example:

How many months in a year have 30 days?

(A) 6 (B) 4 (C) 7 (D) 5

(E) None of these

Answer (B)

Explanation: The month which have 30 days are April, June, September and November.

Example:

Two seats were reserved for a couple on the second of November 2011. Which one of the following dates represents the date on the printed ticket?

(A) 2/2011/11 (B) 2/11/2011

(C) 10/2/2011 (D) 2.11/2011

(E) None of these

Answer (B)

Explanation: Second of November means November 2.

As we know, the correct form of date is: date/month/year or month/date/year or year/month/date. Therefore, printed date for second November 2011 is 2/11/2011 or 11/2/2011 or 2011/11/2.

Common Year and Leap Year

A common year is a calendar year with exactly 365 days. The common year of 365 days has exactly 52 weeks and one day. A leap year is a year containing one additional day. A leap year has 366 days where the month of February is of 29 days instead of 28 days. A leap year occurs every four years. 2001, 2002, 2011, 2015 are common year while 2000, 2004, 2008, 2012, 2016 are leap years.

Calendar Facts

- There are 7 days in a week.
- There are 12 months in a year.
- In a leap year, February has 29 days.
- There are 4 months have 30 days in a year.
- There are 7 months have 31 days in a year.
- The shortest month of all in a year is February.
- A year will be leap year if it is divisible by 4 but not by 100. For example, 2008 is a leap year.
- A year will be leap year if it is divisible by 4 and 400 separately. For example, 2000 is a leap year because it is divisible by 4 and 400 separately, but 1900 is not a leap year because it is only divisible by 4 but not by 400.
- 14 days of a month make one fortnight.
- A leap year comes in every four years.

Problems Based on Time and Calendar

Some problems based on time and calendar are given below. Let us study these examples.

Example:

Susan was in hospital from 7th October to 27th October last year. She was in hospital for:

(A) 19 days (B) 21 days (C) 23 days (D) 20 days

(E) None of these

Answer (B)

Explanation: On counting the number of days from 7th October to 27th October including 7th and 27th, the number of days = 21

Example:

On the basis of clock time, which one of the following is a wrong statement?

(A) Monica takes her breakfast at 7 : 30 am

(B) Dinner is served at 8 : 30 am

(C) My lunch break starts at 12 : 30 pm

(D) The sun rises at 5 am daily.

(E) None of these

Answer (B)

Explanation: 8 : 30 am means morning time. Dinner is served at 8 : 30 pm at night.

Example:

Sum of the numbers of days of the months begin their name with the letter "J" is:

(A) 90 (B) 91 (C) 92 (D) 93

(E) None of these

Answer (C)

Explanation: Months start with letter "J" are: January (31), June (30), July (31).

Sum of the numbers of days = 31 + 30 + 31 = 92

Example:

Two-third of the number of days in a leap year is:

(A) 183 days (B) 122 days (C) 244 days (D) 300 days

(E) None of these

Answer (C)

Explanation: Number of days in a leap year = 366

$\frac{2}{3}$ of 366 = 366 × $\frac{2}{3}$ = 122 × 2 = 244

Example:

Mona started picking apples in an orchard at 10 : 30 am. She filled 3 buckets in 4 hours and then stopped. What time was it when Mona stopped picking apples?

(A) 10 : 30 pm (B) 2 : 30 pm

(C) 3 : 30 pm (D) 1 : 30 pm

(E) None of these

Answer (B)

Explanation: Starting time = 10 : 30 am

Time after 4 hours = 10 : 30 am + 4 hours = (10 + 4) : 30 hours

= 14 : 30 hours = (14 – 12) : 30 pm = 2 : 30 pm

Summary

- **Time** is the ongoing sequence of events and it is passing non-stop. We use a clock or a watch to measure time.
- Time is measured in seconds, minutes, hours, days, weeks, months and years with clocks and calendars.
- If we divide a clock into four equal parts, each part will be a **quarter**.
- '**Quarter past**' means the hour that the clock has crossed. '**Quarter to**' means the hour it is going to complete.
- The first half of the day starting from 12 midnight to 12 noon is called **Ante Meridiem** or **Ante Meridian** or **AM**.
- The second half of day starting from 12 noon to 12 midnight is called **Post Meridiem** or **Post Meridian** or **PM**.
- In 24-hour clock, the day runs from midnight to midnight and it is divided in 24 hours.
- **Calendar** is a chart or series of pages showing the days, weeks, and months of a particular year.

Did You Know?

- The Latin word 'Meridiem' or 'Meridian' means 'Midday'.
- Our 24-hour day comes from the ancient Egyptians who divided day-time in 10 hours.
- Egyptians used sundials that divided a sunlit day into 10 parts plus two 'twilight hours' in the morning and evening.
- Europeans were first made the mechanical clock very similar to that we use today.

Solved Problems

1. In a year, a month is of 31 days which comes in between the months those have 30 days. The name of the month is:

(A) December (B) May

(C) February (D) September

(E) None of these

Answer (B)

Explanation: April comes just before May which has 30 days and June comes just after May which has 30 days.

Therefore, May is the month of 31 days which comes in between the months those have 30 days.

2. Which one of the following years had 366 days?

(A) 2010 (B) 2006

(C) 2008 (D) 2014

(E) None of these

Answer (C)

Explanation: The year 2008 has exactly divisible by 4 and also not divisible by 100. Therefore, 2008 was a leap year and which had 29 days in the month of February or 366 days in the year.

3. How many days are there in the month which comes in between the month of October and December?

(A) 28 (B) 31

(C) 30 (D) 29

(E) None of these

Answer (C)

Explanation: The month which comes in between October and December is November and there are 30 days in the month of November.

4. 13 hours before 7 : 30 pm is:

(A) 6 : 30 pm (B) 10 : 30 am

(C) 5 : 30 am (D) 6 : 30 am

(E) None of these

Answer (D)

Explanation: Here, 7 : 30 pm when converted in 24 hour,

7 : 30 pm = (7 + 12) : 30 hours = 19 : 30 hours

Now, the time difference is as follow:

H : M
19:30
−13:00
6:30

Now, when 6 : 30 hours is converted in am/pm

it is: (6: 30) hours = (6 – 0): 30 am = 6 : 30 am

5. Kanika said that the time is 9 : 30 in her clock. Which of the following clocks is Kanika's clock?

(A) 

(B) 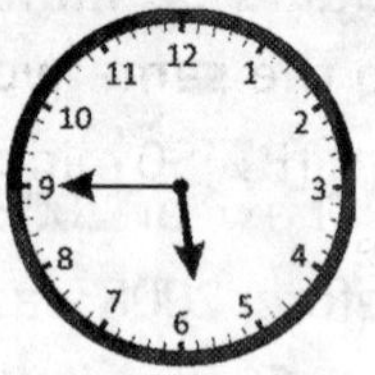

(C) 

(D) 

(E) None of these

Answer (C)

Explanation: Time shown by clock given in option (C) is 9 : 30 because its minute hand is at 6 which shows 30 minutes and its hour hand is at 9.

6. Amit's birthday is on October 23, 20XX. Rahul's birthday is just five days before Amit's birthday. When is the Rahul's birthday?

October 20XX

Sun	Mon	Tue	Wed	Thu	Fri	Sat
			1	2	3	4
5	6	7	8	9	10	11
12	13	14	15	16	17	18
19	20	21	22	23	24	25
26	27	28	29	30	31	

(A) October 17 (B) October 18 (C) October 28 (D) October 25
(E) None of these

Answer (B)

Explanation: Amit's birthday is on October 23. Five days before Amit's birthday is October (23 – 5) = October 18. Therefore, Rahul's birthday is on October 18.

7. Raman takes 4 hours 50 minutes to do a work and Mohan takes 5 hours 40 minutes to do the same work. How much more time does Mohan take?

(A) 40 minutes (B) 50 minutes (C) 45 minutes (D) 55 minutes
(E) None of these

Answer (B)

Explanation: Time taken by Raman = 4 hours 50 minutes = 4 : 50 hours.

Time taken by Mohan = 5 hours 40 minutes = 5 : 40 hours.

So, the time difference is as follow:

(4) (100)
H : M
5 : 40
– 4 : 50
0 : 50

Therefore, Mohan takes 50 minutes more to do the same work.

8. A train starts everyday at 7 : 05 am from New Delhi Railway Station and reaches the Howrah Railway Station at 6 : 40 am next day. How much time does it take to reach Howrah Railway Station?

(A) 23 hours 35 minutes

(B) 40 hours 25 minutes

(C) 42 hours 15 minutes

(D) 19 hours 35 minutes

(E) None of these

Answer (A)

Explanation: Here, 7 : 05 am when converted in 24-hour clock, it is 7 : 05 hours. 6 : 40 am when converted in 24-hour clock, it is 6 : 40 hours. Now, as the train reaches Howrah next day, we add 24 hours to its arrival time that is: (6 + 24) : 40 hours = 30 : 40 hours

$$\begin{array}{r} 30:40 \text{ hours} \\ -\ 7:05 \text{ hours} \\ \hline \end{array}$$

Therefore, the required time difference = 23 : 35 hours

So, the train takes 23 hours 35 minutes to reach the Howrah Railway Station.

9. In a mathematics test paper, the maximum time to solve the paper is 45 minutes. If the test starts at 10 : 55 am, at what time does it end?

(A) 9 : 40 am

(B) 11 : 40 am

(C) 11 : 50 am

(D) 11 : 30 am

(E) None of these

Answer (B)

Explanation: Given that the test starts at 10 : 55 am.

Now in 24-hour clock, it is 10 : 55 hours.

So, the maximum time for the test = 45 minutes

H : M
10 : 55
+ 0 : 45
10 : 100

Therefore, the end time for test = 10 : 100

Or, end time = 10 : 100 = (10 + 1) : (100 – 60) am = 11 : 40 am

So, at 11 : 40 am the test will end.

10. Susan spent 21 days at summer camp. How many weeks did she spend at the camp?

(A) 2 weeks

(B) 3 weeks

(C) 4 weeks

(D) 5 weeks

(E) None of these

Answer (B)

Explanation: As we know, there are 7 days in a week. Susan spent 21 days at the camp. Therefore, the required number of weeks = 21 ÷ 7 = 3

We have, Susan spend 3 weeks at the summer camp.

Practice Exercise 5

1. **Yesterday was Thursday. What day will be the 4th day after tomorrow?**

(A) Sunday
(B) Tuesday
(C) Wednesday
(D) Thursday
(E) None of these

2. **Rahul's birthday falls on the day just before 3rd Monday of the April 20XX. When is Rahul's birthday?**

April 20XX

S	M	T	W	T	F	S
	1	2	3	4	5	6
7	8	9	10	11	12	13
14	15	16	17	18	19	20
21	22	23	24	25	26	27
28	29	30				

(A) April 18, 20XX
(B) April 14, 20XX
(C) April 15, 20XX
(D) April 16, 20XX
(E) None of these

3. **4 hours after the time shown by the clock given below is:**

(A) 6 : 20
(B) 4 : 20
(C) 5 : 40
(D) 3 : 40
(E) None of these

4. **Peter is making the calendar for bulletin board as shown below. Which day of the week will be on March 17, 20XX?**

March 20XX

Sun	Mon	Tue	Wed	Thu	Fri	Sat
			1	2	3	4
5	6	7	8	9	10	11

(A) Thursday (B) Wednesday
(C) Friday (D) Saturday
(E) None of these

5. **How many days are there in 7 weeks?**

(A) 51 days (B) 47 days (C) 48 days (D) 46 days
(E) None of these

6. **If we add 3 hours 45 minutes in the time shown by the given 24-hours clock, the new time in am/pm will be:**

(A) 7 : 35 pm (B) 10 : 35 pm (C) 9 : 45 am (D) 11 : 45 pm
(E) None of these

7. **Rahul said that the time is 2 : 40 in his clock. Which of the following clocks is Rahuls's clock?**

(A) 

(B) 

(C) 

(D) 

(E) None of these

8. Sum of the numbers of days of the last three months in a year is:

(A) 91 days (B) 92 days

(C) 90 days (D) 93 days

(E None of these

9. A bus started from a town X at 6 : 45 am and reached another town Y at 10 : 20 am. How much time did it take to reach the town Y?

(A) 3 hours 35 minutes

(B) 2 hours 55 minutes

(C) 3 hours 45 minutes

(D) 3 hours 55 minutes

(E) None of these

10. In a year, Monday is the first day of the month of March. Which one of the following sets of dates comes on Monday in the same month?

(A) 1, 8, 16, 22, 29

(B) 17, 16, 23, 30

(C) 1, 8, 15, 22, 29

(D) 2, 9, 16, 23, 30

(E) None of these

Chapter 6

Money

Learning Objectives

- Introduction
- Indian Currency
- Conversion of Rupees and Paise
- Addition Involving Money
- Subtraction Involving Money
- Bills and Rate Charts
- Word Problems Involving Money

Introduction

Money involves earning spending and saving. In ancient world, coins were made up of gold and silver. Now a days, money is available in two forms: Coins and Banknotes or Notes. The value of money is denominated on the notes and coins. in this chapter, we will learn about money and its calculation.

Indian Currency

Currency is a generally accepted form of money, including coins and paper notes. Different countries use different currencies. Indian currency is known as **Rupees**. Symbol for Indian rupees is '₹' and Symbol for Indian paise is 'p'. We write 78 rupees as ₹ 78 and 50 paise as 50 p. There are 100 paise in one rupee. Suppose we have rupees one hundred four and twenty five paise. We can express the amount by using decimal notation also as ₹ 104.25.

In India, the denominated coins are: 50 p, ₹ 1, ₹ 2, ₹ 5, ₹ 10, ₹ 20, ₹ 50, ₹ 100, ₹ 200, ₹ 500 and ₹ 2000. In international market, Indian rupees is known as **INR (Indian Rupees)**.

Look at the following pictures of denominated Indian coins:

Paise 50

Rupee. 1

Rupee. 2

Rupees 5

Rupees 10

Look at the following pictures of denominated Indian rupees:

₹ 5

₹ 10

₹ 20

₹ 50

₹ 100

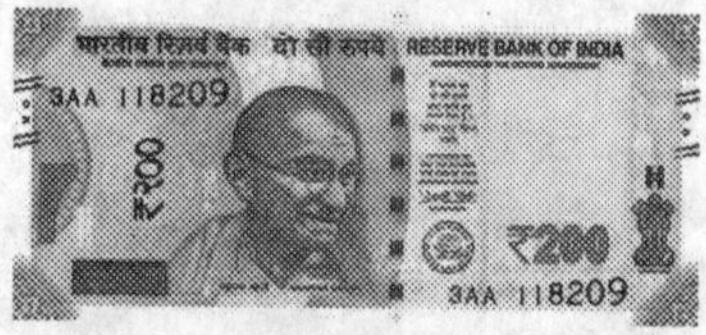

₹ 200

₹ 500

₹ 2000

Example:

Which one of the following is *incorrect*?

(A) All countries use the different currency.

(B) When we buy some items, we get some money.

(C) Spending all our money leaves we with no saving.

(D) Saving regularly helps to take care of sudden expenses.

(E) None of these

Answer (B)

Explanation: When we buy some items, we give some money.

Conversion of Rupees and Paise

As we know, 1 rupee is equal to 100 paise. Let us convert 350 paise into rupees. 350 paise = (100 + 100 + 100 + 50) paise

= (1 + 1 + 1) rupees + 50 paise = 3 rupees + 50 paise = 3.50 rupees

We can convert rupees and paise by multiplying and dividing also. Let us study the following rules.

Conversion of Rupees into Paise

To convert rupees into paise, we multiply the amount in rupees by 100. For example, ₹ 3 = 3 × 100 paise = 300 paise

Conversion of Rupees and Paise into Paise

To convert rupees and paise into paise, we multiply the amount in rupees by 100 and add it to the number of paise. For example, ₹ 7.50 = ₹ 7 and 50 p

= (7 × 100 + 50) paise = (700 + 50) paise = 750 paise

Conversion of Paise into Rupees and Paise

To convert paise into rupees, we have a dot (.) after two digits from the given number showing paise. The number on the left of the dot shows the number of rupees and that of its right shows the number of paise.

For example, 350 p = ₹ 3.50 = ₹ 3 and 50 p = 3 rupees 50 paise

Example:

Change ₹ 6.50 into paise.

(A) 600 paise
(B) 650 paise
(C) 65 paise
(D) 6500 paise
(E) None of these

Answer (B)

Explanation: Here, conversion is as follow: ₹ 6.50 = ₹ 6 and 50 p

= (6 × 100 + 50) paise = (600 + 50) paise = 650 paise

Also, ₹ 6.50 = 6 rupees + 50 paise = (1 + 1 + 1 + 1 + 1 + 1) rupees + 50 paise

= (100 + 100 + 100 + 100 + 100 + 100) paise + 50 paise

= 600 paise + 50 paise = 650 paise

Example:

Change 450 paise into rupees.

(A) ₹4 (B) ₹45 (C) ₹5.40 (D) ₹4.50

(E) None of these

Answer (D)

Explanation: Here, conversion is as follow: 450 paise = 400 paise + 50 paise

= (100 + 100 + 100 + 100) p + 50 p = ₹(1 + 1 + 1 + 1) + 50 p

= ₹4 + 50 p = ₹4.50

Also, 450 paise = 400 paise + 50 paise = ₹ $\frac{400}{100}$ + 50 p = ₹4 + 50 p = ₹4.50

Addition Involving Money

To add the given amount of money, steps are given below:

Step 1: First, express the given amount in figures and use dot (.) showing paise.

Step 2: Arrange the given amounts in a column in such a way that all the dots (.) fall in one column.

Step 3: Then, add the digits of amounts.

Step 4: Put the dot (.) in dot's column when the sum is obtained.

Step 5: Take the sum as amount.

Example:

Find the amount in rupees of the sum given below.

(38 rupees 50 paise + 30 rupees 25 paise)

(A) ₹68.75 (B) ₹67.50 (C) ₹68.50 (D) ₹69.25

(E) None of these

Answer (A)

Explanation: We have, 38 rupees 50 paise

= ₹38 + 50 p = ₹(38 + 0.50) = ₹38.50

And, 30 rupees 25 paise = ₹30 + 25 p = ₹(30 + 0.25) = 30.25

Now, the sum of amounts is as follow:

```
  ₹38.50
 +₹30.25
 -------
  ₹68.75
 -------
```

Hence, the required sum = ₹ 38 .50 + ₹ 30.25 = ₹ (38.50 + 30.25) = ₹ 68.75

Subtraction Involving Money

To subtract the given amount of money steps are given below:

Step 1 : First, express the given amounts in figures and use dot (.) showing paise.

Step 2 : Arrange the given amounts in a column in such a way that all the dots (.) fall in one column.

Step 3 : Then, subtract the digits of amounts.

Step 4 : Put the dot (.) in dot's column when the difference is obtained.

Step 5 : Take the difference as amount.

Example:

Find the amount in rupees of the difference given below.

(29 rupees 45 paise – 18 rupees 65 paise)

(A) ₹ 10.20 (B) ₹ 9.80

(C) ₹ 10.80 (D) ₹ 11.20

(E) None of these

Answer (C)

Explanation: We have, 29 rupees 45 paise = ₹ 29 + 45 p = ₹ (29 + 0.45)

= ₹ 29.45

And, 18 rupees 65 paise = ₹ 18 + 65 p = ₹ (18 + 0.65) = ₹ 18.65

Now, the difference in amounts is as follow:

```
     (8) (14)
  ₹ 2 9 . 4 5
 -₹ 1 8 . 6 5
 ------------
  ₹ 1 0 . 8 0
 ------------
```

Hence, the required difference = ₹ 29.45 – ₹ 18.65 = ₹ 10.80

Bills and Rate Charts

A bill is a written or printed statement showing how much money you two for goods or services. Bill is a very important part of buying and selling. Look at the following example.

Priyanka went to a garment shop with her father. She bought the following items.

Garment Store

245, Bhikaji Cama Place, Delhi

Date : 25/07/2016 Bill no. 342

S. No.	Item	Rate per Item	₹	p
1.	2 Salwar suit	500	1000	00
2.	3 T-shirt	200	600	00
3.	1 Jacket	700	700	00
4.	2 Jeans	800	1600	00
5.	5 Pair of shoks	40	200	00
		Total	4100	00

Signature of Shopkeeper

Look at the bill prepared by the shopkeeper. Here, the shopkeeper made a proper bill mentioning the items, quantity and rates. Name and address of the shop, date of purchase, bill number, signature of the shopkeeper all these are parts of a bill. The bill shown above contains everything that is required. Let us look at the following examples based on bills and rate charts.

Example:

Joseph went for shopping for the Christmas party. He bought the items for which the bill is given below:

S. No.	Item	Rate per Item	₹	p
1.	1 Hat	135	135	00
2.	3 Packets of balloons	20	60	00
3.	50 Paper plates	4	200	00
		Total		

How much money did Joseph left with him if he gave the shopkeeper a ₹500 note?

(A) ₹135 (B) ₹105 (C) ₹115 (D) ₹95
(E) None of these

Answer (B)

Explanation: Here, total bill amount = ₹135 + ₹60 + ₹200 = ₹395

Now, Joseph give the shopkeeper = ₹500

Therefore, money left with Joseph = ₹500 – ₹395 = ₹105

Example:

Observe the menu given below and answer the following questions.

Food's Corner	
SNACKS	
Vada Pav	₹60.00
Tomato Soup	₹40.00
Mixed Salad	₹20.00
DESSERTS	
Chocolate	₹45.00
Lassi	₹30.00
Fruit Salad	₹25.00
DRINKS	
Milk	₹20.00
Cold Drink	₹18.00

1. **Amit ordered one Vada Pav, one Tomato Soup and one glass of Lassi. How much did he spend in all?**

(A) ₹110 (B) ₹120 (C) ₹200 (D) ₹130
(E) None of these

Answer (D)

Explanation: Here, the sum amount as per their rates is as follow:

Vada Pav	=	₹60.00
Tomato Soup	=	₹40.00
Lassi	=	₹30.00
Total	=	₹130.00

Therefore, Amit spent total ₹130.00 on all three items.

2. **Rahul ordered the most expensive food from each course and a Fruit Salad. How much money did he left with him if he gave a ₹500 note?**

(A) ₹350 (B) ₹250

(C) ₹380 (D) ₹410

(E) None of these

Answer (A)

Explanation: The rate of most expensive food from each course and the rate of fruit salad and their sum amount is as follow:

Vada Pav	=	₹ 60.00
Chocolate	=	₹ 45.00
Milk	=	₹ 20.00
Fruit Salad	=	₹ 25.00
Total	=	₹ 150.00

Here, Rahul spent in all = ₹ 150

Therefore, money left with Rahul = ₹ 500 – ₹ 150 = ₹ 350

3. **If three friends ordered everything on the menu, how much would they spend altogether?**

(A) ₹848 (B) ₹784

(C) ₹774 (D) ₹814

(E) None of these

Answer (C)

Explanation: Three friends ordered everything on the menu. The sum amount is as follow:

Total amount = ₹ 60 + ₹ 40 + ₹ 20 + ₹ 45 + ₹ 30 + ₹ 25 + ₹ 20 + ₹ 18 = ₹ 258

Therefore, they spent altogether = ₹ 258 + ₹ 258 + ₹ 258 = ₹ 774

Word Problems Involving Money

In this section, we will solve the word problems involving money which include addition and subtraction. Let us study the following examples.

Example:

Ankita went to a stationary shop. She bought the things shown below. How much did she pay to the shopkeeper?

₹40.50

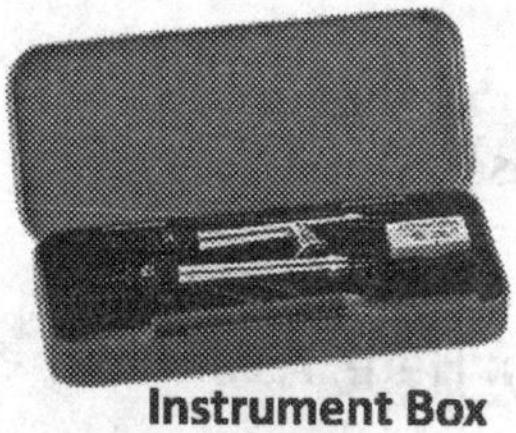

Instrument Box

₹55.75

(A) ₹98.75 (B) ₹96.25 (C) ₹97.65 (D) ₹95.35
(E) None of these

Answer (B)

Explanation: Here, the cost of Notebook = ₹40.50

The cost of Instrument box = ₹55.75

Now, addition is as fallow:

₹ p
40.50
55.75
96.25

Therefore, Ankita has to pay the sum amount = ₹96.25

Example:

Rohit has ₹720. He wants to buy a cricket bat that costs ₹1150. How much more money does he need to buy the bat?

(A) ₹410 (B) ₹440 (C) ₹430 (D) ₹490
(E) None of these

Answer (C)

Explanation: Rohit has amount = ₹720. Cost of the bat = ₹1150

As we know, subtraction is the inverse process of addition.

Hence, the more money that Rohit needs to buy the bat is:

₹1150 – ₹720 = ₹430

Example:

Aslam had ₹ 115. His mother gave him ₹ 85. How much money does Aslam have now?

(A) ₹ 210 (B) ₹ 190 (C) ₹ 250 (D) ₹ 200
(E) None of these

Answer (D)

Explanation: Here, Aslam had ₹ 115. His mother gave him ₹ 85.

Now, Aslam has a total sum money = ₹ 115 + ₹ 85 = ₹ (115 + 85) = ₹ 200

Example:

A packet of 1 kg sugar costs ₹ 52. What will be the cost of 4 such packets?

(A) ₹ 204 (B) ₹ 208 (C) ₹ 156 (D) ₹ 210
(E) None of these

Answer (B)

Explanation: Here, the cost of packet of sugar = ₹ 52

Therefore, the cost of 4 such packets = ₹ 52 + ₹ 52 + ₹ 52 + ₹ 52

= ₹ (52 + 52 + 52 + 52) = ₹ 208

Summary

- Money involves earning, spending and saving.
- Money is available in two forms: Coins and Banknotes or Notes.
- The value of money is denominated on the Notes and Coins.
- Indian currency is known as rupees (₹) and paise (p).
- In India, the denominated coins are: 50 paise, ₹ 1, ₹ 2, ₹ 5, ₹ 10, while the denominated notes are: ₹ 1, ₹ 2, ₹ 5, ₹ 10, ₹ 20, ₹ 50, ₹ 100, ₹ 200, ₹ 500 and ₹ 2000.

- There are 100 paise in one rupee.
- Rupees are converted into paise by multiplying 100 and paise are converted into rupees by dividing 100.

Did You Know ?

- The students or the collectors of coins are known as 'Numismatists'.
- Coins of silver and gold were used for money in ancient times.
- Indians are believed to be the first people who used silver and gold coins.
- First Indian coin was introduced by Sher Shah Suri. He introduced copper coins called 'dam' and gold coins called 'mohur'.
- The word rupee comes from Sanskrit word 'Rupya'.

Solved Problems

1. How many coins of 50 paise make a sum amount of ₹7.50?

(A) 17 coins (B) 15 coins

(C) 16 coins (D) 14 coins

(E) None of these

Answer (B)

Explanation: As we know, there are 100 paise in one rupee.

Now, the given sum amount = ₹7.50 = ₹7 and 50 p = 700 paise + 50 paise

Since, two coins of 50 paise make 100 paise. Therefore, 14 coins of 50 paise make 700 paise.

So, the required number of coins = (14 + 1) coins = 15 coins

2. How much money should be added to ₹130.50 to get 280?

(A) ₹149.50 (B) ₹151.50

(C) ₹148 (D) ₹154

(E) None of these

Answer (A)

Explanation: As we know, subtraction is the inverse process of addition. To know how much money should be added, we have to find the difference amount.

Here, difference is as follow:

(9)
(7)(10) (10)
₹ 2 8 0 . 0 0
₹ 1 3 0 . 5 0
₹ 1 4 9 . 5 0

Therefore, ₹ 149.50 should be added to ₹ 130.50 to get ₹ 280.

Verification: ₹ 130.50 + ₹ 149.50 = ₹ (130.50 + 149.50) = ₹ 280.00 = ₹ 280

3. How much money should be subtracted from ₹ 120.50 to get ₹ 49?

(A) ₹ 72.50
(B) ₹ 69.50
(C) ₹ 71.50
(D) ₹ 79.50
(E) None of these

Answer (C)

Explanation: As we know, subtraction is the inverse process of addition. To find how much money should be subtracted, we have to find the difference amount.

Here, difference is as follow:

(11) (10)
₹ 1 2 0 . 5 0
₹ 4 9 . 0 0
₹ 7 1 . 0 0

Therefore, ₹ 71.50 should be subtracted from ₹ 120.50 to get ₹ 49.

Verification: ₹ 120.50 – ₹ 71.50 = ₹ (120.50 – 71.50) = ₹ 49.00 = ₹ 49

4. If you have three ₹ 50 note, which of the following items can you buy?

(A) 

₹ 160

(B) 

₹ 140

(C) 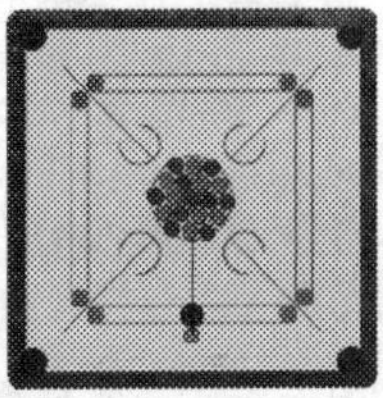

₹ 200

(D) 

₹ 180

(E) None of these

Answer (B)

Explanation: Here, three ₹ 50 note is equal to ₹ 50 + ₹ 50 + ₹ 50 = ₹ 150

So, we have a sum amount of ₹ 150. Now, we can buy an item which costs less than or equal to ₹ 150.

Cost of items given in option (A), (C) and (D) are more than ₹ 150. Therefore, we can buy the air bag which costs ₹ 140 that is less than ₹ 150.

5. What would be the total cost of 4 pens and 5 erasers?

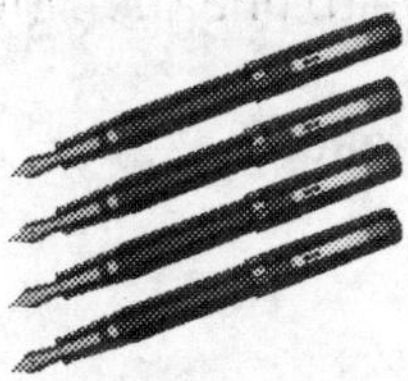

Pens: ₹ 21 each

Erasers: ₹ 5 each

(A) ₹ 110 (B) ₹ 111 (C) ₹ 112 (D) ₹ 109

(E) None of these

Answer (D)

Explanation: Here, the cost of 1 pen = ₹ 21

Therefore, the cost of 4 pens = ₹ (21 + 21 + 21 + 21) = ₹ 84

Now, the cost of 1 eraser = ₹ 5

Therefore, the cost of 4 erasers = ₹ (5 + 5 + 5 + 5 + 5) = ₹ 25

So we have, the total cost of 4 pens and 5 erasers

= ₹ 84 + ₹ 25 = ₹ (84 + 25) = ₹ 109

6. If Rahul bought five T-shirts at the price shown below, then how much he has to pay including the given offer?

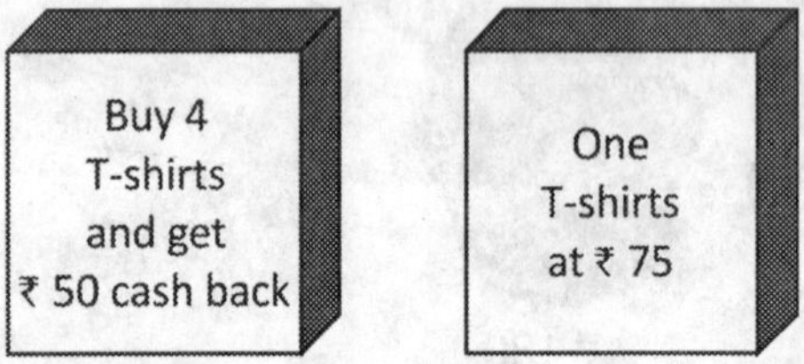

(A) ₹ 450 (B) ₹ 325

(C) ₹ 375 (D) ₹ 350

(E) None of these

Answer (B)

Explanation: Since, Rahul bought five T-shirts at ₹ 75.

Therefore, the cost of 5 T-shirts = ₹ 75 + ₹ 75 + ₹ 75 + ₹ 75 + ₹ 75 = ₹ 375

Now, given offer is ₹ 50 cashback on buying 4 T-shirts.

Therefore, Rahul has to pay including given offer = ₹ 375 – ₹ 50 = ₹ 325

7. How much money is paid for 30 balloons costing 50 p each?

(A) ₹ 15 (B) ₹ 18

(C) ₹ 20 (D) ₹ 12

(E) None of these

Answer (A)

Explanation: Cost of 1 balloon = 50 p

Cost of 30 balloons = 50 p + 50 p + 50 p + 50 p . . . . . up to 30 times

= (50 × 30) p = 1500 p

Since, 100 paise make one rupee. Therefore, 1500 p = ₹ $\left(\frac{1500}{100}\right)$ = ₹ 15

8. Ramesh has ₹ 240. He wants to buy a toy that costs ₹ 310. How much more money does he need to buy the toy?

(A) ₹ 60 (B) ₹ 70

(C) ₹ 80 (D) ₹ 90

(E) None of these

Answer (B)

Explanation: Here, Ramesh has money = ₹ 240. Cost of toy = ₹ 310

Now, difference in amounts = ₹ 310 – ₹ 240 = ₹ 70

So, Ramesh needs ₹ 70 more to buy the toy.

9. This is the box of chocolates. Which of these can be found out from the information on it?

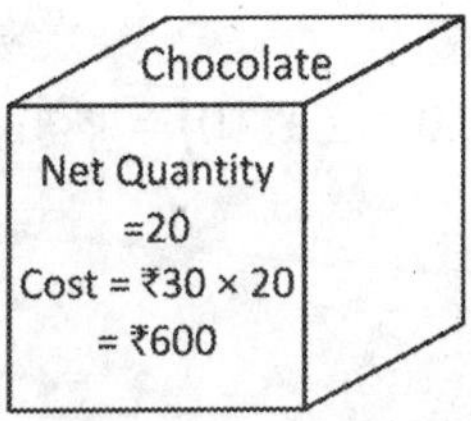

(A) It contains 20 chocolates.

(B) Each chocolate costs ₹ 600.

(C) Cost of 20 chocolates = ₹ 50.

(D) All chocolates are of different cost.

(E) Cannot be determined

Answer (A)

Explanation: All the informations given on the box of chocolate are as follow:

(1) It contains 20 chocolates.

(2) Each chocolate costs ₹ 30.

(3) Cost of 20 chocolates is ₹ 600.

(4) All the chocolates are of same cost.

Therefore, the information given in option (A) is correct.

10. Total value of the coins shown here is:

(A) ₹32 (B) ₹31

(C) ₹35 (D) ₹33

(E) None of these

Answer (C)

Explanation: Sum of rupees = ₹(1 + 1 + 5 + 2 + 2 + 10 + 2 + 10) = ₹33

Sum of paise = (50 + 50 + 50 + 50) p = 200 p = ₹2

Therefore, the value of all coins = ₹33 + ₹2 = ₹35

Practice Exercise 6

1. **Karan has a ₹50 note with him. Which of the following items he can buy?**

(A) 

₹60

(B) 

₹40

(C) 

₹110

(D) 

₹90

(E) None of these

2. **Manoj bought 40 packets of cream rolls for a party. The total cost for cream rolls was ₹600. The cost of one packet of cremroll is:**

(A) ₹12 (B) ₹15

(C) ₹30 (D) ₹20

(E) None of these

3. **Calculate the amount for 13 coins of 50 paise in rupees and paise.**

(A) ₹6 (B) ₹5 and 50 p

(C) ₹6 and 50 p (D) ₹7

(E) None of these

4. **How much money should be added to ₹130.90 to get ₹500?**

(A) ₹369.10

(B) ₹327.10

(C) ₹432.50

(D) ₹330.90

(E) None of these

5. Rahul has some money in his piggi bank as shown below.

His mother has some rupees notes with her and she wants to exchange with Rahul. Which of the total amounts shown below is same as Rahul's mother amount?

(A) 

(B) 

(C) 

(D) 

(E) None of these

6. If Sumit bought 5 pants each for ₹ 600, how much he has to pay including the offer given below?

Offer !
Buy 1 pant, get ₹50 back
Buy 2 pants, get ₹200 back
Buy 3 pants, get ₹500 back

(A) ₹ 2300 (B) ₹ 2800 (C) ₹ 2500 (D) ₹ 2000
(E) None of these

7. Which of the following sets of notes has the greatest value?

(A) 

(B) 

(C) 

(D) 

(E) 

8. Sandeep has ₹ 175 to spend on snacks at a theme park. Which two things can he buy with this money?

(A) 

₹ 180

(B) 

₹ 210

(C) 

₹ 190

(D) 

₹ 205

(E) None of these

9. Mohit bought these four things:

₹850

₹110

₹190

₹450

What was the total cost of these four items?

(A) ₹1500 (B) ₹1550

(C) ₹1600 (D) ₹1750

(E) None of these

10. Sangeeta went to a cake shop. She bought some items as shown in the given bill. If she gave the shopkeeper a ₹500 note, how much did she get back?

S.No.	Item	Rate per Item	₹	p
1. 2. 3.	1 Chocolate 2 Jam bottles 1 Cherry knobs	₹80.50 ₹40.50 ₹50.50	80 81 50	50 00 50
		Total		

(A) ₹248 (B) ₹288

(C) ₹272 (D) ₹314

(E) None of these

Chapter

7 Unitary Method

Learning Objectives

- Introduction
- Unitary Method
- Rules Applied in Unitary Method
- Problems Based on Unitary Method

Introduction

Unitary means 'of one' or of 'single unit', mathematically it means '1'. When we go to market to buy an article, we ask the shopkeeper to tell the price of the article. This price is called **unit price**. We calculate the price of numbers of articles, which we want to buy, by using this unit price. Sometimes we calculate unit price when the price of more than one article is given. This method is known as **unitary method**. In this chapter, we will learn about unitary method and its uses.

What is Unitary Method

Unitary method is also known as **method of one**. The term 'Unitary Method' is a technique which has evolved from the concept of **'unit'** which means 'of one'.

In Unitary Method:

- To get more value we multiply.
- To get less value we divide.

Example:

If the weight of 4 coins is 152 grams, then what is the weight of 1 such coin?

(A) 32 grams (B) 38 grams (C) 36 grams (D) 34 grams
(E) None of these

Answer (B)

Explanation: Here, the weight of 4 coins is given and we have to find out the weight of 1 such coin. Therefore, we divide the weight of 4 coins by 4.

Hence, the weight of 4 coins = 152 grams

So, the weight of 1 coin = (152 ÷ 4) = 38 grams

Example:

If the price of one bicycle is ₹ 1200, then what is the price of such 5 bicycles?

(A) ₹ 1700 (B) ₹ 4000 (C) ₹ 5600 (D) ₹ 6000
(E) None of these

Answer (D)

Explanation: Here, price of one bicycle is ₹ 1200 and we have to find out the price of 5 such bicycles. Therefore, we multiply the price of 1 bicycle by 5.

Hence, the price of 1 bicycle = ₹ 1200

So, the price of 5 bicycles = ₹ (1200 × 5) = ₹ 6000

Rules Applied in Unitary Method

Rule 1 : If we know the value of one then to find the value of many, we do multiplication.

Rule 2 : If we know the value of many then to find the value of one, we do division.

Rule 3 : If we know the value of many then to find the value of more than given or less than given, we first need to calculate the value of one.

Example:

If the cost of 2 apples is ₹ 24, then find the cost of 3 such apples.

(A) ₹ 36 (B) ₹ 42 (C) ₹ 32 (D) ₹ 27
(E) None of these

Answer (A)

Explanation: As the cost of 2 apples = ₹ 24

Therefore, the cost of 1 apple = ₹ (24 ÷ 2) = ₹ 12

So, the cost of 3 apples = ₹ (12 × 3) = ₹ 36

Problems Based on Unitary Method

Some examples of problems based on unitary method are given below. Let us study the following examples.

Example:

If 4 litres of petrol is consumed by a car in covering a distance of 80 km, then how many kilometres will it go in 5 litres of petrol?

(A) 140 km (B) 90 km (C) 100 km (D) 120 km

(E) None of these

Answer (C)

Explanation: As we know, if the value of many is given, then to find out the value of more than given or less than given, we first need to calculate the value of one.

Here, in 4 litres of petrol, the car covered the distance = 80 km

Therefore, in 1 litre of petrol, the car will cover the distance

= (80 ÷ 4) km = 20 km

So, in 5 litres of petrol, the car will cover the distance = (20 × 5) km = 100 km

Example:

If the cost of 10 kilograms of rice is ₹ 90, then what is the cost of 560 kilograms of rice?

(A) ₹ 5400 (B) ₹ 5040 (C) ₹ 4050 (D) ₹ 4500

(E) None of these

Answer (B)

Explanation: Here, to find out the value of more than given or less than given, first we need to find out the value of one.

Since, the cost of 10 kilograms of rice = ₹ 90

So, the cost of 1 kilogram of rice = ₹ 90 ÷ 10 = ₹ 9

Therefore, the cost of 560 kilograms of rice = ₹ (9 × 560) = ₹ 5040

Summary

- The term **unitary method** is a technique which has evolved from the concept of '**unit**' which means 'of one'. Therefore, the unitary method is also known as the **method of one**.
- In unitary method: to get more value we multiply and to get less value we divide.
- If we know the value of one then to find the value of more than one, we do multiplication.
- If we know the value of many then to find the value of one, we do division.
- If we know the value of many then to find the value of more than given or less than given, we first need to calculate the value of one.

Did You Know?

- Unitary method has several uses in our daily life, when we talk about speed, rate, time and work, we invariably relate to unitary method.
- Unitary method is a technique in elementary algebra which deals relations with the general properties of numbers and relations between them.
- Elementary algebra began in ancient Egypt and Babylon.

Solved Problems

1. Rohit bought 5 pens each for ₹12 and 3 pencils each costing ₹7. How much he has to pay?

(A) ₹120 (B) ₹96 (C) ₹84 (D) ₹81
(E) None of these

Answer (D)

Explanation: As the cost of 1 pen = ₹12

So, the cost of 5 pens = ₹(12 × 5) = ₹60

Now, the cost of 1 pencil = ₹7

So, the cost of 3 pencils = ₹(7 × 3) = ₹21

Therefore, Rohit has to pay = ₹60 + ₹21 = ₹81

2. If the cost of 9 litres of milk is ₹378, then what will be the cost of 5 litres of milk?

(A) ₹200 (B) ₹210 (C) ₹240 (D) ₹280
(E) None of these

Answer (B)

Explanation: As the cost of 9 litres of milk = ₹378

So, the cost of 1 litre of milk = ₹(378 ÷ 9) = ₹42

Therefore, the cost of 5 litres of milk = ₹(42 × 5) = ₹210

3. A carpenter is buying 54 metres of oak boards to build 9 tables. How many metres would he have needed to buy if he wanted to build 7 such tables?

(A) 30 metres (B) 42 metres (C) 45 metres (D) 60 metres
(E) None of these

Answer (B)

Explanation: As to build 9 tables, the required oak boards = 54 metres

So, to build 1 table, the required oak boards = (54 ÷ 9) metres = 6 metres

Therefore, to build 7 tables, the required oak boards = (6 × 7) metres = 42 metres

So, the carpenter have needed 42 metres of oak boards to build 7 tables.

4. A car travels a distance of 240 kilometres in 2 hours. At the same speed, the distance covered by the car in 30 minutes will be:

(A) 60 kilometres (B) 72 kilometres

(C) 54 kilometres (D) 84 kilometres

(E) None of these

Answer (A)

Explanation: There are 60 minutes in 1 hour.

As the distance covered by the car in 2 hours = 240 kilometres

So, the distance covered by the car in 1 hour

= (240 ÷ 2) kilometres = 120 kilometres

So, the distance covered by the car in 60 minutes = 120 kilometres

Therefore, the distance covered by the car in 1 minute

= (120 ÷ 60) kilometres = 2 kilometres

So we have, the distance covered by the car in 30 minutes

= (2 × 30) kilometres = 60 kilometres

5. If ▲ represents 4 items, and the cost of ▲▲▲▲▲▲ = ₹72, then the cost of ▲▲▲▲ will be:

(A) ₹42 (B) ₹54 (C) ₹48 (D) ₹60

(E) None of these

Answer (C)

Explanation: Given that ▲ represents 4 items.

Therefore, ▲▲▲▲▲▲ represent (4 × 6) items = 24 items

And, ▲▲▲▲ represent (4 × 4) items = 16 items

Now, the cost of 24 items = ₹72

So, the cost of 1 item = ₹(72 ÷ 24) = ₹3

Therefore, the cost of 16 items = ₹(3 × 16) =₹48

Hence, the cost of ▲▲▲▲ is ₹48

6. **If the total weight of the apples shown below is 984 grams, then the weight of 5 such apples will be:**

(A) 720 grams (B) 615 grams (C) 725 grams (D) 675 grams
(E) None of these

Answer (B)

Explanation: Here, the number of apples = 8

Now, as the total weight of 8 apples = 984 grams

So, the weight of 1 apple = (984 ÷ 8) grams = 123 grams

Therefore, the total weight of 5 apples = (123 × 5) grams = 615 grams

7. **Eight baskets of fruits cost ₹2568. Then the cost of 1 such basket of fruits will be:**

(A) less than ₹320 (B) more than ₹320
(C) equal to ₹320 (D) equal to ₹160
(E) Cannot be determined

Answer (B)

Explanation: As the cost of 8 baskets of fruits = ₹2568

So, the cost of 1 basket of fruits = ₹(2568 ÷ 8) = ₹321 > ₹320

Therefore, the cost of 1 basket of fruits is more than ₹320

8. **A man works for 6 days and earns ₹780. How much does he earn in a day?**

(A) ₹128 (B) ₹120 (C) ₹140 (D) ₹130
(E) None of these

Answer (D)

Explanation: Earning of the man in 6 days = ₹780

Earning of the man in 1 day = ₹780 ÷ 6 = ₹130

9. **The value of ▲ + ▲ + ▲ = 21 and the value of ● + ● + ● + ● = 24, so the value of ▲ + ● will be:**

(A) 14 (B) 12 (C) 13 (D) 15
(E) None of these

Answer (C)

Explanation: As the value of ▲ + ▲ + ▲ = 21

Or, the value of three triangles = 21. So, the value of one triangle = 21 ÷ 3 = 7

So we have, the value of ▲ = 7

Now, the value of ● + ● + ● + ● = 24

Or, the value of four triangles = 24. So, the value of one triangle = 24 ÷ 4 = 6

So we have, the value of ● = 6

Therefore, the value of ▲ + ● = 7 + 6 = 13

10. If the cost of half dozen guavas is ₹72, then what is the cost of 9 such guavas?

(A) ₹108 (B) ₹96 (C) ₹60 (D) ₹84

(E) None of these

Answer (A)

Explanation: Half dozen = 6

As the cost of half dozen guavas = ₹72

So, the cost of 6 guavas = ₹72

Therefore, the cost of 1 guava = ₹(72 ÷ 6) = ₹12

Hence, the cost of 9 guavas = ₹(12 × 9) = ₹108

Practice Exercise 7

1. **If the cost of 7 stickers is ₹91, then the cost of 98 such stickers is:**

   (A) ₹1080 (B) ₹1464

   (C) ₹1274 (D) ₹1262

   (E) None of these

2. **If the value of ○ + ○ + ○ = 39 and the value of □ + □ + □ + □ = 48, then find the value of ○ + □ + ○.**

   (A) 32 (B) 38

   (C) 36 (D) 42

   (E) None of these

3. **If the cost of 9 pencils is ₹63, then the cost of 63 such pencils is:**

   (A) ₹504 (B) ₹567

   (C) ₹441 (D) ₹378

   (E) None of these

4. **If the half dozen eggs cost ₹24, then the cost of one and half dozen eggs is:**

   (A) ₹72 (B) ₹54

   (C) ₹84 (D) ₹60

   (E) None of these

5. **How many seconds are there in 2 hours?**

   (A) 3600 seconds

   (B) 7600 seconds

   (C) 5400 seconds

   (D) 7800 seconds

   (E) None of these

6. If  represents 171 articles, then the number of articles represented by the given symbols will be:

(A) 1477 (B) 1288

(C) 1368 (D) 1378

(E) None of these

7. If 8 erasers cost ₹ 24, then the cost of 12 such erasers is:

(A) ₹ 36 (B) ₹ 32

(C) ₹ 48 (D) ₹ 72

(E) None of these

8. Weight of 65 books is 13 kg. How many such books weigh 5 kg?

(A) 21 (B) 24

(C) 35 (D) 25

(E) None of these

9. If 6 notebooks cost ₹ 78, then find the cost of 9 such notebooks.

(A) ₹ 124 (B) ₹ 121

(C) ₹ 119 (D) ₹ 117

(E) None of these

10. John types 360 words in half an hour. How many words would he type in 40 minutes?

(A) 480 words (B) 420 words

(C) 440 words (D) 460 words

(E) None of these

Chapter 8

Measurement

Learning Objectives

- Introduction
- Units of Measurement
- Measurement of Length and Distance
- Measurement of Long Distance
- Operations with Measured Lengths
- Measurement of Mass
- Operations with Measured Masses
- Measurement of Capacity (Volume)
- Operations with Measured Capacities (Volume)

Introduction

The act or process of measuring something is called measurement. Measurement is the elementary information about everything. Length, width, height and capacity (volume) of a thing are measured in appropriate units. In this chapter, we will learn about the concept of measurement.

Units of Measurement

The metric system was introduced to measure length, mass (weight) and capacity (volume). The modern form of the metric system is known as **SI Unit** or the **International System of Units**.

SI Units or Base Units

Physical Quantity	SI Unit
Length	Metre (m)
Mass	Kilogram (kg)
Time	Second (s)

Some units of measurement obtained by multiplication or division of the SI units and are called derived units. For example, unit of speed is metre per second (m/s) or kilometre per hour (km/ h) is a derived unit.

Measurement of Length and Distance

The shape and size of everything are measured by a measuring instrument. Rulers are well known devices for the measurement of length. Measured lengths are expressed in units. The units for measured lengths are kilometre (km), metre (m), centimetre (cm) and millimetre (mm). Small lengths are measured in metre, centimetre and millimertre. The length of our one finger is measured in inches, centimetres or in millimetres but the distance between two cities is measured in kilometres. The standard unit used to measure any length or distance is the metre for which we use 'm'. To convert metres into centimetres we multiply metre by 100, therefore, 100 cm = 1 m. To convert kilometres into metres, we multiply kilometre by 1000, thus 1000 m = 1 Kilometre.

Conversion Table for Length and Distance

10 millimetres (mm)	1 centimetre (cm)
10 centimetres (cm)	1 decimetre (dm)
10 decimetres (dm)	1 metre (m)
10 metres (m)	1 decametre (dam)
10 decametres (dam)	1 hectometre (hm)
10 hectometres (hm)	1 kilometre (km)

Example:

Convert 45 metres into centimetres and choose the correct option.

(A) 5400 cm (B) 4500 cm (C) 240 cm (D) 450 cm

(E) None of these

Answer (B)

Explanation: Since, 1 metre = 100 centimetres

Therefore, 45 metres = (45 × 100) centimetres = 4500 centimetres

Conversion of Metres and Centimetres

Metres are converted into centimetres by multiplying 100 and centimetres are converted into metres by dividing 100. Therefore, 100 cm = 1 m and 1 cm = $\frac{1}{100}$ m.

Example:

If we convert 3445 metres into centimetres, the number of digits in centimetres will be:

(A) 4 (B) 5 (C) 6 (D) 7

(E) None of these

Answer (C)

Explanation: Since, 1 m = 100 cm

Therefore, 3445 m = (3445 × 100) cm = 344500 cm

Hence, the number of digits = 6

Conversion of a Mixed Units of Measure (Metres and Centimetres) into a Single Unit

To convert a mixed unit of metres and centimetres, we either convert metres into centimetres by multiplying 100 or we convert centimetres into metres by dividing 100. After that, we add them and express the sum in a single unit.

Example:

Convert 85 m 55 cm into centimetres.

(A) 2500 cm (B) 8500 cm (C) 8555 cm (D) 5585

(E) None of these

Answer (C)

Explanation: Here, 85 m will be converted into centimetres by multiplying 100. Therefore, (85×100) cm = 8500 cm

Now, the required conversion is $(8500 + 55)$ cm = 8555 cm

Example:

Convert 85 m 55 cm into metres.

(A) 85 m (B) 85.55 m (C) 55.85 m (D) 14 m

(E) None of these

Answer (B)

Explanation: Here, we will convert 55 cm into metres by dividing 100.

Therefore, 55 cm = $\frac{55}{100}$ m = 0.55 m

Now, the required conversion is $(85 + 0.55)$ m = 85.55 m

Measurement of Long Distance

Distance between two cities in a country is very long as compare to the distance between two walls of a room, therefore, a long distance is measured in kilometres. Greater unit of length can be converted into smaller unit and smaller unit into greater unit. Number of digits for the representation of a long distance in smaller unit takes more space and it is not a simple process, therefore, long distance are usually expressed in greater units.

Conversion of Kilometres and Metres

Kilometres are converted into metres by multiplying 1000 and metres are converted into kilometres by dividing 1000.

Therefore, 1000 m = 1 km and, 1 m = $\frac{1}{1000}$ km

Example:

Distance between two colonies in a city is 15 km 540 m. Express the distance in metres.

(A) 14460 m (B) 15540 m (C) 15054 m (D) 54015 m

(E) None of these

Answer (B)

Explanation: 15 km 540 m = (15 × 1000) m + 540 m = (15 × 1000 + 540) m
= (15000 + 540) m = 15540 m

Example:

Distance between two railway stations is 27 km 72 m. Express the distance in kilometres.

(A) 27.72 km (B) 270.20 km (C) 2.772 km (D) 27.072 km
(E) None of these

Answer (D)

Explanation: 27 km 72 m = 27 km + $\left(\frac{72}{1000}\right)$ km

= (27 + 0.072) km = 27.072 km

Conversion of Mixed Unit of Measure (Kilometres and Metres) into a Single Unit

To convert a mixed unit of kilometres and metres, we either convert kilometres into metres by multiplying 1000 or we convert metres into kilometres by dividing 1000. After that, we add them and express the sum in a single unit.

Example:

Convert 35 km 41 m into metres.

(A) 3541 m (B) 35041 m (C) 35410 (D) 350041 m
(E) None of these

Answer (B)

Explanation: Here, 35 km will be convert into metres by multiplying 1000.

Therefore, 35 km = (35 × 1000) m = 35000 m

Now, the required conversion is (35000 + 41) m = 35041 m

Example:

Convert 35 km 41 m into kilometres.

(A) 35.41 km (B) 3504.1 km (C) 35.041 km (D) 3.541 km
(E) None of these

Answer (C)

Explanation: Here, 41 m will be convert into kilometres by dividing 1000.

Therefore, 41 m = $\left(\frac{41}{1000}\right)$ km = 0.041 km

Now, the required conversion is (35 + 0.041) km = 35.041 km

Operations with Measured Lengths

Addition of Measured Lengths with Conversion

Following steps are used for the addition of measured lengths:

Step 1 : Convert the metres into centimetres if the given lengths are in metres and centimetres.

Step 2 : Add the centimetres.

Step 3 : Convert the sum back to metres.

Example:

Add 65 m 38 cm and 26 m 45 cm.

(A) 91 m 83 cm (B) 98 m 13 cm

(C) 159 m 27 cm (D) 113 m 46 cm

(E) None of these

Answer (A)

Explanation: Here, addition is as follow:

65 m 38 cm	=	65 38 cm
26 m 45 cm	=	+ 26 45 cm
		91 83 cm

Therefore, the required sum is 91 m 83 cm.

Addition of Measured Lengths without Conversion

Following steps are used for the addition of measured lengths:

Step 1 : Arrange the numbers in metres (m) and centimetres (cm) columns if the given lengths are in metres and centimetres.

Step 2 : Add them together.

Step 3 : If carry is generated then add them to the next addition.

Example:

Add 48 m 65 cm and 83 m 70 cm.

(A) 134 m 45 cm (B) 132 m 61 cm

(C) 132 m 35 cm (D) 98 m 41 cm

(E) None of these

Answer (C)

Explanation: Here, addition is as follow:

	m	cm
	48	65
+	83	70
	132	35

Therefore, the required sum is 132 m 35 cm.

Subtraction of Measured Lengths with Conversion

Following steps are used for the subtraction of measured lengths:

Step 1 : Convert the metres into centimetres if the given lengths are in metres and centimetres.

Step 2 : Subtract the centimetres.

Step 3 : Convert back to metres and centimetres.

Example:

Subtract 7 m 17 cm from 11 m 14 cm.

(A) 3 m 97 cm (B) 5 m 29 cm

(C) 17 m 31 cm (D) 4 m 3 cm

(E) None of these

Answer (A)

Explanation: Here, subtraction is as follow:

11 m 14 cm = 11 14 cm

7 m 17 cm = − 7 17 cm

3 97 cm

Therefore, the required difference is 3 m 97 cm.

Subtraction of Measured Lengths without Conversion

Following steps are used for the subtraction of measured lengths:

Step 1 : Arrange the numbers in metres (m) and centimetres (cm) columns if the given length are in metres and centimetres.

Step 2 : Subtract the numbers.

Step 3 : If borrowing is needed, borrow them from the next place of digit.

Example:

Subtract 13 m 27 cm from 95 m 15 cm.

(A) 88 m 81 cm (B) 89 m 42 cm

(C) 87 m 86 cm (D) 81 m 88 cm

(E) None of these

Answer (D)

Explanation: Here, subtraction is as follow:

m	cm
95	15
−13	27
81	88

Therefore, the required difference is 81 m 88 cm.

Multiplying the Measured Length

Following steps are used for multiplying the measured length:

Step 1 : Arrange the numbers in metres (m) and centimetres (cm) columns if the given length is in metres and centimetres.

Step 2 : Multiply the numbers by given multiplier.

Step 3 : Product so obtained is the required length.

Example:

Multiply 17 m 28 cm by 9.

(A) 156 m 51 cm (B) 152 m 55 cm

(C) 155 m 52 cm (D) 153 m 37 cm

(E) None fo these

Answer (C)

Explanation: Here, multiplication is as follow:

m	cm
17	28
	× 9
155	52

Therefore, the required length is 155 m 52 cm.

Division of Measured Length

Following steps are used for the division of measured length:

Step 1 : Arrange the numbers in metres (m) and centimetres (cm) columns if the given length is in metres and centimetres.

Step 2 : Divide the number by simple division method.

Step 3 : Quotient so obtained is the part of the given length.

Example:

Find the one-fourth part of 288 m 24 cm.

(A) 76 m 12 cm (B) 72 m 6 cm

(C) 77 m 13 cm (D) 71 m 66 cm

(E) None of these

Answer (B)

Explanation: One-fourth part means division by 4. Here, division is as follow:

```
     m    cm
4) 2 8 8  2 4 (72 m 06 cm
  -2 8↓
     ×8
     -8   ↓↓
       × 2 4
        -2 4
           ×
```

Therefore, the required part of length is 72 m 06 cm = 72 m 6 cm

Measurement of Mass

The standard unit for the measurement of mass is kilogram (kg). The other units for measuring mass are grams (g) and milligrams (mg). Mass of small thing is usually measured in grams. To convert kilograms into grams, we multiply kilogram by 1000, therefore, one gram is thousandth part of a kilogram.

Conversion Table for Mass

10 milligrams (mg)	1 centigram (cg)
10 centigrams (cg)	1 decigram (dg)
10 decigram (dg)	1 gram (g)
10 grams (g)	1 decagram (dag)
10 decagram (dag)	1 hectogram (hg)
10 hectogram (hg)	1 kilogram (kg)

Example:

Convert 45 kilograms into grams.

(A) 450 grams
(B) 4500 grams
(C) 45000 grams
(D) 450000 grams
(E) None of these

Answer (C)

Explanation: Since, 1 kilogram = 1000 grams

Therefore, 45 kilograms = (45 × 1000) grams = 45000 grams

Operations with Measured Masses

Addition of Measured Masses with Conversion

Following steps are used for the addition of measured masses:

Step 1 : Convert the kilograms into grams if the given masses are in kilograms and grams.

Step 2 : Add the grams.

Step 3 : Convert the sum back to kilograms.

Example:

Add 6 kg 924 g and 5 kg 334 g.

(A) 11 kg 352 g (B) 12 kg 258 g

(C) 13 kg 476 g (D) 12 kg 367 g

(E) None of these

Answer (B)

Explanation: Here, addition is as follow:

6kg 924g	=	6 924g
5kg 334g	=	+5 334g
		12 258g

Therefore, the required sum is 12 kg 258 g.

Addition of Measured Masses without Conversion

Following steps are used for the addition of measured masses:

Step 1 : Arrange the numbers in kilograms (kg) and grams (g) columns if the given masses are in kilograms and grams.

Step 2 : Add them together.

Step 3 : If carry is generated then add them to the next addition.

Example:

Add 17 kg 315 g and 11 kg 788 g.

(A) 28 kg 109 g (B) 27 kg 127 g

(C) 26 kg 207 g (D) 29 kg 103 g

(E) None of these

Answer (D)

Explanation: Here, addition is as follow:

17 kg	315 g
+11 kg	788 g
29 kg	103 g

Therefore, the required sum is 29 kg 103 g.

Subtraction of Measured Masses with Conversion

Following steps are used for the subtraction of measured masses:

Step 1: Convert the kilograms in grams if the given masses are in kilograms and grams.

Step 2 : Subtract the grams.

Step 3 : Convert back to kilograms and grams.

Example:

Subtract 86 kg 48 g from 93 kg 43 g.

(A) 7 kg 991 g
(B) 6 kg 995 g
(C) 6 kg 993 kg
(D) 7 kg 995 g
(E) None of these

Answer (B)

Explanation: Here, the subtraction is as follow:

93 kg 43 g	=	93 043 g
86 kg 48 g	=	− 86 048 g
		6 995 g

Therefore, the required difference is 6 kg 995 g.

Subtraction of Measured Masses without Conversion

Following steps are used for the subtraction of measured masses:

Step 1 : Arrange the numbers in kilograms (kg) and grams (g) columns if the given masses are in kilograms and grams.

Step 2 : Subtract the numbers.

Step 3 : If borrowing is needed borrow them from the next place of digit.

Example:

Subtract 27 kg 39 g from 39 kg 27 g.

(A) 18 kg 943 g
(B) 13 kg 992 g
(C) 12 kg 981 g
(D) 11 kg 988 g
(E) None of these

Answer (D)

Explanation: Here, subtraction is as follow:

	kg	g
	39	027
−	27	039
	11	988

Therefore, the required difference is 11 kg 988 g.

Multiplying the Measured Mass

Following steps are used for multiplying the measured mass:

Step 1 : Arrange the numbers in kilograms (kg) and grams (g) columns if the given mass is in kilograms and grams.

Step 2 : Multiply the numbers by given multiplier.

Step 3 : Product so obtained is the required mass.

Example:

Multiply 83 kg 38 g by 7.

(A) 581 kg 266 g (B) 589 kg 256 g

(C) 668 kg 259 g (D) 523 kg 289 g

(E) None of these

Answer (A)

Explanation: Here, multiplication is as follow:

kg	g
83	038
	× 7
581	266

Therefore, the required mass is 581 kg 266 g.

Division of Measured Mass

Following steps are used for the division of measured mass:

Step 1 : Arrange the numbers in kilograms (kg) and grams (g) column if the given mass is in kilograms and grams.

Step 2 : Divide the number by simple division method.

Step 3 : Quotient so obtained is the required part of given mass.

Example:

Find the one-third part of 39 kg 93 g.

(A) 11 kg 23 g (B) 17 kg 27 g

(C) 13 kg 31 g (D) 23 kg 13 g

(E) None of these

Answer (C)

Explanation: One-third part means division by 3. Here, division is as follow:

```
    kg    g
3) 39 093 (13 kg 031 g
  -3↓
   ×9
  -9    ↓
     × 9
     -9 ↓
      × 3
      - 3
        0
```

Therefore, one-third part of the given mass is 13 kg 31 g.

Measurement of Capacity (Volume)

The capacity of a container is the maximum quantity of liquid that container can contain. If the capacity of a container is 1 litre then it means, it can hold the volume 1 litre of liquid inside it. The standard unit for the measurement of liquid is litre. The larger volume of liquid is measured in litres and the smaller volume is in millilitres. One litre is equal to 1000 millilitres. Therefore, one millilitre is the thousandth part of a litre. litre is denoted by letter of English alphabet (l) or (L) and millilitre is denoted by (ml).

Conversion Table for Capacity

10 millilitres (ml)	1 centilitre (cl)
10 centilitres (cl)	1 decilitre (dl)
10 decilitres (dl)	1 litre (L)
10 litres (L)	1 decalitre (dal)
10 decalitre (dal)	1 hectolitre (hl)
10 hectolitre (hl)	1 kilolitre (kl)

Example:

Convert 39 litres into millilitres.

(A) 390 millilitres (B) 3900 millilitres

(C) 39000 millilitres (D) 390000 millilitres

(E) None of these

Answer (C)

Explanation: Since, 1 litre = 1000 millitres.

Therefore, 39 litres = (39 × 1000) millilitres = 39000 millilitres

Operations with Measured Capacities

Addition of Measured Capacities with Conversion

Following steps are used for the addition of measured capacities:

Step 1 : Convert the litres in millilitres if the given capacities are in litres and millilitres.

Step 2 : Add the millilitres.

Step 3 : Convert the sum back to litres.

Example:

Add 7 L 912 ml and 2 L 134 ml.

(A) 8 L 36 ml (B) 9 L 34 ml (C) 11 L 56 ml (D) 10 L 46 ml

(E) None of these

Answer (D)

Explanation: Here, addition is as follow:

7 L 912 ml	=	7912 ml
2 L 134 ml	=	+ 2134 ml
		10046 ml

Therefore, the required sum is 10 L 046 ml = 10 L 46 ml

Addition of Measured Capacities without Conversion

Following steps are used for the addition of measured capacities:

Step 1 : Arrange the numbers in litres (L) and millilitres (ml) columns if the given capacities are in litres and millilitres.

Step 2 : Add them together.

Step 3 : If carry is generated then add them to the next addition.

Example:

Add 27 L 314 ml and 13 L 745 ml.

(A) 41 L 59 ml (B) 43 L 57 ml

(C) 40 L 49 ml (D) 42 L 39 ml

(E) None of these

Answer (A)

Explanation: Here, addition is as follow:

L	ml
27	314
+ 13	745
41	059

Therefore, the required sum is 41 L 059 ml = 41 L 59 ml

Subtraction of Measured Capacities with Conversion

Following steps are used for the subtraction of measured capacities:

Step 1 : Convert the litres in millilitres if the given capacities are in litres and millilitres.

Step 2 : Subtract the millilitres.

Step 3 : Convert back to litres and millilitres.

Example:

Subtract 68 L 84 ml from 86 L 48 ml.

(A) 27 L 952 ml (B) 17 L 964 ml (C) 27 L 964 ml (D) 17 L 954 ml

(E) None of these

Answer (B)

Explanation: Here, subtraction is as follow:

86 L 48 ml = 86 048 ml
68 L 84 ml = − 68 084 ml
17 964 ml

Therefore, the required difference is 17 L 964 ml

Subtraction of Measured Capacities without Conversion

Following steps are used for the subtraction of measured capacities:

Step 1 : Arrange the numbers in litres (L) and millilitres (ml) columns if the given capacities are in litres and millilitres.

Step 2 : Subtract the numbers.

Step 3 : If borrowing is needed, borrow them from the next place of digit.

Example:

Subtract 17 L 93 ml from 29 L 37 ml.

(A) 12 L 944 ml (B) 12 L 954 ml
(C) 11 L 956 ml (D) 11 L 944 ml
(E) None of these

Answer (D)

Explanation: Here, subtraction is as follow:

	L	ml
	29	037
−	17	093
	11	944

Therefore, the required difference is 11 L 944 ml.

Multiplying the Measured Capacity

Following steps are used for multiplying the measured capacity:

Step 1 : Arrange the numbers in litres (L) and millilitres (ml) if the given capacity is in litres and millilitres.

Step 2 : Multiply the numbers by given multiplier.

Step 3 : Product so obtained is the required capacity.

Example:

Six times of a capacity 38 L 283 ml will be:

(A) 232 L 98 ml (B) 229 L 698 ml
(C) 238 L 980 ml (D) 230 L 98 ml
(E) None of these

Answer (B)

Explanation: Here, multiplication is as follow:

```
  L   ml
 38  283
     × 6
---------
229  698
```

Therefore, the required capacity is 229 L 698 ml.

Division of Measured Capacity

Following steps are used for the division of measured capacity:

Step 1 : Arrange the numbers in litres (L) and millilitres (ml) columns if the given capacity is in litres and millilitres.

Step 2 : Divide the numbers by simple division method.

Step 3 : Quotient so obtained is the required part of the given capacity.

Example:

Find the one-fourth part of 39 L 180 ml.

(A) 9 L 795 ml (B) 8 L 45 ml

(C) 9 L 245 ml (D) 7 L 885 ml

(E) None of these

Answer (A)

Explanation: One-fourth part means division by 4. Here, division is as follow:

```
    L    ml
4 ) 3 9  1 8 0 ( 9 L 795 ml
   −3 6 ↓
    ×3 1
    −2 8↓
     × 3 8
      −3 6 ↓
       × 2 0
       − 2 0
         0 0
```

Therefore, one-fourth part of the given capacity is 9 L 795 ml.

Summary

- Act or process of measuring something is called **measurement**.
- **Metric system** was introduced to measure length, mass and capacity (volume).
- **Standard unit** to measure length is metre (m), where 1 metre is the thousand part of 1 kilometre (km).
- Small lengths are measured in metres, centimetres and millimetres and long distances are measured in kilometres.
- Standard unit to measure or weigh mass is kilogram (kg) where 1 kilogram is thousand times of 1 gram (g).
- Kilogram is used to weigh large quantities and gram is used to weigh small quantities.
- **Capacity** of a container is the maximum quantity of liquid that container can contain.
- Standard unit to measure capacity is litre (L) where 1 litre is thousand times of 1 millilitre (ml).
- Litre (L) is used to measure small quantities and kilolltre (kl) is used to measure very large quantities while millilitre (ml) is used to measure very small quantities.

Did You Know?

- Grain was the earliest unit for the measurement of mass.
- Metric system was first adopted by France.
- Metre is little more than one yard and one kilometre is less than a mile.
- Foot as a unit of length is defined today as 0.3048 metres or 30.48 centimetres.
- One litre is the volume of a cube with sides 10 cm.
- Kilolitres, megalitres and gigalitres are commonly used for measuring water consumption, reservoir capacities, river flows and swimming pools.
- In some countries, a teaspoon is a unit of volume.

Solved Problems

1. What should be subtracted from 45 m 15 cm to get 15 m 45 cm?

(A) 30 m 80 cm (B) 29 m 60 cm

(C) 30 m 75 cm (D) 29 m 70 cm

(E) None of these

Answer (D)

Explanation: As we know, subtraction is the inverse process of addition.

Here, subtraction is as follow:

	m	cm
	45	15
−	15	45
	29	70

When, 15 m 45 cm is subtracted from 45 m 15 cm, the difference is 29 m 70 cm. Thus, the required length is 29 m 70 cm.

2. What should be added to 35 m 20 cm to get 120 m 35 cm?

(A) 110 m 45 cm (B) 85 m 15 cm

(C) 95 m 35 cm (D) 80 m 85 cm

(E) None of these

Answer (B)

Explanation: As we know, the inverse process of addition is subtraction.

Here, subtraction is as follow:

	m	cm
	120	35
−	35	20
	85	15

Therefore, 85 m 15 cm should be added to 35 m 20 cm to get 120 m 35 cm.

3. Maria has a rope 7 m 35 cm long and Jenny has another rope 8 m 80 cm long. What is the total length of both ropes?

(A) 15 m 45 cm (B) 16 m 15 cm (C) 15 m 95 cm (D) 16 m 95 cm

(E) None of these

Answer (B)

Explanation: Here, addition is as follow:

$$\begin{array}{rr} \text{m} & \text{cm} \\ 7 & 35 \\ -\ 8 & 80 \\ \hline 16 & 15 \\ \hline \end{array}$$

Therefore, total length of both the ropes is 16 m 15 cm.

4. If the length of a bed is 2 m 30 cm and its breath is 1 m 45 cm, then by how much is the length exceed the breath?

(A) 85 cm (B) 75 cm (C) 1 m 5 cm (D) 1 m 15 cm

(E) None of these

Answer (A)

Explanation: Here, subtraction is as follow:

$$\begin{array}{rr} \text{m} & \text{cm} \\ 2 & 30 \\ -\ 1 & 45 \\ \hline \times & 85 \\ \hline \end{array}$$

Therefore, the length exceed the breath by 85 cm.

5. Peter travels 6 km 200 m by bus and 2 km 850 m by auto to reach the school from his house. How far is Peter's school from his home?

(A) 8 km 950 m (B) 9 km 50 m

(C) 9 km 500 m (D) 8 km 50 m

(E) None of these

Answer (B)

Explanation: On adding the both distances, we get 6 km 200 m + 2 km 850 m

= 6000 m + 200 m + 2000 m + 850 m = 9050 m = 9 km 50 m

Therefore, Peter's school from his home is at 9 km 50 m.

6. **Aman covers a distance of 5 km 350 m in first hour and 3 km 550 m in the next hour. Total distance covered by Aman in two hours is:**

(A) 8 km 850 m (B) 9 km 950 m
(C) 9 km 800 m (D) 8 km 900 m
(E) None of these

Answer (D)

Explanation: Here, addition is as follow:

```
 km   m
  5  350
+ 3  550
---------
  8  900
---------
```

Therefore, total distance covered by Aman is 8 km 900 m.

7. **A 35 m 80 cm long electric wire is cut into four equal parts. The length of each part is:**

(A) 7 m 20 cm (B) 8 m 20 cm (C) 7 m 85 cm (D) 8 m 95 cm
(E) None of these

Answer (D)

Explanation: Four equal parts means, whole length is divided by 4.

Here, division is as follow:

```
    m   cm
 4) 3 5 8 0 ( 8 m 95 cm
   -3 2 ↓
   -------
    × 3 8
    - 3 6 ↓
    -------
        2 0
      - 2 0
      -----
        0 0
      -----
```

Therefore, the required length is 8 m 95 cm.

8. **An electrician needs 14 m 25 cm of electric wire for internal wiring of a room. How long wire does he need for internal wiring of 5 such rooms?**

(A) 71 m 25 cm (B) 70 m 75 cm
(C) 72 m 25 cm (D) 69 m 75 cm
(E) None of these

Answer (A)

Explanation: Here, multiplication is as follow:

m	cm
14	25
	× 5
71	25

When 14 m 25 cm is multiplied by 5, the product is 71 m 25 cm.

Therefore, the required length of wire is 71 m 25 cm

9. What should be added to 19 kg 310 g to get 91 kg 130 g?

(A) 72 kg 440 g
(B) 71 kg 820 g
(C) 70 kg 840 g
(D) 69 kg 480 g
(E) None of these

Answer (B)

Explanation: As we know, subtraction is the inverse process of addition. Here, subtraction is as follow:

kg	g
91	130
– 19	310
71	820

Therefore, 71 kg 820 g should be added to 19 kg 310 g to get 91 kg 130 g.

10. What should be subtracted from 53 kg 410 g to get 35 kg 140 g?

(A) 18 kg 270 g
(B) 16 kg 390 g
(C) 17 kg 550 g
(D) 19 kg 720 g
(E) None of these

Answer (A)

Explanation: As we know, subtraction is the inverse processs of addition. Here, subtraction is as follow:

kg	g
53	410
– 35	140
18	270

Therefore, 18 kg 270 g should be subtracted from 53 kg 410 g to get 35 kg 140 g

11. Susan bought 7 kg 500 of apples, 9 kg 300 g of oranges and 3 kg 800 g of grapes. Find the weight of all fruits.

(A) 21 kg 400 g (B) 19 kg 700 g

(C) 20 kg 600 g (D) 22 kg 800 g

(E) None of these

Answer (C)

Explanation: Here, addition is as follow:

```
   7  500 g
   9  300 g
 + 3  800 g
 ----------
  20  600 g
 ----------
```

On adding all the weights, the sum weight = 20 kg 600 g

Therefore, all fruits weigh 20 kg 600 g.

12. 15 kg 220 g of flour is removed from a drum containing 51 kg 770 g of flour. The left flour in the drum is:

(A) 35 kg 50 g (B) 36 kg 550 g

(C) 34 kg 500 g (D) 37 kg 450 g

(E) All of these

Answer (B)

Explanation: Here, subtraction is as follow:

```
   kg   g
   51  770
 – 15  220
 ---------
   36  550
 ---------
```

Therefore, the left flour in the drum is 36 kg 550 g.

13. There are 8 tea bags in a pack. If each bag contains 1 g 850 mg of tea leaves, the pack is of:

(A) 15 g 500 mg (B) 13 g 750 mg

(C) 12 g 450 mg (D) 14 g 800 mg

(E) None of these

Answer (D)

Explanation: Here, multiplication is as follow:

```
  g  mg
  1  850
   ×   8
 14  800
```

Therefore, the pack is of 14 g 800 mg.

14. If 1 kg 620 g of cashew nuts distribute among 9 boys, then each boy will get:

(A) 130 g of cashew nuts (B) 140 g of cashew nuts

(C) 180 g of cashew nuts (D) 190 g of cashew nuts

(E) None of these

Answer (C)

Explanation: Here, division is as follow:

```
9) 1 6 2 0 (180 g
  −9 ↓
   ×7 2
   −7 2
    0 0
```

Therefore, each boy will get 180 g of cashew nuts.

15. What should be added to 18 L 27 ml to get 27 L 18 ml?

(A) 19 L 991 ml (B) 8 L 981 ml

(C) 8 L 991 ml (D) 9 L 927 ml

(E) None of these

Answer (C)

Explanation: As we know, subtraction is the inverse process of addition.

Here, subtraction is as follow:

```
   L   ml
  27  018
− 18  027
   8  991
```

Therefore, 8 L 991 ml should be added to 18 L 27 ml to get 27 L 18 ml.

16. What should be subtracted from 63 L 25 ml to get 36 L 52 ml?

(A) 25 L 937 ml (B) 26 L 973 ml
(C) 25 L 963 ml (D) 26 L 953 ml
(E) None of these

Answer (B)

Explanation: As we know, subtraction is the inverse process of addition.

Here, subtraction is as follow:

	L	ml
	63	025
−	36	052
	26	973

When 36 L 52 ml is subtracted from 63 L 25 ml, the difference is 26 L 973 ml.
Therefore, 26 L 73 ml is subtracted from 63 L 25 ml to get 36 L 52 ml.

17. When 2100 ml of water is added to 34 L 200 ml of water, the total volume of water is:

(A) 34 L 400 ml (B) 36 L 100 ml
(C) 36 L 300 ml (D) 34 L 300 ml
(E) None of these

Answer (C)

Explanation: On adding, we get

34 L 200 ml + 2100 ml = 34000 ml + 200 ml + 2100 ml = 36300 ml = 36 L 300 ml

18. A bottle contains 3 L 230 ml of milk. Another bottle contains 2 L 850 ml of milk. When the milk of bottles poured into a pot, total milk in the pot will be:

(A) 6 L 80 ml (B) 5 L 800 ml
(C) 6 L 180 ml (D) 5 L 620 ml
(E) None of these

Answer (A)

Explanation: Here, addition is as follow:

	L	ml
	3	230
+	2	850
	6	080

Therefore, 3 L 230 ml of milk when added to 2 L 850 ml of milk, total milk in the pot is 6 L 80 ml.

19. 9 bottles of water can fill a bucket. If each bottle can hold 1 L 125 ml of water, how much water can hold the bucket?

(A) 9 L 750 ml (B) 10 L 825 ml

(C) 9 L 225 ml (D) 10 L 125 ml

(E) None of these

Answer (D)

Explanation: Here, multiplication is as follow:

L	ml
1	125
	× 9
10	125

The bucket can hold (1 L 125 ml) × 9 of water or, 10 L 125 ml of water.

20. 7 bottles of water can fill a bucket. If the bucket can hold maximum 12 L 250 ml of water, then each bottle can hold:

(A) 1 L 250 ml of water

(B) 1 L 750 ml of water

(C) 1 L 125 ml of water

(D) 2 L 25 ml of water

(E) None of these

Answer (B)

Explanation: Here, division is as follow:

```
7)12 250(1 L 750 ml
 - 7 ↓
   5 2
  -4 9↓
     3 5
    -3 5
     0 0
```

Therefore, 12 L 250 ml of water when poured into 7 bottles, each bottle can hold 1 L 750 ml of water.

Practice Exercise 8

1. **If 1 orange + 1 orange + 1 orange = 423 grams, then one orange = ?**

   (A) 139 grams (B) 121 grams (C) 141 grams (D) 132 grams
   (E) None of these

2. **If**  =  +  +  + **, and**  **= 750 ml, then what is the capacity of**  **?**

   (A) 6 L (B) 3 L (C) 4.5 L (D) 3.5 L
   (E) None of these

3. **If**  +  +  +  +  **= 180 grams, then**  +  **= ?**

   (A) 72 grams (B) 68 grams (C) 84 grams (D) 90 grams
   (E) None of these

4. **A copper wire of length 68 m is cut into 8 equal piece. How long is each piece of wire?**

   (A) 8 m (B) 8.5 m (C) 7 m (D) 7.5 m
   (E) None of these

5. **Distance between two colonies in a city is 18 km 500 m. Express the distance in metres.**

   (A) 1850 m (B) 18500 m (C) 185 m (D) 18500 m
   (E) None of these

6. **One-fifth of 5000 metres is:**

   (A) 5 km (B) 10 km (C) 1 km (D) $\frac{1}{2}$ km
   (E) None of these

7. **Subtract 17 grams from 17 kilograms.**

   (A) 16 kg 83 g (B) 17 kg 17 g (C) 15 kg 83 g (D) 16 kg 983 g
   (E) None of these

8. **Nine times of a capacity 2 L 240 ml is:**
(A) 20 L 160 ml (B) 17 L 920 ml
(C) 18 L 216 ml (D) 19 L 320 ml
(E) None of these

9. **What should be subtracted from 11 km to get 11 m?**
(A) 10 km 909 m (B) 9 km 899 m
(C) 10 km 989 m (D) 11 km 909 m
(E) None of these

10. **What should be added to 17 kg 11 g to get 71 kg 17 g?**
(A) 52 kg 66 g (B) 53 kg 8 g
(C) 54 kg 6 g (D) 55 kg 84 g
(E) None of these

11. **The weight of 7 coins is 84 grams. What is the weight of such 6 coins?**
(A) 72 grams (B) 60 grams (C) 68 grams (D) 48 grams
(E) None of these

12. **A bucket contains 6 litres of water. How much water do 67 such buckets contain?**
(A) 420 litres (B) 402 litres
(C) 368 litres (D) 396 litres
(E) None of these

13. **Susan has a rope 3 m 35 cm long and Garima has another rope 4 m 65 cm long. What is the total length of both ropes?**
(A) 8 m (B) 7 m 300 cm
(C) 7 m (D) 8 m 900 cm
(E) None of these

14. **If the length of a dining table is 7 m 50 cm and its breath is 3 m 45 cm, by how much does the length exceed the breath?**
(A) 3 m 50 cm (B) 4 m 50 cm
(C) 4 m 5 cm (D) 3 m 5 cm
(E) None of these

15. 3.7 kilometres is equal to:

(A) 370 metres
(B) 37000 metres
(C) 370.7 metres
(D) 37.7 metres
(E) None of these

16. Peter covers a distance 7 km 70 m in first hour and 6 km 77 m in the next hour. Total distance covered by Peter in two hours is:

(A) 13 km 147 m
(B) 14 km 47 m
(C) 13 km 84 m
(D) 14 km 147 m
(E) None of these

17. The sum weight of 7 kg 300g, 3 kg 700 g and 37 kg and 730 g is:

(A) 43 kg 740 g
(B) 48 kg 730 g
(C) 47 kg 330 g
(D) 46 kg 460 g
(E) None of these

18. There are 6 tea bags in a pack. If each bag contains 1 g 760 mg of tea leaves, the pack is of:

(A) 10 g 560 mg
(B) 8 g 320 mg
(C) 9 g 420 mg
(D) 11 g 760 mg
(E) None of these

19. If 5 L of milk distribute equally among 8 boys, each boy gets:

(A) 750 ml of milk
(B) 625 ml of milk
(C) 450 ml of milk
(D) 525 ml of milk
(E) None of these

20. A drum contains 8 kg 500 g of wheat. Another drum contains 11 kg 800 g of wheat. How much wheat is there in two drums?

(A) 21 kg 600 g
(B) 19 kg 800 g
(C) 20 kg 300 g
(D) 21 kg 300 g
(E) None of these

Chapter 9

Geometrical Shapes

Learning Objectives

- Introduction
- Classifying Shapes
- Basic Geometric Elements
- Polygon
- Triangle
- Rectangle and Square
- Perimeter

Introduction

There are shapes all around us. Shapes can be plane and solid. Lines, rays, line segments are basic concept of geometrical shapes. Geometry is a part of Mathematics which deals with points, lines, rays, and line segments. The word 'Geometry' comes from the Greek word 'Geo' means earth and 'Metria' means measure. In this chapter, we will learn about the basic geometrical shapes.

Classifying Shapes

We recognize geometrical shapes by their appearances without paying attention to their component parts such as sides and angles.

Plane Shapes and Solid Shapes

Shapes can be either plane or solid. Let us compare the plane shapes and solid shapes.

Plane Shapes	Solid Shapes
a) They are two dimensional (2D) shapes.	a) They are three dimensional (3D) shapes.
b) They have only one length and breadth but no thickness.	b) They have lenght breadth and thickness.
c) They have only one face.	c) They have many faces.
d) They do not occupy volume.	d) They occupy volume.
e) For example: 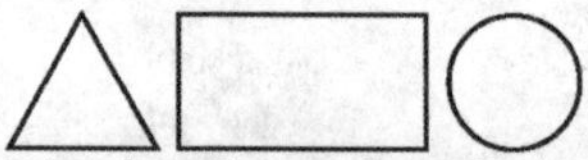 Triangle Rectangle Circle	e) 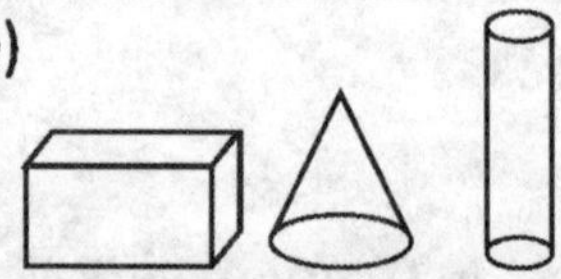 Cuboid Cone Cylinder

Solid Geometrical Shapes

Cube, cuboid, cylinder, sphere and cone are examples of solid geometrical shapes.

Cube:

A cube has 6 faces of the same shape and size. It has 12 equal edges and 8 vertices (corners).

Cuboid:

A cuboid has 6 faces in which the opposite faces are of the same shape and size. It has 12 edges where opposite edges are of the same size. It has 8 vertices.

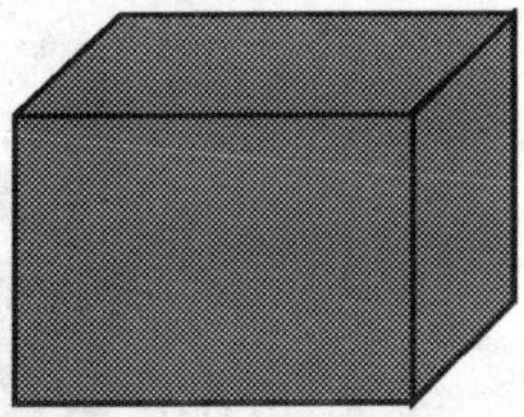

Cylinder:

A cylinder has 3 faces, 2 planes and 1 curved surface. It has 2 round edges and has no vertex or corner.

Sphere:

A sphere has 1 face or 1 curved surface. It has no edge and no vertex.

Cone:

A cone has 2 faces, 1 plane and 1 curved surface and 1 vertex.

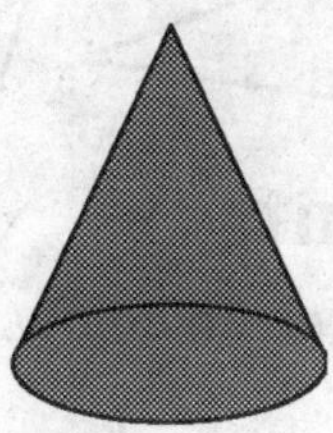

Example:

Which one of the following has a cylindrical shape?

(A) 

(B) 

(C) 

(D) 

(E) None of these

Answer (D)

Explanation: Figure given in option (D) has a cylindrical shape.

Regular Shapes and Irregular Shapes

Regular Shapes: Regular shapes have sides that are equal and interior (inside) angles that are all equal. In the given figures below, equilateral triangle, regular pentagon and regular hexagon are examples of regular shapes.

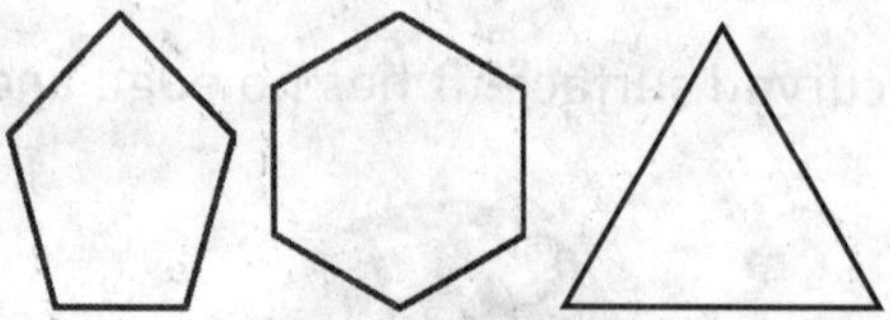

Irregular Shapes: Irregular shapes have sides and angles of different length and size. In the figures given below, scalene triangle, irregular quadrilateral and irregular pentagon are examples of irregular shapes.

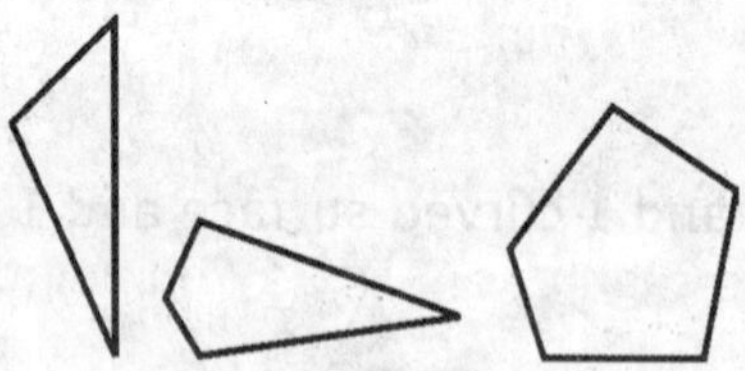

Basic Geometric Elements

Some basic geometric elements are given below. Let us study about these geometric elements.

Point

A point has no dimensions. It has only position. It is denoted by a dot (.). For example, point A is marked in the given figure. A point is generally represented by a capital letter.

Line Segment

A line segment is a straight path between 2 points. It has a fixed length. In the given figure, a line segment BC or CD is given which is denoted as $\overline{BC}$ or $\overline{CB}$.

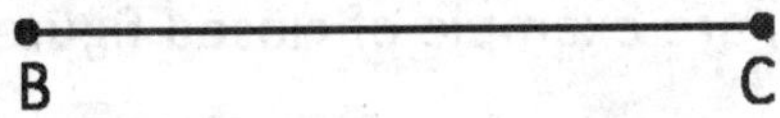

Line

A line is a straight path that goes on forever in both directions. It does not have fixed length. In the figure given below, a line PQ or QP is given which is denoted as $\overleftrightarrow{PQ}$ or $\overleftrightarrow{QP}$.

Example:

A line segment is defined by:

(A) 4 points (B) 3 points

(C) 2 points (D) 1 point

(E) None of these

Answer (C)

Explanation: A line segment has two end points.

Example:

Consider the following two statements:

Statement 1: A line segment has only one end point.

Statement 2: A line does not have a fixed length.

Which one of the following options is correct for the above statements?

(A) Statement 1 is true and 2 is false.

(B) Statement 2 is true and 1 is false.

(C) Both the statements 1 and 2 are true.

(D) Both the statements 1 and 2 are false.

(E) Cannot be determined

Answer (B)

Explanation: A line segment has two ends points and these end points make a segment or a part of a line.

Closed Figure and Open Figure

Closed Figure: A closed figure is figure which can be traced using the same starting and stopping points, and without crossing or retracing any section of the figure. Square, triangle, circle, etc, are example of closed figures.

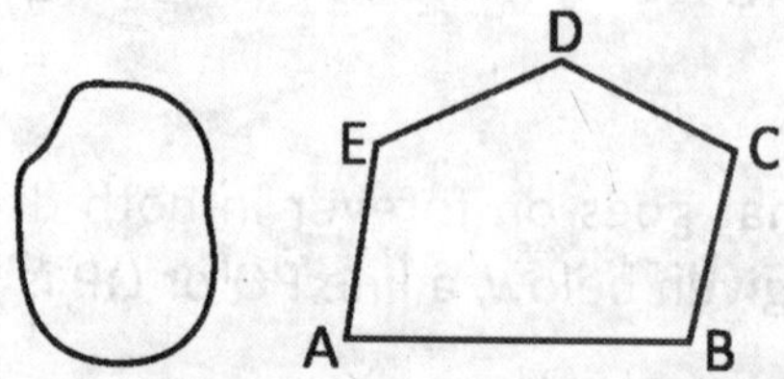

Open Figure: An open figure is figure which can be traced using the different starting and stopping points. Given figures are examples of open figures which have an opening.

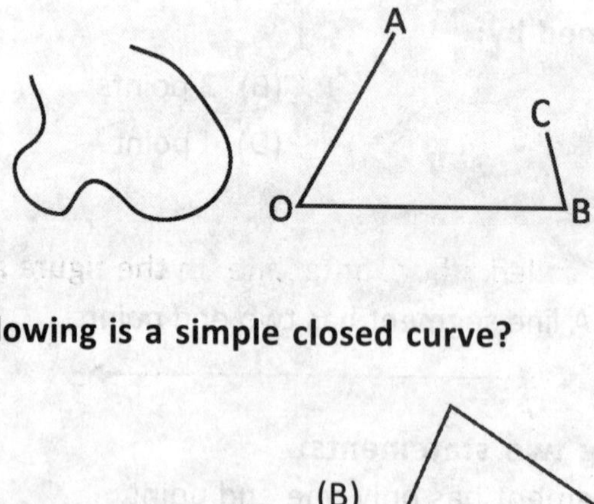

Example:

Which one of the following is a simple closed curve?

(A) 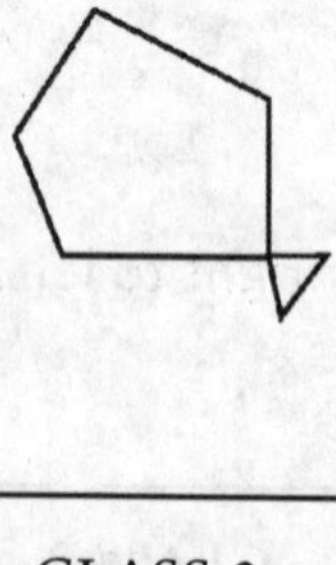

(B) 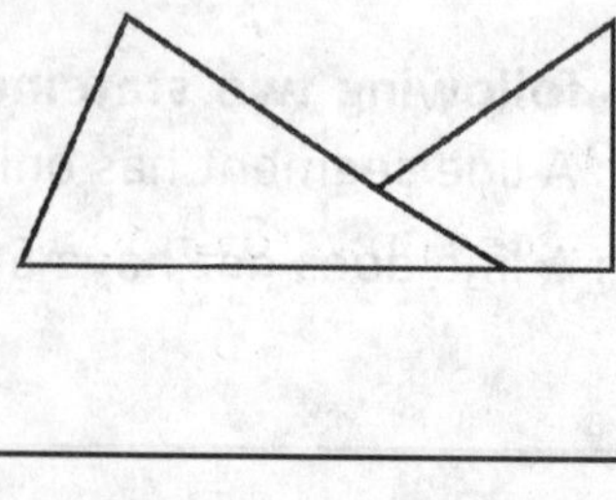

(C) 

(D) 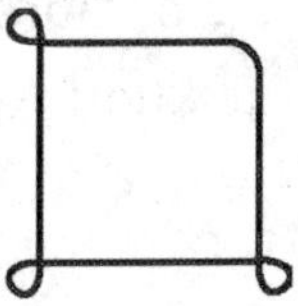

(E) None of these

Answer (C)

Explanation: A simple closed curve is a figure which can be traced using the same starting and stopping points, and without crossing or retracing any section of the figure. Figure given in option (C) is a simple closed curve.

Ray

A ray is a straight path that goes on forever in one direction. It has only one end point. In the figure given below, a ray AB is given which is denoted by $\overrightarrow{AB}$.

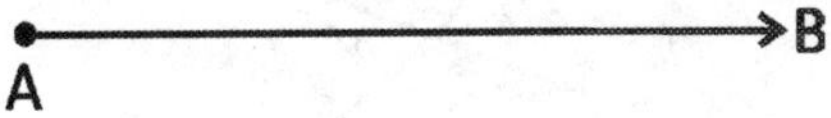

Vertical Line

An upright line is called a vertical line. In the figure given below, line AB is a vertical line.

Horizontal Line

A straight line across is called a horizontal line. In the figure given below, line AB is a horizontal line.

Slanting Line

A slanting line goes upward or downward from left to right or right to left.

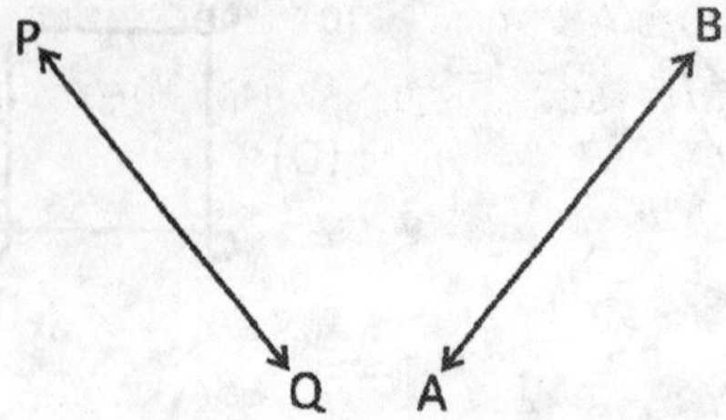

In the figures given above, line PQ and line AB are slanting lines. A slanting line is also called a **sloping line** or **oblique line**.

Curved Line

A **straight line** is nothing but a line with no curve. Most of times when we say about lines, we are talking about straight lines. A line that is not straight is called a **curved line**. But in geometry, a line is always straight, not curved.

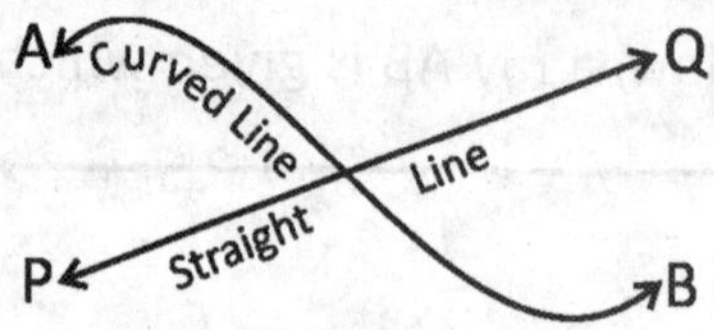

In the given figure above, AB is a curved line and PQ is a straight line or a line.

Parallel Lines

Two or more than two lines are called parallel lines if the distances between them remain the same, no matter how much you extend the lines.

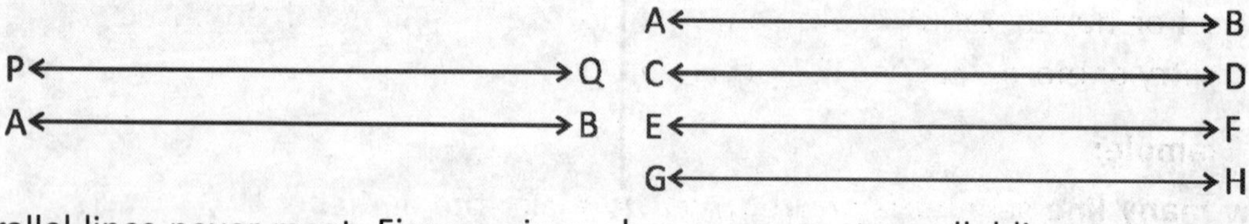

Parallel lines never meet. Figures given above represent parallel lines.

Intersecting Lines

Intersecting lines are two lines that share exactly one point. The shared point is called the **point of intersection**.

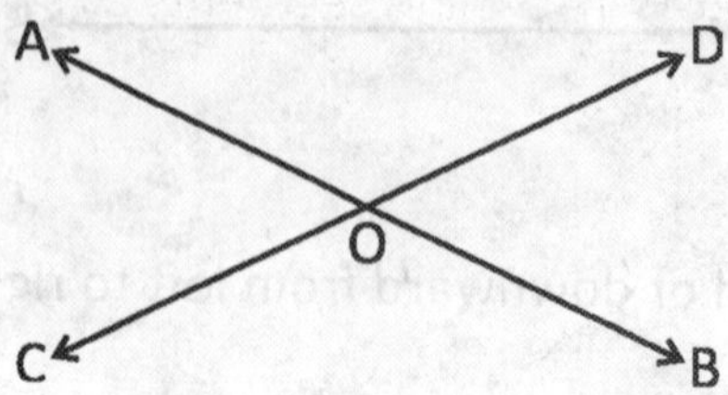

In the given figure above, lines AB and CD intersect each other at the point O. Here, line AB and CD are called **intersecting** lines and the point O is called the **point of intersection**.

Line of Symmetry

Look the figure given below. A dotted line PQ divides the figure in the middle to get two equal halves.

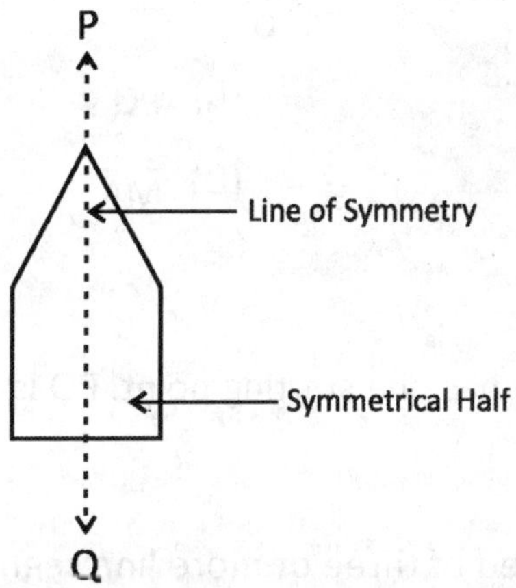

When a line divides a figure in the middle to get two equal halves, the halves are said to be symmetrical. Line which divides the figure is called the **line of symmetry.** In the given figure above, PQ is the line of symmetry. The line of symmetry can be vertical or horizontal. A figure can have no line of symmetry, exactly one line of symmetry or more than one line of symmetry.

Example:

How many line segments are required to make the alphabet W?

(A) 6 (B) 4 (C) 3 (D) 5

(E) None of these

Answer (B)

Explanation: Letter W has 4 line segments as shown below:

W ⇒ 

Example:

Which one of the following is *not* a ray in the given figure?

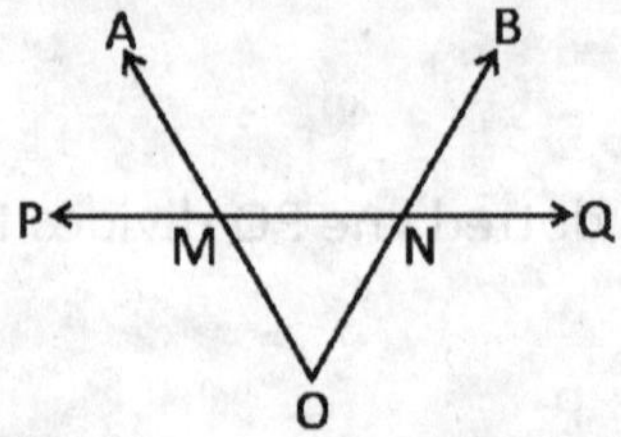

(A) $\overrightarrow{OA}$ (B) $\overrightarrow{PQ}$

(C) $\overrightarrow{OB}$ (D) $\overrightarrow{MA}$

(E) None of these

Answer (B)

Explanation: A ray has one starting point. PQ is a line with no starting point.

Polygon

A simple closed figure formed of three or more line segments is called a polygon. In the given figure, triangle, quadrilateral, pentagon and hexagon, all are examples of polygon.

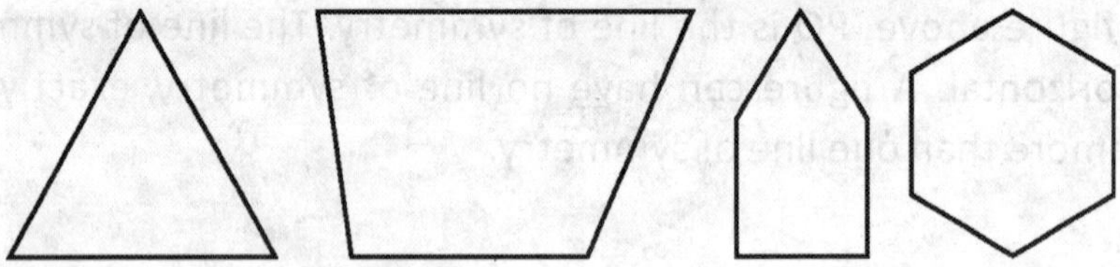

Regular and Irregular Polygon

A regular polygon has all sides equal and all angles equal, otherwise, it is an irregular polygon.

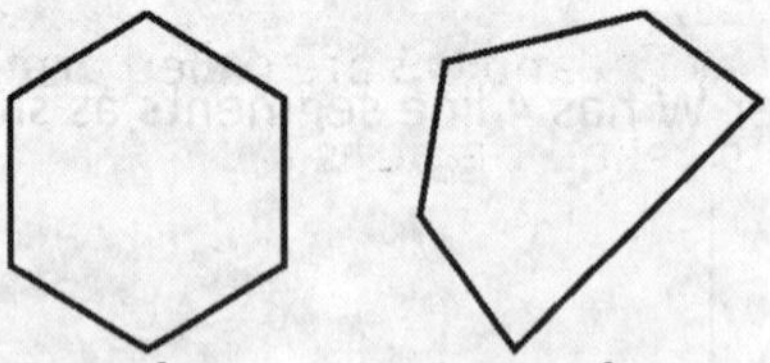

Regular polygon **Irregular polygon**

Simple and Complex Polygon

A simple polygon has only one boundary and it does not cross over itself. A complex polygon intersects itself.

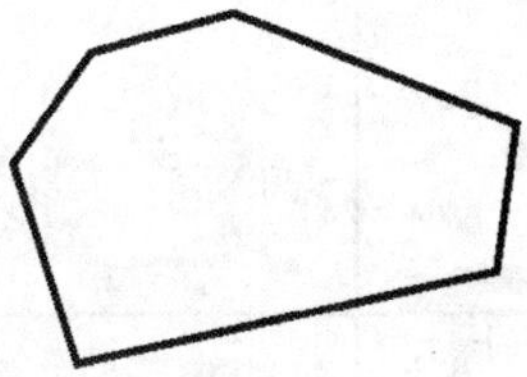

Simple polygon

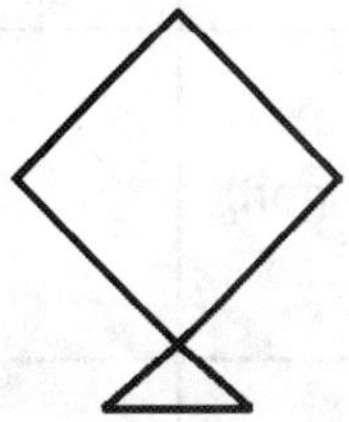

Complex polygon

Vertex and Angle

A point where two or more straight lines meet is called its **vertex**. The plural of word 'vertex' is **vertices**. A vertex is also known as **corner**.

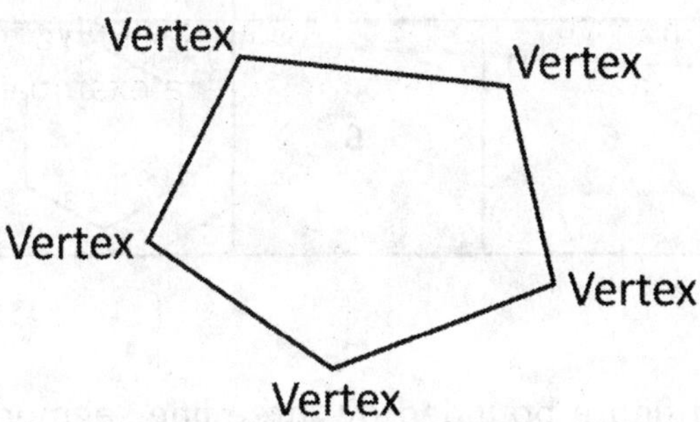

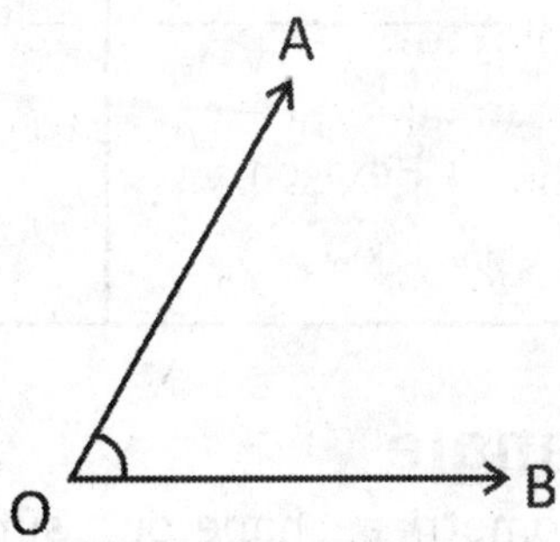

Inclination between two rays having the common end point is called an angle. In the figure given above, OA and OB are two rays which have a common end point O. The inclination between the rays OA and OB is an angle AOB and it is denoted as $\angle AOB$. Point O is called **vertex** and ray OA and OB are called **arms** of the angle AOB. Angles are usually measured in units called **degrees (°)**.

Names of Polygons

Names of polygons based on their number of sides are given in the following table.

Name	Number of Sides	Number of vertices	Number of Angles	Shape
Triangle (or Trigon)	3	3	3	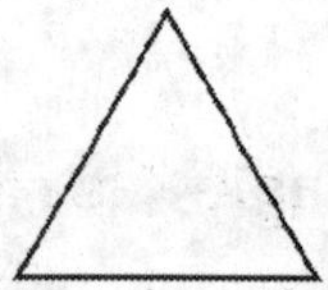
Quadrilateral (or Tetragon)	4	4	4	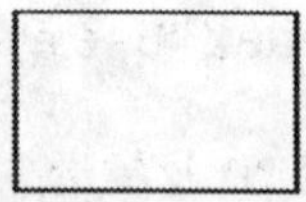
Pentagon	5	5	5	
Hexagon	6	6	6	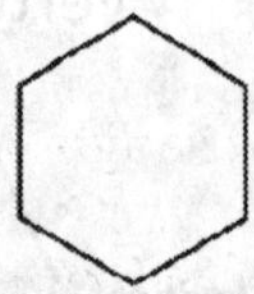

Triangle

A geometrical shape or a simple closed figure bounded by three line segments is called a triangle. The line segments are called sides of the triangle.

Parts of a Triangle

- A triangle has three sides. In the triangle ABC given below, sides are AB, BC and CA.
- A triangle has three vertices. In the given triangle ABC, vertices are A, B and C.
- A triangle has three angles. Angles are always formed at the vertices.

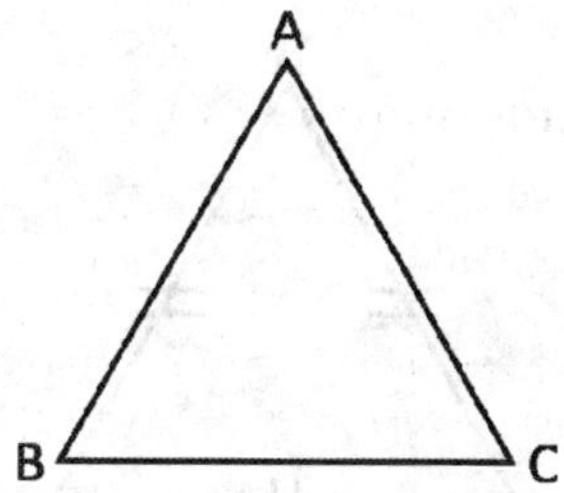

Triangle Classification

The basic elements of any triangle are its sides and angles. Let us study the types of triangles that classified on the basis of their sides.

Scalene Triangle

A triangle whose all sides are of different length is called a scalene triangle. No angles are equal in a scalene triangle.

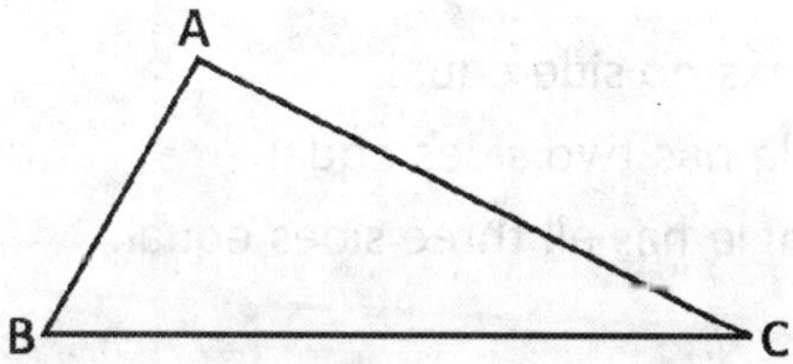

In the triangle ABC given above, side AB, BC and AC are not equal.

Isosceles Triangle

A triangle whose any two sides are of equal length is called an isosceles triangle. Opposite angles of equal sides of an isosceles triangle are equal.

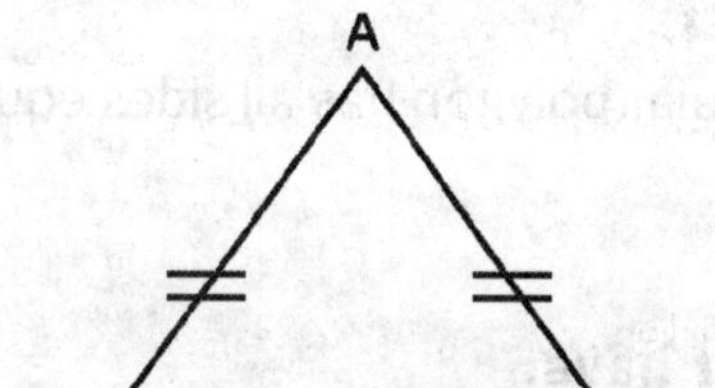

In the triangle ABC given above, side AB and AC are equal.

Equilateral Triangle

A triangle whose all three sides are of equal length is called an equilateral triangle. All three angles of an equilateral triangle are of 60°. An equilateral triangle is also known as an equiangular triangle.

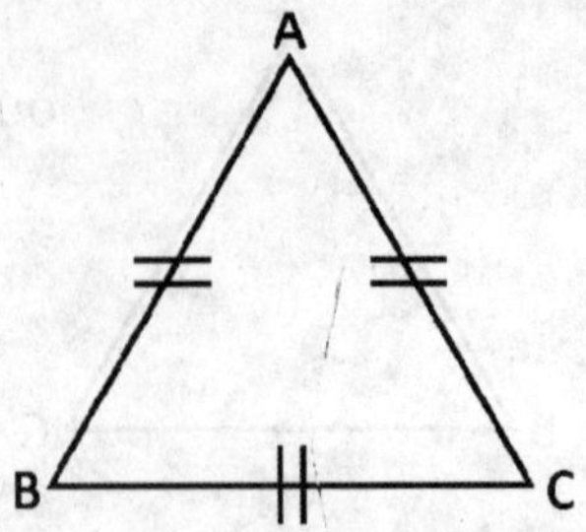

In the triangle ABC given above, sides AB, BC and AC are equal.

Properties of Triangle

- A triangle has three sides, three angles and three vertices.
- The sum of all three angles of a triangle is equal to 180°.
- If two angles of a triangle are equal then the angles opposite to them are also equal.
- A scalene triangle has no side equal.
- An isosceles triangle has two sides equal.
- An equilateral triangle has all three sides equal.

Example:

A polygon which has no equal side is called a/an:

(A) regular polygon (B) irregular polygon
(C) complex polygon (D) non-polygon
(E) None of these

Answer (B)

Explanation: A regular polygon has all sides equal otherwise, it is an irregular polygon.

Example:

A regular hexagon does *not* have:

(A) six equal sides (B) six equal angles
(C) six vertices (D) six pairs of parallel sides
(E) None of these

Answer (D)

Explanation: A regular hexagon has six equal sides, six equal angles and has six vertices. A regular hexagon has three pairs of parallel sides.

Rectangle and Square

A geometrical shape or a simple closed figure bounded by four line segments is called a **quadrilateral**. There are many different types of quadrilateral which can be classified by the relationship of their sides and angles. The two special types of quadrilateral are rectangle and square.

Rectangle

A rectangle is a special type of quadrilateral in which:

(a) opposite sides are equal.

(b) both diagonals are equal, and

(c) each angle is a right angle (90°).

In the rectangle ABCD given above, AB = CD and AD = BC

Diagonals AC = BD and each angle is of 90°.

Square

A square is a special type of quadrilateral in which:

(a) all four sides are equal

(b) both diagonals are equal, and

(c) each angle is a right angle (90°).

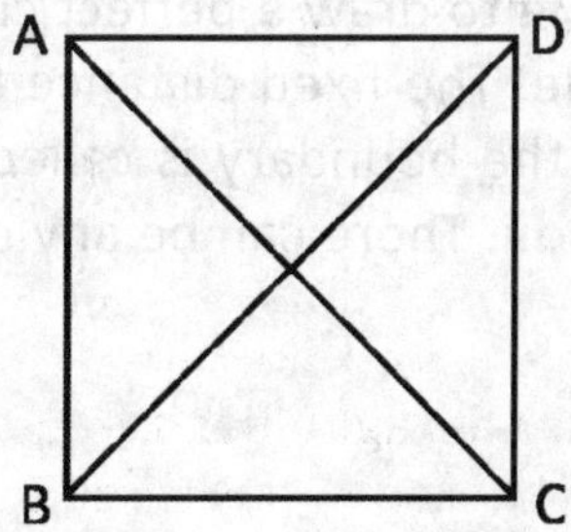

In the square ABCD given above, AB = BC = CD = AD and diagonal, AC = BD. Each angle is of 90°. A square is a special type of rectangle, but not every rectangle is a square.

Example:

The shapes given below are:

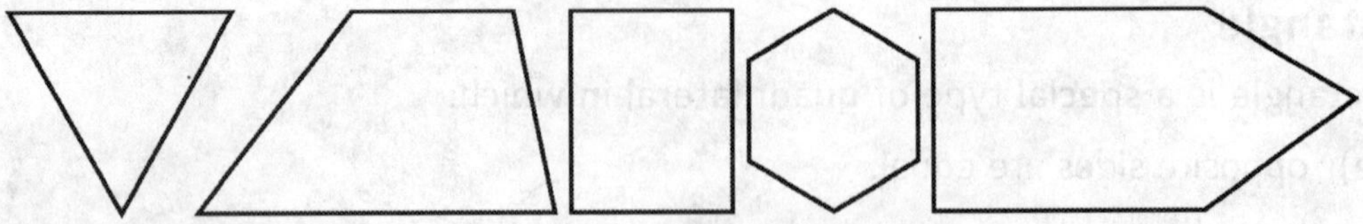

(A) triangles
(B) quadrilaterals
(C) polygons
(D) pentagons
(E) None of these

Answer (C)

Explanation: All of the given shapes are polygons.

Circle

A circle is a simple closed shape with curved boundary each of whose points is at the same distance from a fixed point inside it. A circle has no sides or corners, like the square, rectangle and triangle.

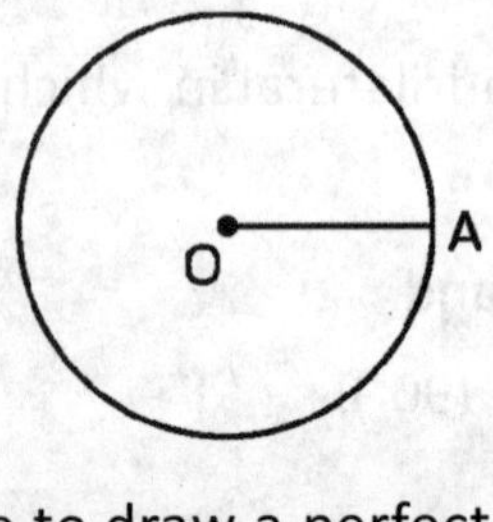

We need a fixed point to be able to draw a perfect circle around it. This fixed point is called the **centre** of the circle. The fixed distance from centre O, as given in the figure above, to any point on the boundary is called the **radius** of the circle. The plural of the word 'radius' is **radii**. There can be any number of radii. All the radii of a circle are equal in length.

Example:

Which one of the following shapes is different from other?

(A) 

(B) 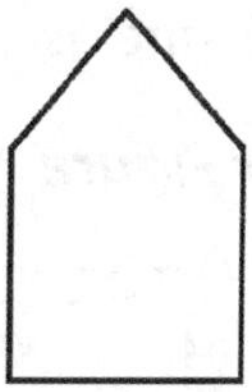

(C) 

(D) 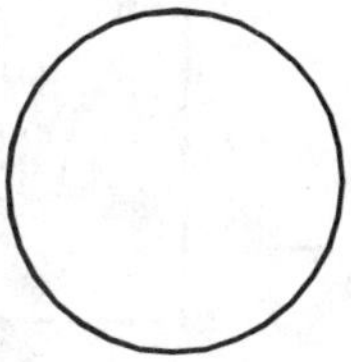

(E) 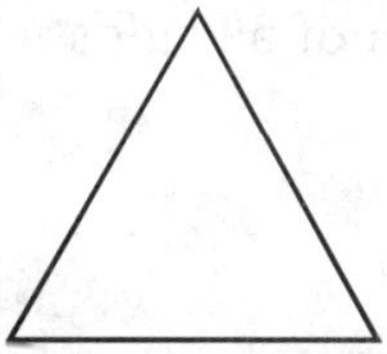

Answer (D)

Explanation: Figures given in option (A), (B), (C) and (E) have vertices but the given circle in option (D) has no vertex or no corner.

Perimeter

A plane figure bounded by line segments and composed of angular corners is called a **rectilinear figure**. Triangles, quadrilateral, pentagons and hexagons are examples of rectilinear figures. A circle is not a rectilinear figure.

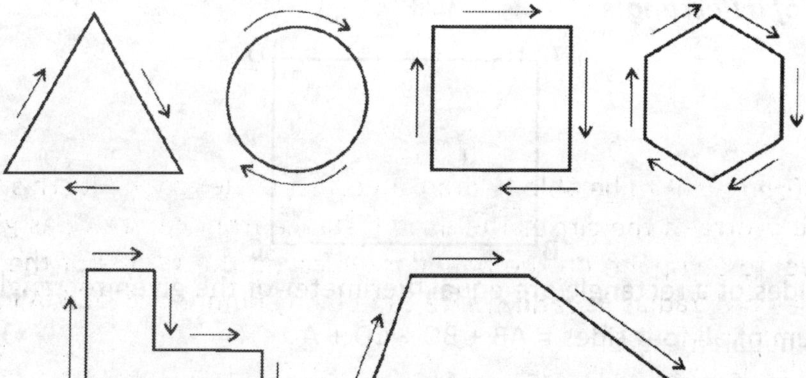

The length of the total boundary of a closed figure is called its **perimeter**. To find the perimeter of a rectilinear figure, we need to know the length of its side. The metric unit of perimeter is same as the unit of length.

Perimeter of a Rectilinear Figure

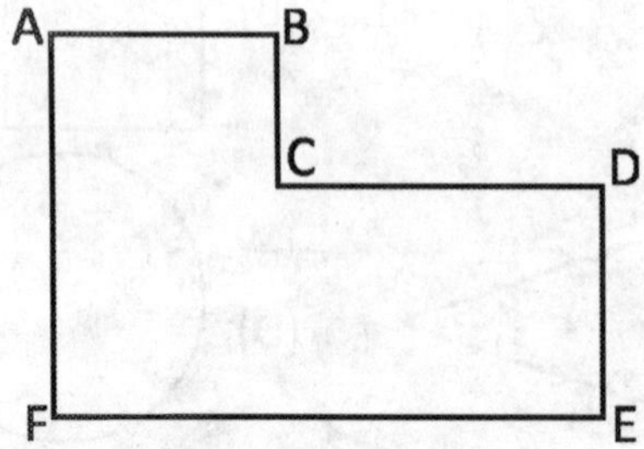

Perimeter of the given rectilinear figure ABCDEF = The sum of all sides

= AB + BC + CD + DE + EF + AF

Perimeter of a Triangle

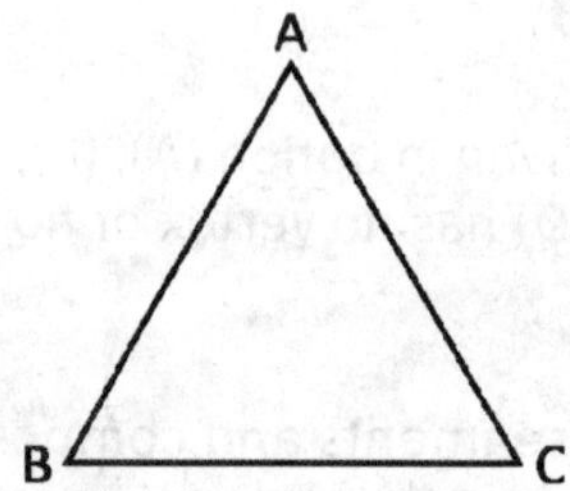

Perimeter of the given triangle ABC = Sum of all three sides = AB + BC + AC

Perimeter of a Rectangle

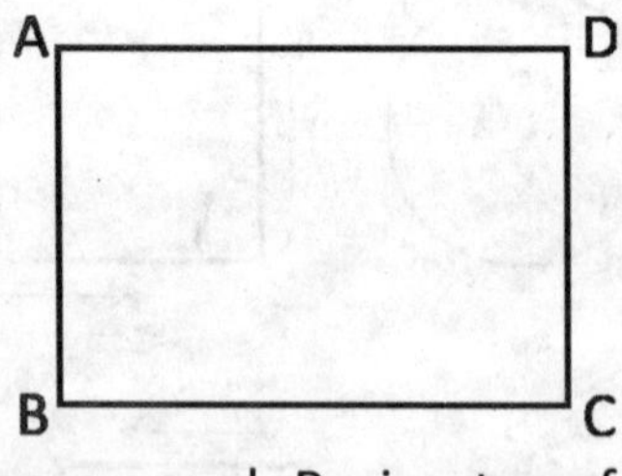

Opposite sides of a rectangle are equal. Perimeter of the given rectangle ABCD

= Sum of all four sides = AB + BC + CD + AD

Or, perimeter of a rectangle = (Sum of two unequal sides) × 2

Perimeter of a Square

All four sides of a square are equal.

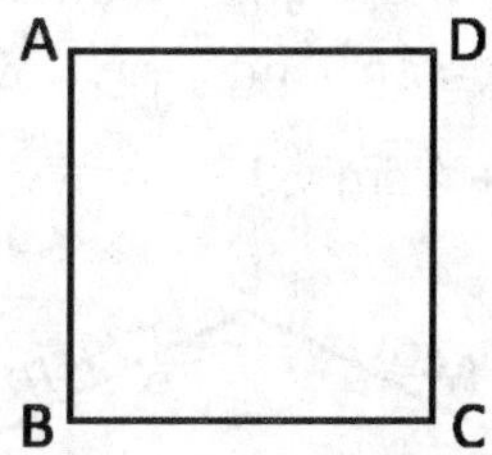

Perimeter of the given square ABCD

= Sum of all four sides = AB + BC + CD + AD = 4 × One side

Perimeter of a Circle

Perimeter of a circle is the length of its circular boundary. The circular boundary is known as its **circumference**.

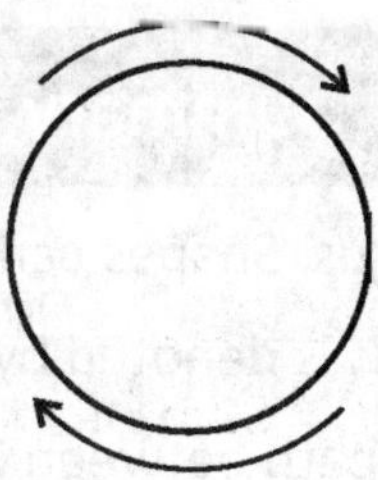

Example:

Find the perimeter of the given diamond.

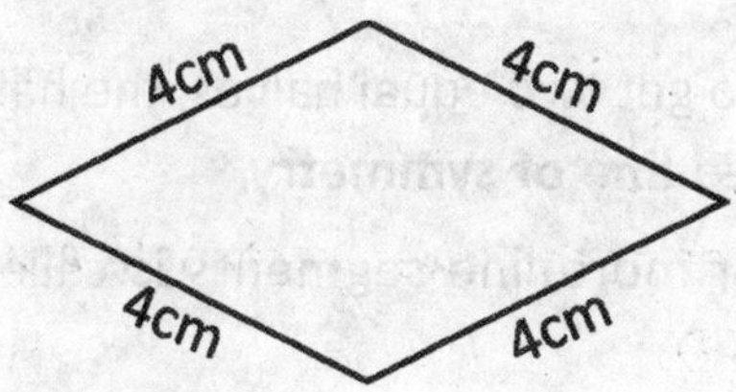

(A) 20 cm (B) 16 cm

(C) 12 cm (D) 8 cm

(E) None of these

Answer (B)

Explanation: Perimeter of the given diamond ABCD

= Sum of all four sides = AB + BC + CD + AD

= 4 cm + 4 cm + 4 cm + 4 cm = 16 cm

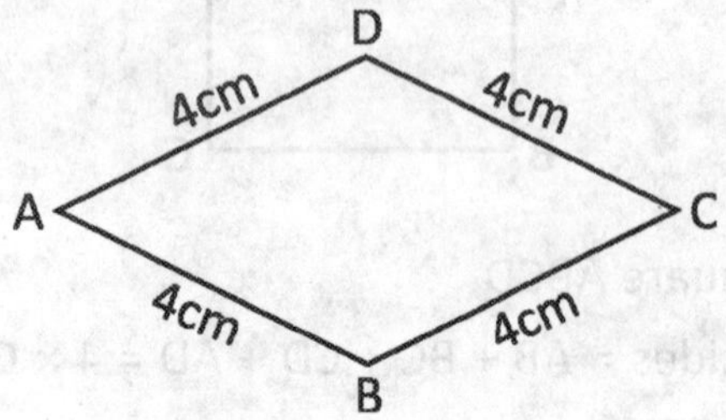

Summary

- There are shapes all around us. Shapes can be plane and solid.
- A **point** has no dimensions. It is denoted by a dot (.) and it has only position.
- A **line segment** is a straight path between 2 points. It has a fixed length.
- A **ray** is a straight path that goes on forever in one direction. It has only one end point.
- A **line** is a straight path that goes on forever in both directions. It does not have a fixed length.
- When a line divides a figure in the middle to get two equal halves, the halves are said to be symmetrical. The line is called **line of symmetry.**
- A simple closed figure formed of three or more line segments is called a **polygon**.
- The length of the total boundary of a closed figure is called its **perimeter.**

Did You Know?

- The triangle property 'Sum of all angles of a triangle is 180°' was first described by Greek mathematician 'Pythagoras'.
- Distance between the Sun and the Earth was first calculated by the Greek astronomer 'Aristarchus'.
- Aristarchus realized that when the Moon was exactly half illuminated, it form of right angle with the Earth and the Sun.

Solved Problems

1. Which one of the following is generally used to tell the position of something?

(A) Line segments (B) Rays

(C) Lines (D) Points

(E) None of these

Answer (D)

Explanation: Points are generally used to tell the position of something.

2. How many triangles are there in the given figure?

(A) 4 (B) 8 (C) 12 (D) 16

(E) None of these

Answer (B)

Explanation: Triangles are: Δ ABC, Δ BCD, Δ ADC, Δ BAD and Δ AOB, Δ BOC, Δ COD, Δ AOD.

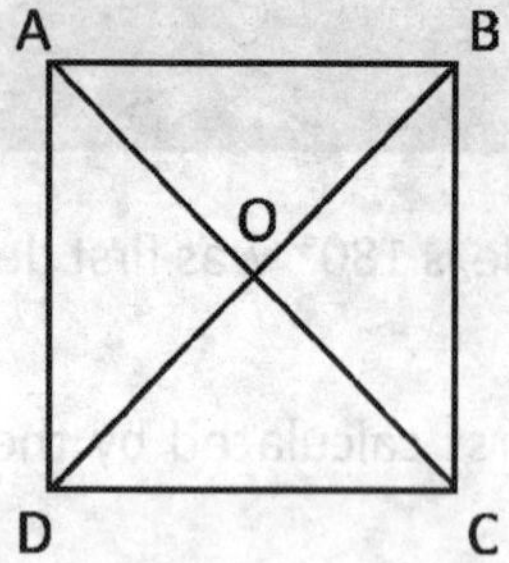

3. Which of the following shapes has *no* pointed corner?

(A) 

(B) 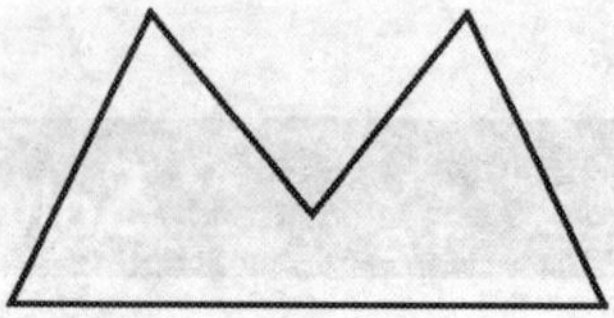

(C) 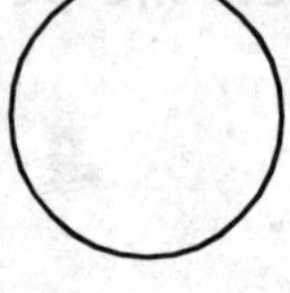

(D) 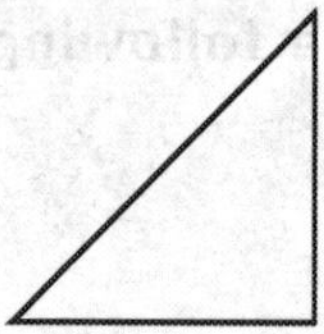

(E) None of these

Answer (C)

Explanation: A circle has no vertex or no pointed corner.

4. How many line segments would needed to make the given figure?

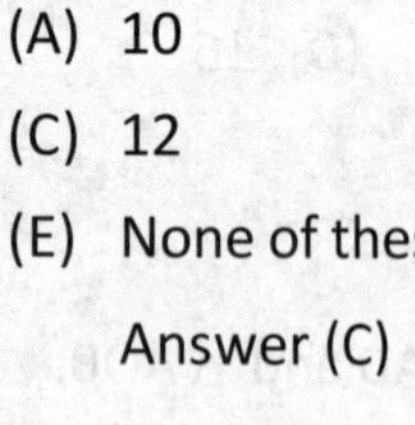

(A) 10
(B) 11
(C) 12
(D) 14
(E) None of these

Answer (C)

Explanation:

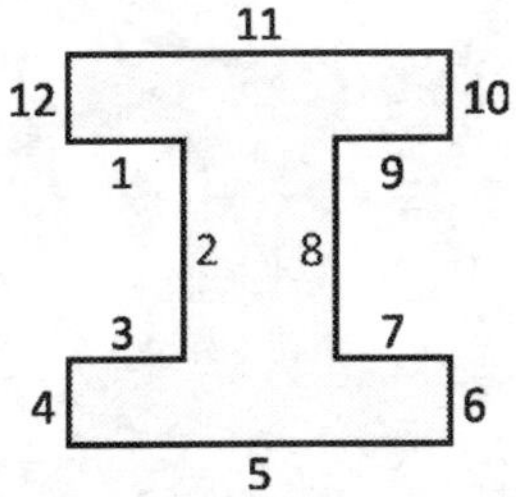

Clearly, the number of line segments needed to make the shaded figure is 12.

5. Which one of the following represents a rectangular solid?

(A) 

(B) 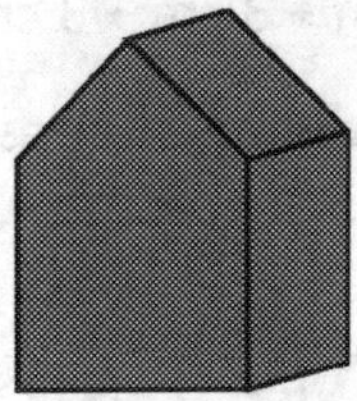

(C) 

(D) 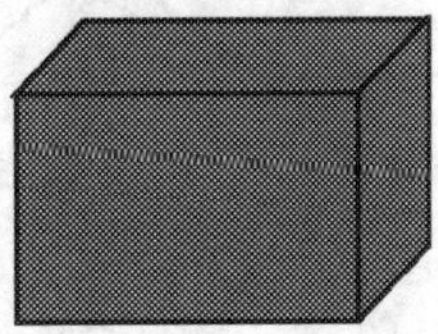

(E) None of these

Answer (D)

Explanation: A cuboid is a rectangular solid. Image given in option (D) shows a rectangular solid or a cuboid.

6. The given figure is made up of 4 squares. Find the perimeter of the figure.

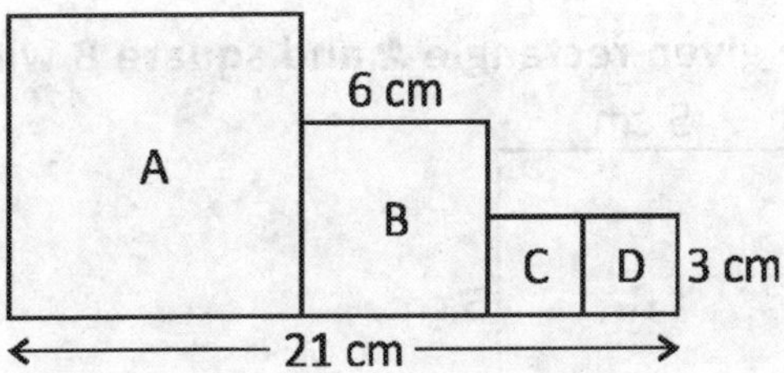

(A) 57 cm (B) 54 cm (C) 60 cm (D) 51 cm

(E) None of these

Answer (C)

Explanation: Here, a = 21 cm – 6 cm – (3 + 3) cm = 21 cm – 12 cm = 9 cm

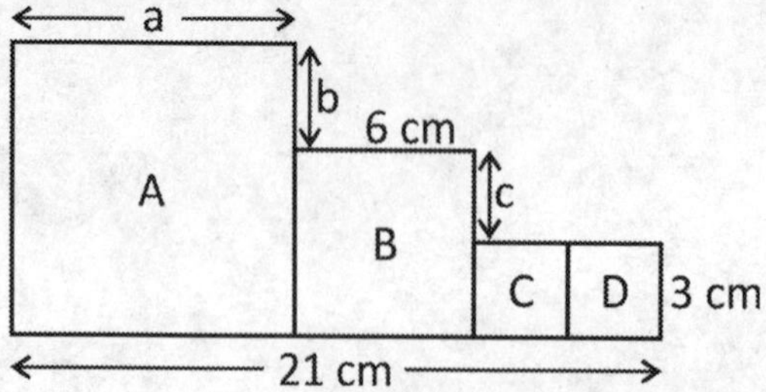

b = 9 cm – 6 cm = 3 cm and, c = 6 cm – 3 cm = 3 cm

Therefore, the required perimeter

= 21 cm + 3 cm + 3 cm + 3 cm + 3 cm + 6 cm + 3 cm + 9 cm + 9 cm = 60 cm

7. Which of the following shapes is a circle?

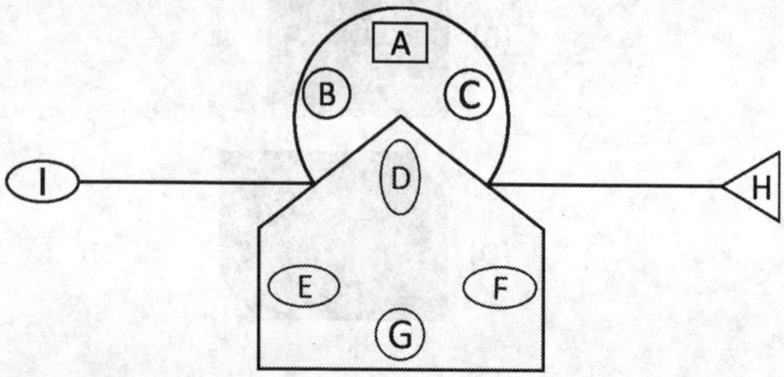

(A) Shape E (B) Shape C (C) Shape A (D) Shape H

(E) None of these

Answer (B)

Explanation: Only the shapes represent B, C and G are the shapes of a circle.

8. Difference of the perimeters of the given rectangle A and square B will be:

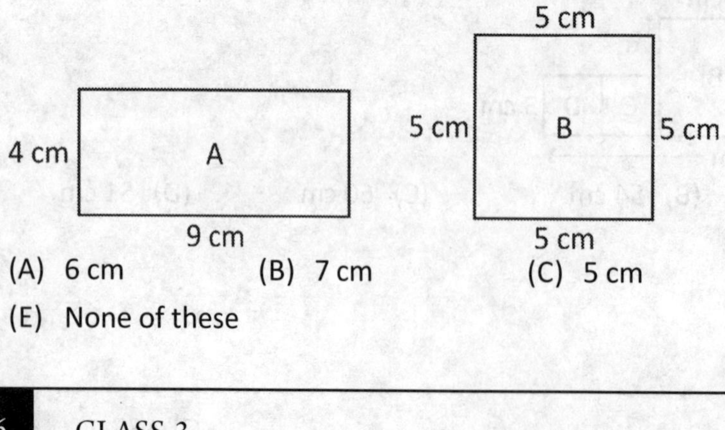

(A) 6 cm (B) 7 cm (C) 5 cm (D) 5 cm

(E) None of these

Answer (A)

Explanation: Perimeter of rectangle A

= Sum of unequal side × 2 = (9 + 4) × 2 cm = 13 × 2 cm = 26 cm

Perimeter of square B = 4 × One side = (5 × 4) cm = 20 cm

Therefore, the required difference = 26 cm – 20 cm = 6 cm

9. How many triangles are there in the given figure?

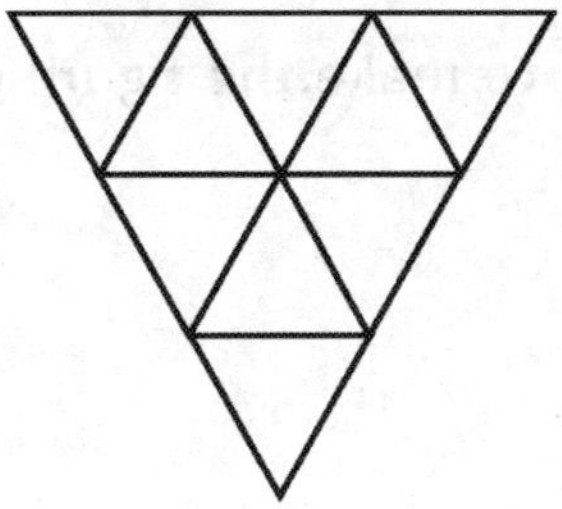

(A) 11 (B) 10 (C) 13 (D) 12

(E) None of these

Answer (C)

Explanation: Clearly, there are 9 + 3 + 1 = 13 triangles in the given figure.

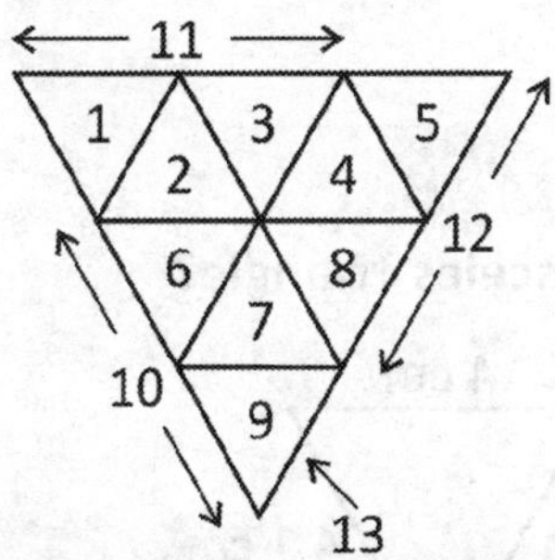

10. Which one of the following has *no* vertex?

(A) Cone (B) Cuboid (C) Cylinder (D) Cube

(E) None of these

Answer (C)

Explanation: A cone has one vertex. A cuboid and a cube have 8 vertices. A cylinder has no vertex.

Practice Exercise 9

1. Which one of the following is a shape with two curricular bases?

(A) Sphere
(B) Cylinder
(C) Cone
(D) Prism
(E) None of these

2. For one cube **, how many cubes are needed to make the figure given below?**

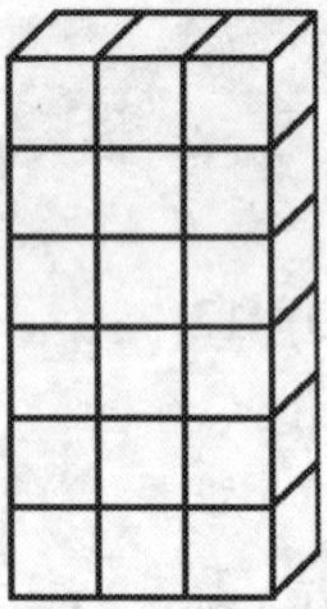

(A) 24
(B) 22
(C) 16
(D) 18
(E) None of these

3. Which of the following shapes is *not* an isosceles triangle?

(A) 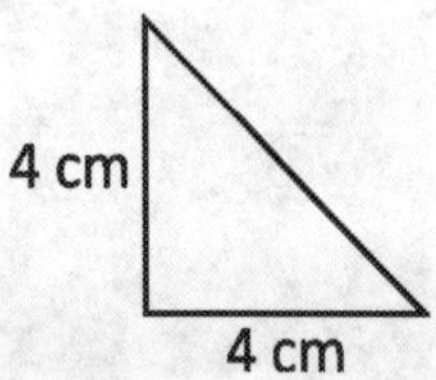

(B) 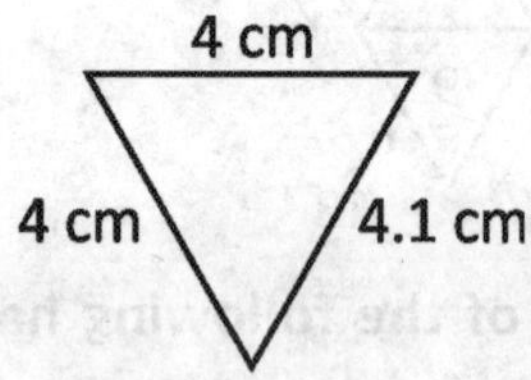

(C) 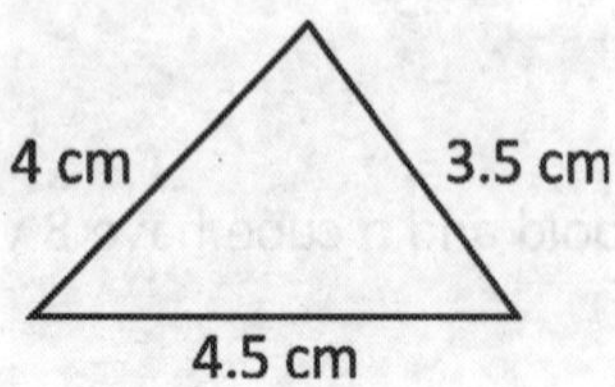

(D) 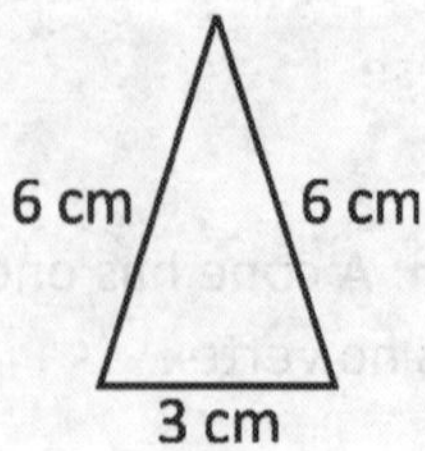

(E) None of these

4. **How many edges are there in the figure given below?**

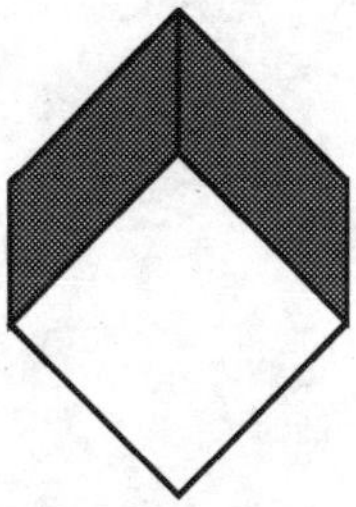

(A) 8 (B) 12 (C) 13 (D) 16
(E) None of these

5. **Number of triangles in the figure given below is:**

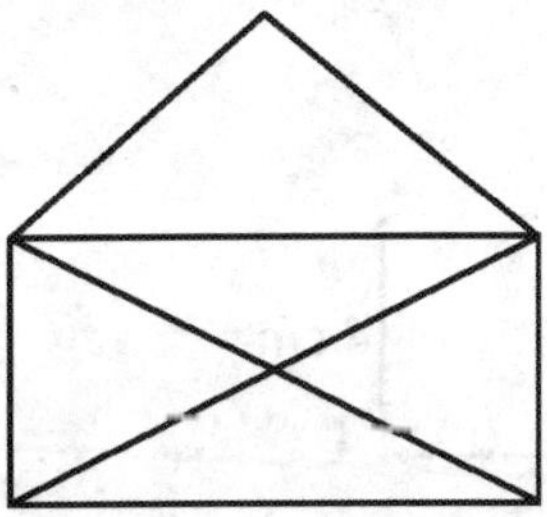

(A) 5 (B) 6 (C) 9 (D) 11
(E) None of these

6. **Which of the following shapes can be the face of a cuboid?**

(A) Circle (B) Rectangle
(C) Triangle (D) Cone
(E) None of these

7. **Find the perimeter of the given figure.**

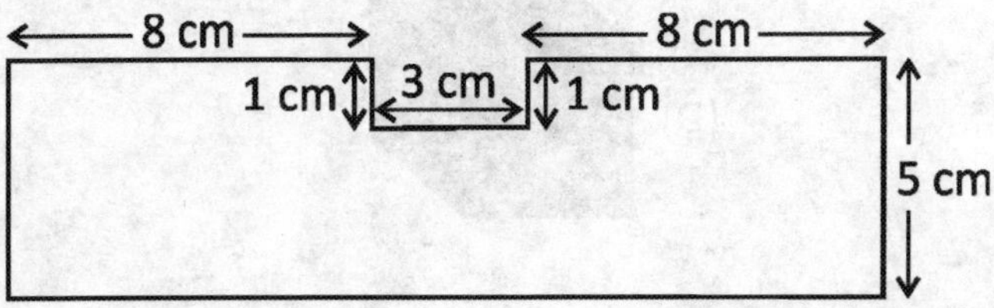

(A) 48 cm (B) 49 cm
(C) 54 cm (D) 50 cm
(E) None of these

8. How many lines are there in the given figure?

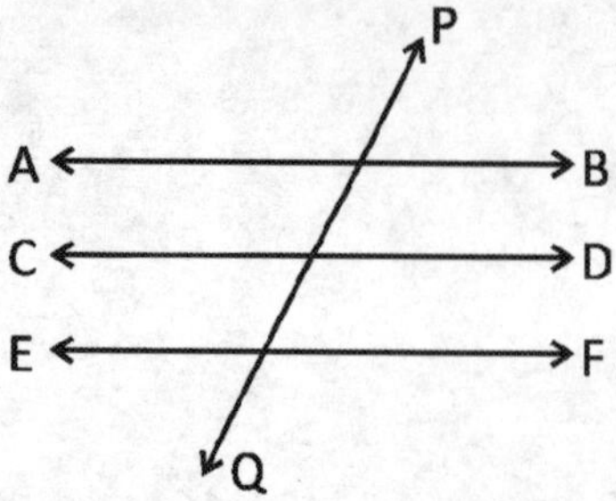

(A) 10 (B) 5 (C) 8 (D) 13

(E) None of these

9. Sum of perimeters of the given square A and rectangle B will be:

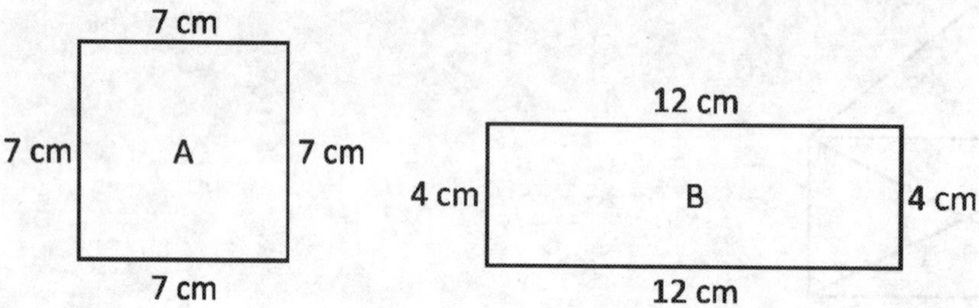

(A) 56 cm (B) 64 cm (C) 67 cm (D) 60 cm

(E) None of these

10. Which one of the following solids has more than one corner?

(A) 

(B) 

(C) 

(D) 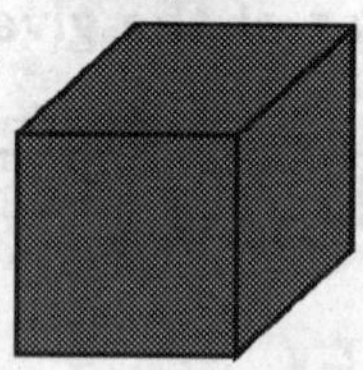

(E) None of these

Chapter 10

Data Handling

Learning Objectives

- Introduction
- Data
- Pictograph
- Bar Graph

Introduction

Everyday we come across a lot of information in the form of numerical figures, tables and graphs. These are provided by newspapers, televisions, magazines and other means of communication. The term **'data handling'** is all about gathering information and representing the same through pictographs and diagrams. In this chapter, we will study about pictograph and bar graph, and how to extract informations contained by the graphs.

Data

A collection of facts, such as numbers, words, measurements, observations or even just descriptions of things is called **data**. Data can be represented graphically to give clear idea of what it represents. It is easier to interpret and organise data using pictorial representation some of the way data can be represented pictorially are:

(1) Pictograph (2) Bar graph

Pictograph

A picture used to represent an item of data is called a symbol. A pictograph is way of showing data using pictures. In a pictograph, lots of simple pictures as symbols are used to give information, where a key is provided to tell what quantity is represented by each symbol. Generally pictographs are used to represent less information. In a pictograph, we will need to look at the key carefully to determine how many items or quantities are represented by each symbol.

Suppose the following data were collected about favourite colours of students of a class.

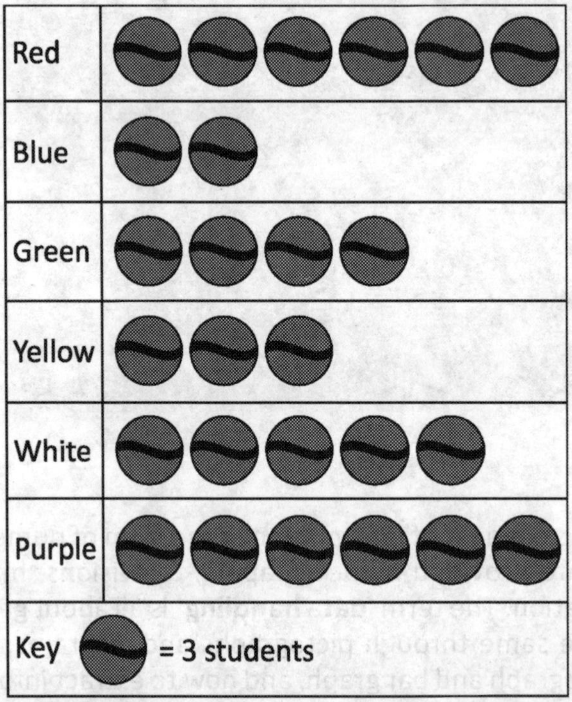

Clearly, here one symbol  represents 3 students. If we observe the given pictograph, we conclude that the largest number of students likes red colour and the least number of students like blue colour.

Reading a Pictograph

Pictograph is the easiest method for representation of data. A pictograph is basically a way to represent data with pictures that relate to data. Let us look at the following word problem that asks to interpret a pictograph. Here we analyse the data and answer the given questions.

Example:

In a school canteen, the number of ice-creams sold during the first six months is represented in the pictograph given below.

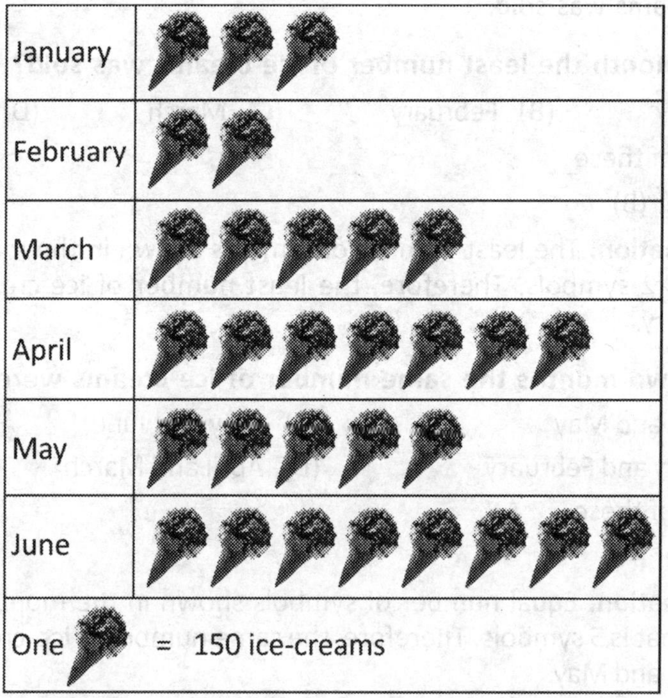

Read the pictograph and answer the following questions:

1. The key signifies that one  **represents:**

(A) 100 ice-creams (B) 120 ice-creams
(C) 150 ice-creams (D) 50 ice-creams
(E) None of these

Answer (C)

Explanation: The key signifies that one  represents 150 ice-creams.

2. In which month, the maximum number of ice-creams was sold?

(A) January (B) April (C) May (D) June

(E) None of these

Answer (D)

Explanation: The maximum number of symbols shown in the month of June that is 8 symbols. Therefore, in the month of June, the maximum number of ice-creams was sold.

3. In which month the least number of ice-creams was sold?

(A) January (B) February (C) March (D) May

(E) None of these

Answer (B)

Explanation: The least number of symbols shown in the month of February that is 2 symbols. Therefore, the least number of ice-creams was sold in February.

4. In which two months the same number of ice-creams were sold?

(A) March and May (B) May and June

(C) January and February (D) April and March

(E) None of these

Answer (A)

Explanation: Equal number of symbols shown in the months of March and May that is 5 symbols. Therefore, the same number of ice-creams was sold in March and May.

5. How many ice-creams were sold in all six months?

(A) 4000 (B) 5500 (C) 4500 (D) 3500

(E) None of these

Answer (C)

Explanation: Total number of symbols from January to June

$= (3 + 2 + 5 + 7 + 5 + 8) = 30$

One symbol = 150 ice-creams

Number of ice-creams sold in all six months = $30 \times 150 = 4500$

Therefore, 4500 ice-creams were sold in all six months.

6. **If one ice-cream costs ₹ 5, then how much had the canteen manager earn in the month of April?**

(A) ₹ 5550 (B) ₹ 5250 (C) ₹ 4250 (D) ₹ 4550

(E) None of these

Answer (B)

Explanation: Number of symbols shown in the month of April = 7

One symbol = 150 ice-creams

Total number of ice-creams sold in April = 7 × 150 = 1050

Cost of 1 ice-cream = ₹ 5. Cost of 1050 ice-creams = ₹ (1050 × 5) = ₹ 5250

Therefore, the canteen manager had earned ₹ 5250 in the month of April.

Bar Graph

We can also represent data pictorially with the help of a bar graph. A bar graph is a chart that uses bars to show comparisons between categories of data. It is another types of graph used to showing data or information in a quick way. The bars can be either horizontal or vertical. Bar graphs with vertical box are sometimes called vertical bar graphs. They are quite simple and easy to draw.

To draw a bar graph, we need two axes: one horizontal axis is called the X-axis and the vertical axis is called the Y-axis. Let us draw a bar graph.

Suppose the following data were collected regarding the number of students in class 1 to 6 of a school.

Class 1	Class 2	Class 3	Class 4	Class 5	Class 6
20	25	15	30	25	10

Let us draw a bar graph to detect this information.

Step 1: Draw a horizontal line OX and a vertical line OY, meeting at a point O.

Step 2: Choose a convenient scale. Along OX and OY, mark point at equal intervals.

Step 3: Now, from the points taken along OX, draw rectangular bars keeping width of the bars and distance between the bars equal. Length (heights) of the bars represent respective observations.

Step 4: Label these rectangular bars with the company they represent and shade the bars.

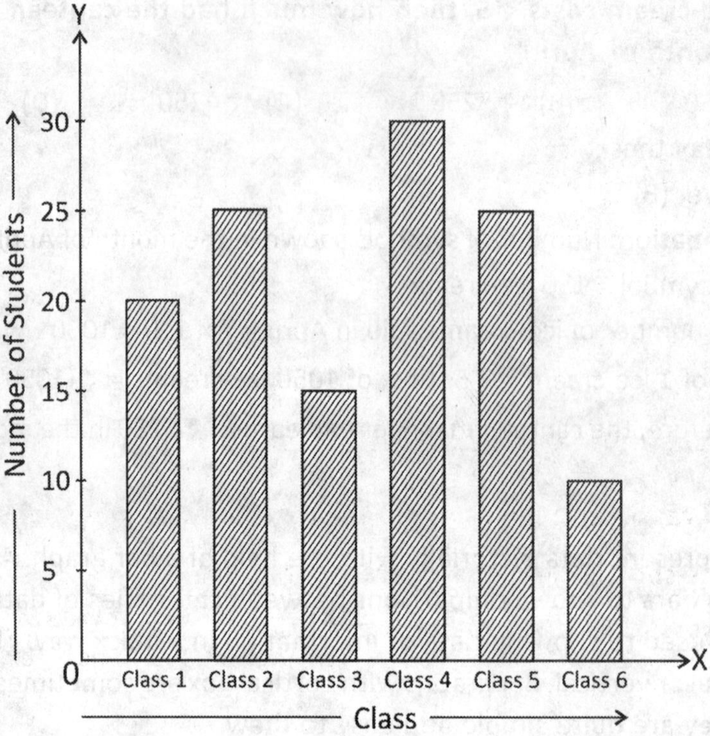

Here, X-axis represents the classes (1 to 6) and Y-axis represents the number of students in each class. Clearly, in the given figure shown above, 5 units on Y-axis represents 5 students, 10 units represents 10 students, and so on. Therefore, we obtained the bar graph to depict the given information.

Reading a Bar Graph

A bar graph displays data visually and it is sometime called a **bar chart**. Data are displayed either horizontally or vertically and allow viewers to compare items displayed. Data displayed will relate to things like amounts, times, number of something, etc. Let us look at the following word problems that ask to interpret a bar graph. Here, we analyse the data and answer the given questions.

Example:

In a school, the students of a particular class come to school by different mode of transport as represented in the following bar graph.

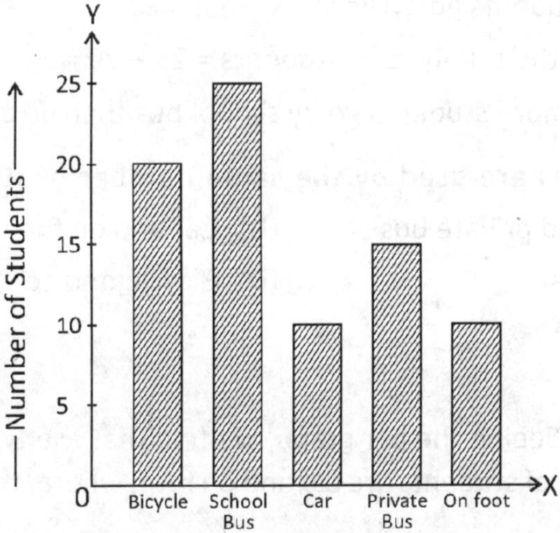

Study the bar graph carefully and answer the following questions:

1. Which axis shows the mode of transport?

(A) X-axis (B) Y-axis

(C) Both X-axis and Y-axis (D) Neither X-axis nor Y-axis

(E) None of these

Answer (A)

Explanation: Seeing the bar graph, we find that X-axis shows the mode of transport.

2. Which axis shows the number of students of the class?

(A) X-axis (B) Y-axis

(C) Both X-axis and Y-axis (D) Neither X-axis nor Y-axis

(E) None of these

Answer (B)

Explanation: Seeing the bar graph, we find that Y-axis shows the number of students of the class.

3. How many more students go by school bus than go cycling to school?

(A) 25 (B) 15 (C) 10 (D) 5

(E) None of these

Answer (D)

Explanation: Number of students go by school bus to school = 25

Number of students go cycling to school = 20

Difference of the numbers of students = 25 – 20 = 5

Therefore, 5 more students go by school bus than go cycling to school.

4. Which two modes are used by the same number of students?

(A) School bus and private bus
(B) Car and on foot
(C) Bicycle and car
(D) Bicycle and school bus
(E) None of these

Answer (B)

Explanation: Seeing the bar graph, we find that the two modes used by the same number of students are car and on foot, where, the number of students is 10.

5. How many students go by private bus to school?

(A) 10
(B) 25
(C) 15
(D) 20
(E) None of these

Answer (C)

Explanation: There are 15 students go by private bus to school.

6. How many students are there in the class altogether?

(A) 70
(B) 80
(C) 90
(D) 75
(E) None of these

Answer (B)

Explanation: Number of students go cycling to school = 20

Number of students go by school bus = 25

Number of students go by car = 10

Number of students go by private bus = 15

Number of students go on foot = 10

Therefore, total number of students in the class altogether

= 20 + 25 + 10 + 15 + 10 = 80

Example:

The following bar graph represents the time taken by five competitors to run 250 metres race.

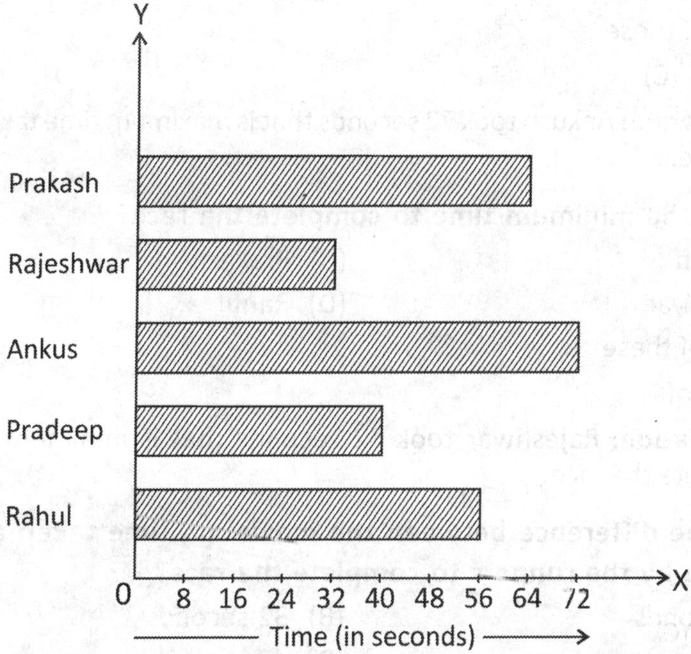

Study the bar graph carefully and answer the following question:

1. Which axis shows the competitors on the graph?

(A) X-axis (B) Y-axis

(C) Both X-axis and Y-axis (D) Neither X-axis nor Y-axis

(E) None of these

Answer (B)

Explanation: Seeing the bar graph, we find that Y-axis shows the competitors on the graph.

2. Which axis shows the time taken in seconds on the graph?

(A) X-axis (B) Y-axis

(C) Both X-axis and Y-axis (D) Neither X-axis nor Y-axis

(E) None of these

Answer (A)

Explanation: Seeing the bar graph, we find that X-axis shows the time taken in seconds on the graph.

3. **Who took the maximum time to complete the race?**

(A) Pradeep (B) Prakash
(C) Ankush (D) Rajeshwar
(E) None of these

Answer (C)

Explanation: Ankush took 72 seconds that is maximum time taken to complete the race.

4. **Who took the minimum time to complete the race?**

(A) Pradeep (B) Prakash
(C) Rajeshwar (D) Rahul
(E) None of these

Answer (C)

Explanation: Rajeshwar took 32 seconds that is minimum time taken to complete the race.

5. **What is the difference between the maximum time taken and minimum time taken by the runners to complete the race?**

(A) 48 seconds (B) 32 seconds
(C) 40 seconds (D) 42 seconds
(E) None of these

Answer (C)

Explanation: Seeing the bar graph, we find that the maximum time taken by Ankush = 72 seconds and the minimum time taken by Rajeshwar = 32 seconds

Therefore, the required time difference

= 72 seconds – 32 seconds = 40 seconds

6. **Who complete the race before Ankush but after Rahul?**

(A) Prakash (B) Pradeep
(C) Rajeshwar (D) All of these
(E) None of these

Answer (A)

Explanation: Prakash complete the race before Ankush but after Rahul, because, Ankush took 72 seconds, Rahul took 56 seconds and Prakash took 64 seconds to complete the race.

7. Who took time more than 32 seconds but less than 52 seconds?

(A) Rajeshwar (B) Prakash

(C) Ankush (D) Pradeep

(E) None of these

Answer (D)

Explanation: Pradeep took 40 seconds to complete the race that is more than 32 seconds but less than 52 seconds.

Summary

- The term '**data handling**' is all about gathering information and representing the same though pictographs and diagrams.
- A collection of facts, such as numbers, words, measurements, observations or even first descriptions of things is called **data**.
- A picture used to represent an item of data is called a **symbol**. Two or more number of the same articles are represented by a symbol.
- A **pictograph** is a way of showing data using pictures. It is the easiest method for representation of data.
- A **bar graph** is a chart that uses bars to show comparisons between categories of data.

Did You Know ?

- Pictogram or pictograph is the oldest method to represent numbers.
- Early written symbols were based on pictographs.
- There is standard representation of pictograph which is accepted globally.
- Bar graph was invented by Scottish engineer 'William Playfair'.

Solved Problems

1. Some notebooks are equally distributed among 5 students in a week as given below. If one symbol represents 2 notebooks, how many notebooks did each student get?

Monday	
Tuesday	
Wednesday	
Thursday	
Friday	
Saturday	

(A) 4　　(B) 5

(C) 6　　(D) 8

(E) None of these

Answer (A)

Explanation:

Total number of symbols = 2 + 1 + 2 + 1 + 1 + 3 = 10

Total number of notebooks = 2 × 10 = 20

Therefore, each student got $\frac{20}{5}$ notebooks = 4 notebooks

2. The trees in a certain area of a forest were represented in a pictograph as given below:

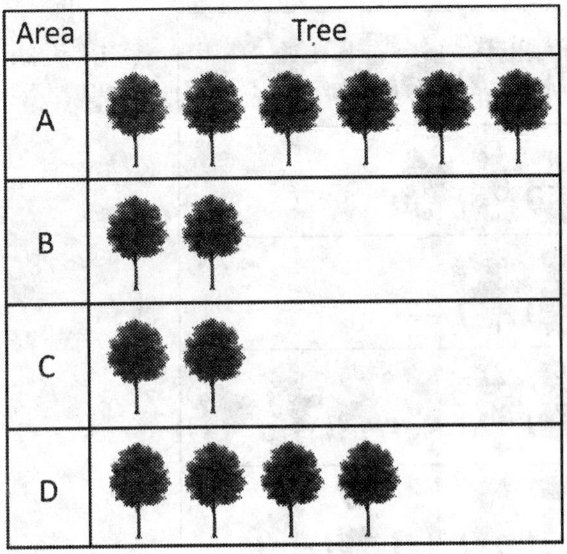

If one symbol  **represents 5,000 trees, then the sum of numbers of trees in both areas B and D will be:**

(A) 30,000

(B) 20,000

(C) 40,000

(D) 25,000

(E) All of these

Answer (A)

Explanation: Number of symbols for area B = 2

Number of trees in area B = 2 × 5,000 = 10,000

Number of symbols for area D = 4

Number of trees for area D = 4 × 5,000 = 20,000

Therefore, the sum of numbers of trees in both areas B and D

= 10,000 + 20,000 = 30,000

3. The picture given table shows the number of toys were sold in a day of a particular week at a toy shop.

Monday	
Tuesday	
Wednesday	
Thursday	
Friday	
Saturday	
One  = 20 toys	

Study the pictograph carefully and answer the following questions:

(a) Which day has the least sale of toys at the shop?

(A) Tuesday

(B) Wednesday

(C) Friday

(D) Saturday

(E) None of these

Answer (B)

Explanation: Number of symbols shown on Wednesday is 2 that is the least number of symbols among all. Therefore, Wednesday has the least sale of toys at the shop.

(b) Which day has the highest sale of toys at the shop?

(A) Monday (B) Tuesday (C) Thursday (D) Friday

(E) None of these

Answer (C)

Explanation: Number of symbols shown on Thursday is 6 that is the highest number of symbols among all. Therefore, Thursday has the highest sale of toys at the shop.

(c) Which two days have same sale?

(A) Tuesday and Wednesday (B) Wednesday and Thursday

(C) Thursday and Tuesday (D) Monday and Friday

(E) None of these

Answer (D)

Explanation: Number of symbols shown on Monday and Friday is same that is equal number of symbols 5. Therefore, Monday and Friday have the same sale of toys.

(d) Which day has sale exact 60 toys?

(A) Monday (B) Tuesday (C) Wednesday (D) Thursday

(E) None of these

Answer (B)

Explanation: Here, 1 symbol represents 20 toys.

Therefore, number of symbols for 20 toys = 60 ÷ 20 = 3

Now, seeing the pictograph, Tuesday has 3 symbols.

So we have, Tuesday has sale of 60 toys.

(e) What was the total sale of toys in the week?

(A) 440 (B) 380 (C) 480 (D) 420

(E) None of these

Answer (E)

Explanation: Here, total number of symbols = 5 + 3 + 2 + 6 + 5 + 4 = 25

One symbol represents 20 toys.

Hence, the total sale of toys in the week = 25 × 20 = 500

4. Production of bicycles at a bicycle manufacturing unit in six months is given below. In which month the product of the company was maximum?

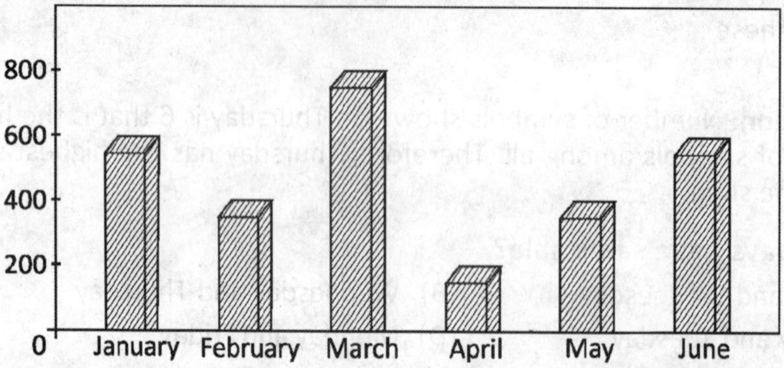

(A) January (B) March (C) February (D) June

(E) None of these

Answer (B)

Explanation: Seeing the graph, we find that the height of bar shown by the month of March is the highest and it is at 800.

Therefore, the production of company was maximum in March.

5. Following bar graph tells us about the marks obtained by Manju in five different subjects in a particular test.

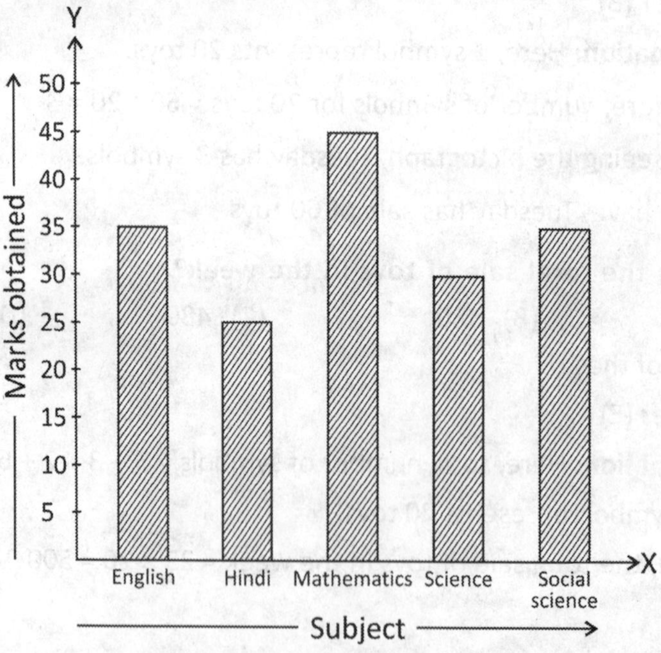

Read the bar graph and answer the following questions:

(a) In which subject Manju scored more than 40 marks?

(A) English (B) Mathematics

(C) Social Science (D) Science

(E) None of these

Answer (B)

Explanation: Seeing the bar graph, we find that in Mathematics, Manju scored more that 40 marks that is 45 marks.

(b) If 20 was the passing marks, which subject did Manju fail in?

(A) Social Science (B) Hindi

(C) Science (D) English

(E) None of these

Answer (E)

Explanation: Passing marks was 20 and Manju scored the least marks in Hindi that is 25 marks. Therefore, Manju did not fail in any subject.

(c) In which two subjects did Manju score equal marks?

(A) Hindi and Science

(B) Science and Mathematics

(C) Mathematics and English

(D) English and Social Science

(E) None of these

Answer (D)

Explanation: Seeing the bar graph, we find that Manju scored equal marks in English and Social Science that is 35 marks.

(d) If 50 was the maximum marks in each subject, what marks did Manju score in English, Mathematics and Science out of 150?

(A) 100 (B) 110 (C) 120 (D) 90

(E) None of these

Answer (B)

Explanation: Sum of marks scored in English, Mathematics and Science

= 35 + 45 + 30 = 110

Therefore, Manju scored 110 marks out of 150 in English, Mathematics and Science.

6. Given bar graph represents the types of Indian dishes that people like the most.

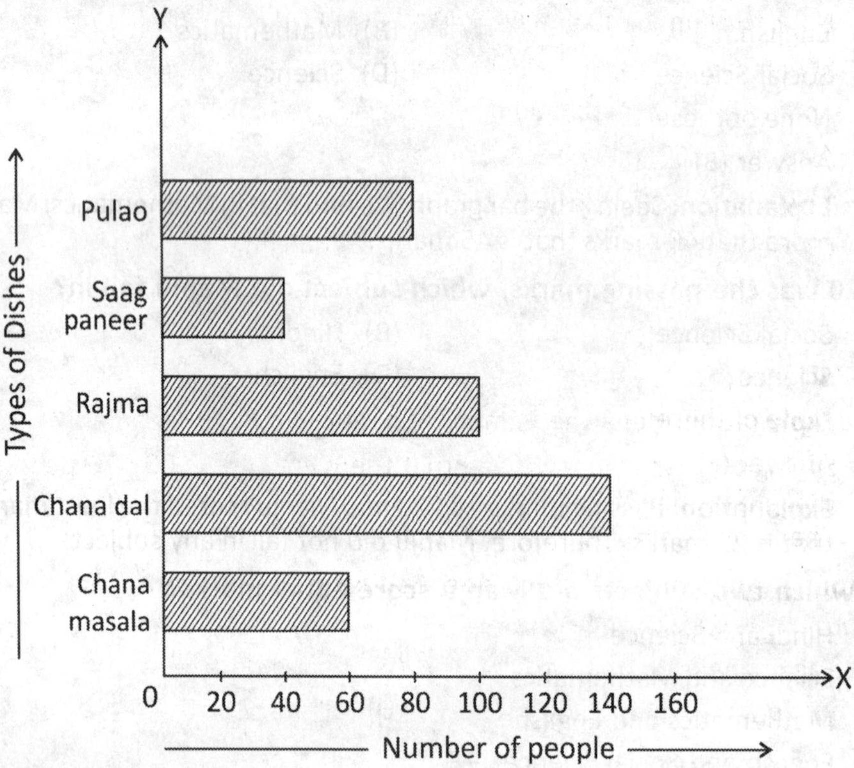

Study the bar graph carefully and answer the following questions:

(a) How many more people like Chana dal than Saag paneer?

(A) 40 (B) 100 (C) 60 (D) 80

(E) None of these

Answer (B)

Explanation: Seeing the bar graph, we find that the number of people who like chana dal = 140 and the number of people who like Saag paneer = 40

Therefore, the difference in the numbers of people = 140 – 40 = 100

Hence, there are 100 more people like Chana dal than Saag paneer.

(b) 60 less people prefer Saag paneer than ______.

(A) Chana dal (B) Chana masala

(C) Pulao (D) Rajma

(E) None of these

Answer (D)

Explanation: Here, the number of people who like Saag paneer = 40

Now, the sum of 40 and 60 = 40 + 60 = 100

Seeing the bar graph, we find that there are 100 people who like Rajma.

Therefore, 60 less people prefer Saag paneer than Rajma.

Also, 100 – 60 = 40 people like Saag paneer.

(c) Total number of people who like Rajma and ______ is 160.

(A) Chana masala (B) Chana dal

(C) Pulao (D) Saag paneer

(E) None of these

Answer (A)

Explanation: Here, the number of people who like Rajma = 100

Seeing the bar graph, we find that there are 160 – 100 = 60 people who like Chana masala. Therefore, the total number of people who like Rajma and Chana masala = 100 + 60 = 160

(d) Among all five dishes, which one dish is less popular than Rajma but more popular than Chana masala?

(A) Sagg paneer (B) Chana dal

(C) Pulao (D) All of these

(E) None of these

Answer (C)

Explanation: Number of people who like Rajma = 100

Number of people who like Chana masala = 60

Now, there are 80 people who like pulao. So, among all five dishes, Pulao is less popular than Rajma but more popular than Chana masala.

Practice Exercise 10

***Direction (1 – 4)*: Following pictograph tells us about the kind of books read by Prashant.**

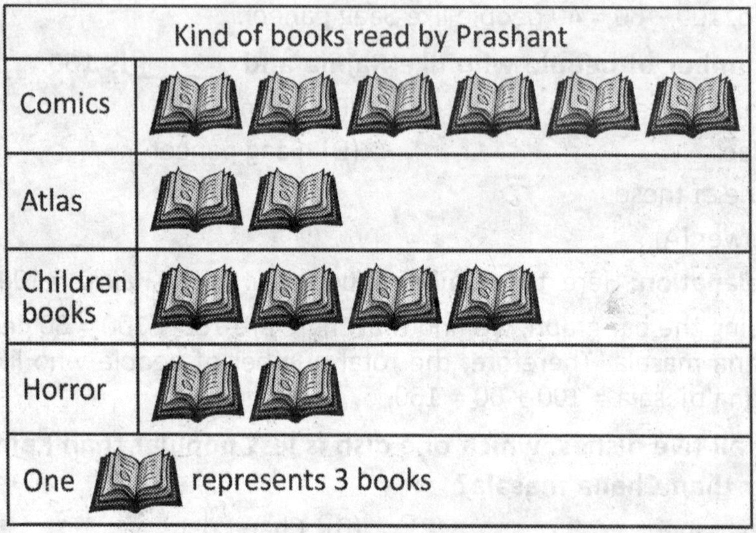

Read the pictograph and answer the following questions:

1. How many children books did Prashant read?

(A) 18 (B) 12 (C) 15 (D) 8

(E) None of these

2. Which two types of books did Prashant read same in number?

(A) Comics and Atlas

(B) Atlas and Horror

(C) Horror and Children books

(D) Children books and Comics

(E) None of these

3. How many more books on comics than Horror books are read by Prashant?

(A) 15 (B) 6 (C) 12 (D) 9

(E) None of these

4. **How many books did Prashant read in all?**

(A) 42

(B) 39

(C) 36

(D) 45

(E) None of these

5. **Given pictograph represents the number of students in the class 1 to 5 of a school.**

Class 1	
Class 2	
Class 3	
Class 4	
Class 5	
One  = 5 students	

How many students are there in all?

(A) 120

(B) 90

(C) 100

(D) 80

(E) None of these

***Direction (6 – 10)*: Given bar graph represents the number of people who were at store in different time intervals during a particular day.**

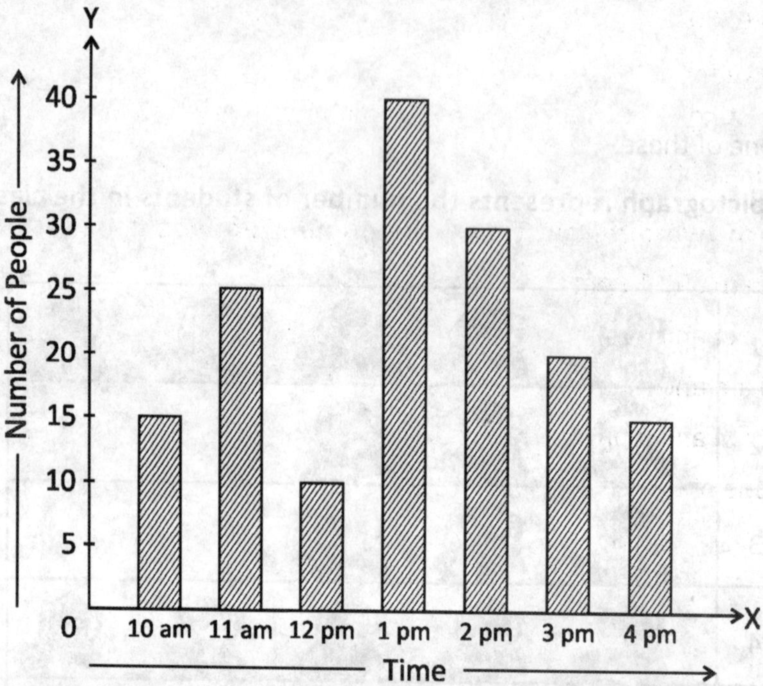

Study the bar graph carefully and answer the following questions:

6. How many people were in the store when it opened?

(A) 10
(B) 15
(C) 5
(D) 20
(E) None of these

7. How many people were in the store when it closed?

(A) 20
(B) 10
(C) 5
(D) 15
(E) None of these

8. What is the busiest time of the day at the store?

(A) 1 pm
(B) 2 pm
(C) 11 am
(D) 10 am
(E) None of these

9. How many people were there at the store in between 1 pm to 2 pm?

(A) 40 to 70

(B) 60 to 80

(C) 30 to 40

(D) 50 to 60

(E) None of these

10. At which two different times, the number of people were same?

(A) 11 am and 12 pm

(B) 12 pm and 4 pm

(C) 10 am and 4 pm

(D) 11 am and 3 pm

(E) None of these

Chapter 11

Reasoning and Aptitude

Learning Objectives

- Introduction
- Alphabet Test and Word Formation
- Analytical Reasoning
- Analogy and Classification
- Grouping Figures
- Possible Combinations
- Geometrical Shapes

Introduction

The process of thinking about something in a logical way in order to form a conclusion is called 'Logical Reasoning'. It is the ability to think and understand things in logical way. In this chapter, we will learn what logical reasoning involves and how to integrate the application of Mathematics to problem solving.

Alphabet Test and word Formation

Following table represents each letter of the English alphabet by a number which corresponds to that letter's position in the alphabet.

A	B	C	D	E	F	G	H	I	J	K	L	M	N	O	P	Q	R
1	2	3	4	5	6	7	8	9	10	11	12	13	14	15	16	17	18

S	T	U	V	W	X	Y	Z
19	20	21	22	23	24	25	26

There are 26 letters in English alphabet. The first letter is A and last letter is Z.

Some Important Tips

1. Arrange the letters in different combinations given in options to find a meaningful word if the numbers are given to the corresponding letters.
2. To form a meaningful word and to find the category of word, arrange the given jumbled letters in meaningful word and identify the category in which formed word lies.
3. To identify the combination of letters that has same number of skipped letters between the adjacent letters, wrlte the alphabetical series in order, then observe carefully all the options.

Example:

Form a meaningful word by arranging the given numbers corresponding to the letters given below:

A	L	Y	P
1	2	3	4

(A) 2, 1, 4, 3 (B) 4, 3, 2, 1

(C) 4, 2, 1, 3 (D) 3, 2, 1, 4

(E) None of these

Answer (C)

Explanation: Option (A): 2, 1, 4, 3 = LAPY

Option (B): 4, 3, 1, 2 = PYAL.

Option (C): 4, 2, 1, 3 = PLAY

Option (D): 3, 2, 1, 4 = YLAP

So, the word formed by the by the series given in option (C) is a meaningful word.

Example:

Form a meaningful word from given jumbled letters and find its category.

RNWBO

(A) Measurement (B) Colour (C) Animal (D) Grain

(E) None of these

Answer (B)

Explanation: Word formed from RNWBO is BROWN which is the name of a colour.

Letter Series

Letter series usually consists of a series of letters which follow a certain pattern, or some letters are missing from the series. These missing letters are then given in a proper sequence as one of the alternatives.

Example:

Which letter will replace the question mark (?) in the letter series given below?

C	F	I	L	O	?

(A) **R** (B) **P** (C) **Q** (D) **M**

(E) None of these

Answer (A)

Explanation: The answer is R, because the pattern is to count forward in three's from the first given letter Ⓒ D E Ⓕ G H Ⓘ J K Ⓛ M N Ⓞ P Q Ⓡ

Analytical Reasoning

The term "analytical reasoning" refers to recognising patterns and connections in a variety of information. It is the logical puzzle based on a given set of conditions. Analytical reasoning test measures our ability to analyze and to draw result from a situation by applying our logic.

Following techniques are used for solving the problems based on analytical reasoning:

- Diagrams
- Ascending and Descending Order
- Line-up Representation
- Math Operators
- Table Representation

Example:

Read the following information carefully.

- **Amit is younger than Rajesh.**
- **Rajesh is younger than Manpreet.**
- **Akash is the eldest.**
- **Mohit is the youngest.**

Based on the above information, answer the given question:

If we arrange their ages in ascending order then who will be in the third place?

(A) Amit (B) Rajesh (C) Manpreet (D) Akash

(E) Mohit

Answer (B)

Explanation: Let us arrange the group of children in ascending order as per their age.

Mohit < Amit < Rajesh < Manpreet < Akash

Therefore, Rajesh will be in the third place.

Directions and Positions

Directions and Positions are used to judge the students ability to trace correctly and to sense correct direction.

There are four main directions: North, East, South and West as shown below.

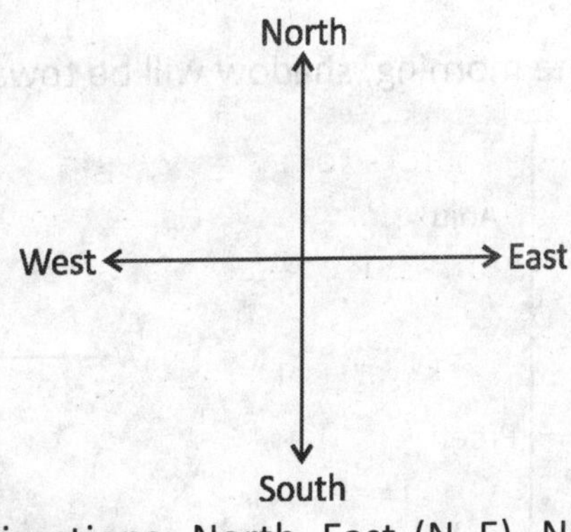

There are four cardinal directions: North–East (N–E), North–West (N–W), South–East (S–E) and South–West (S–W).

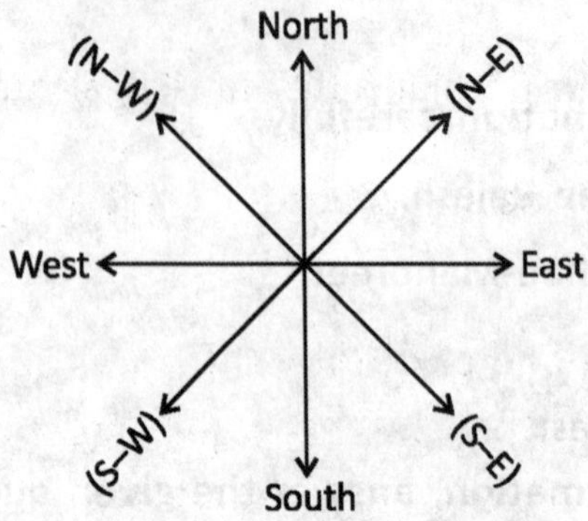

Read the following facts:

- ❖ At the time of sunset, the shadow of an object is always in the East.
- ❖ At the time of sunrise, the shadow of an object is always in the West.
- ❖ If you stand facing the North at the time of sunrise, your shadow will be towards your left and at the time of sunset, it will be towards your right.
- ❖ The rays of the sun are vertically downward at 12:00 noon, so there will be no shadow at 12 : 00 noon.

Example:

One morning Preeti and Anju were talking to each other face to face at a crossing. If Preeti's shadow was exactly to the right of Anju, which direction was Anju facing?

(A) East (B) West

(C) North (D) South

(E) None of these

Answer (D)

Explanation: In the morning, shadow will be towards West direction.

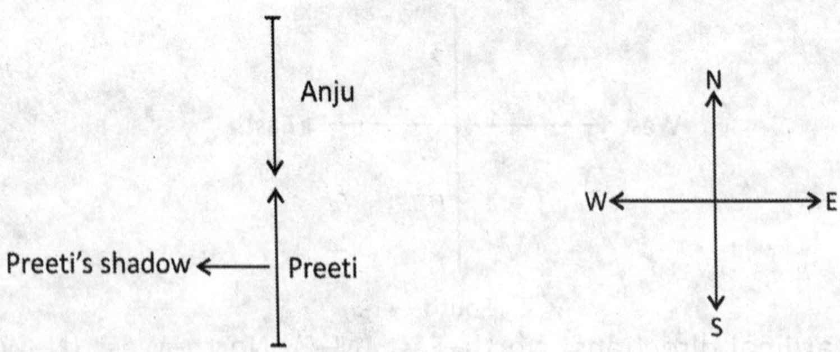

Therefore, Anju was facing South direction.

Odd One Out

'Odd one out' means a person or thing different from all other members of a particular group or set in some way. The object of 'odd one out' is to guess which one of the group of items does not belong and why it does not belong.

Example:

Which of these is the odd one out (different from the rest)?

(A) Oven (B) Computer (C) Gas stove (D) Heater

(E) Refrigerator

Answer (C)

Explanation: Oven, Computer, Heater and Refrigerator run on electricity. Gas stove is different from the others.

Analogy and Classification

Analogy

Analogy is a similarity between like features of two things on which comparison may be based. In analogy-based questions, we will usually be given one pair of images that are connected in a particular way and the first image of the second pair in the same way as the first pair.

Example:

Identify the relationship between the pair of figures given on either side of :: and then find the missing figure.

 :  ::  : ?

(A)  (B) 

(C)  (D) 

(E) None of these

Answer (C)

Explanation: Look carefully at the pair of figures on the left side of :: and consider their relationship to the second pair.

To play hockey, a hockey stick and a ball are required. In the same way, to play badminton, we need to shuttle bat and a shuttlecock. So, the figure given in option (C) is correct.

Example:

Identify the relationship between the pair of figures given on either side of :: and then find the missing figure.

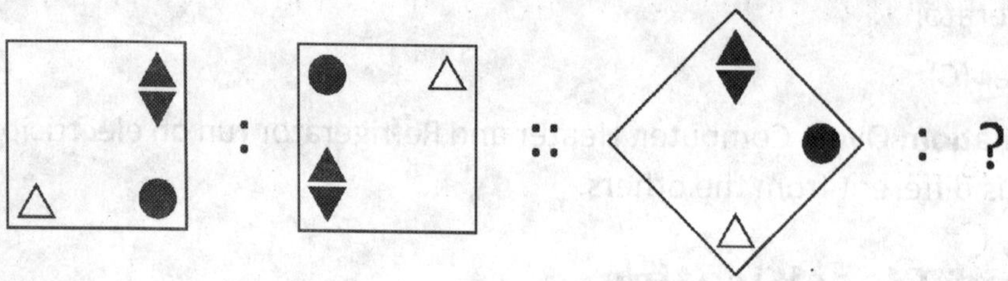

(A) 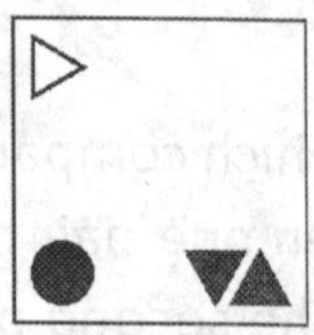

(B) 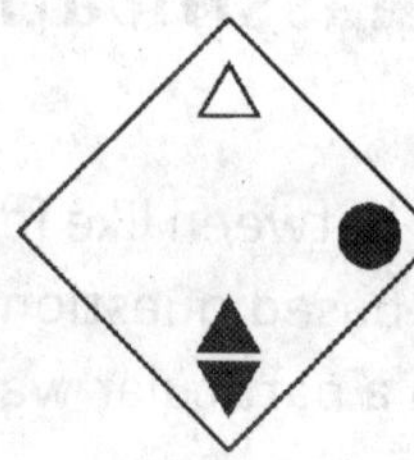

(C) 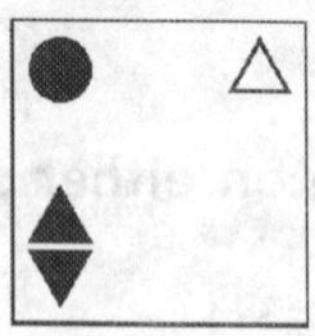

(D) 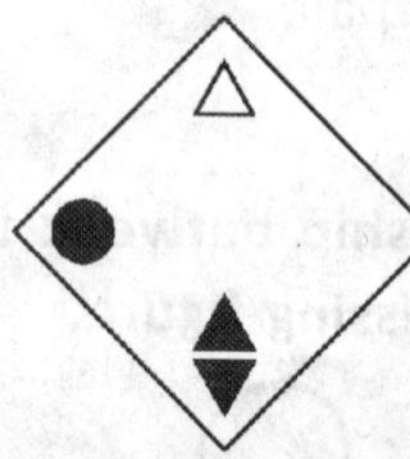

(E) None of these

Answer (D)

Explanation: Look carefully at the pair of figures on the left side of :: and consider their relationship to the second pair.

Shape: Both are of the same shape, and both contain an unshaded triangle, two shaded triangles and one shaded circle.

Position: The position of the one unshaded triangle (△) has changed from bottom of the left side to the top of the right side.

The position of two shaded triangles () has changed from top of the right side to the bottom of the left side.

The position of one shaded circle (●) has changed from bottom of the right side to the top of the left side. Here, also no change in any of the angles, size and in the shading.

Now, on the basis of above, we can predict the second phase in the second pair. Therefore, the figure given in option (D) is correct.

Classification

Classification of the figures or shapes tests our ability to work out, which shapes are similar and which are different in a given set of options. We need to use our observation skill to compare the given shapes, symbols and find the visual link or links.

Example:

Find the odd one out.

(A)

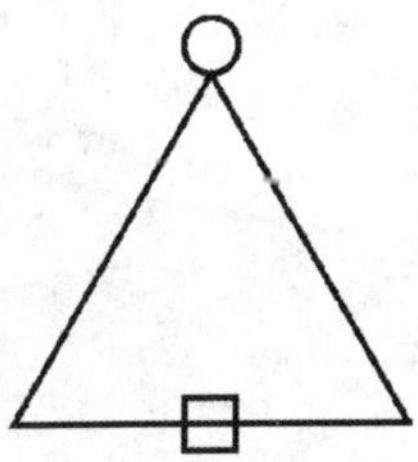

(B)

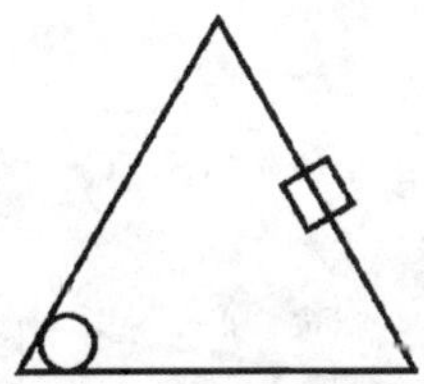

(C)

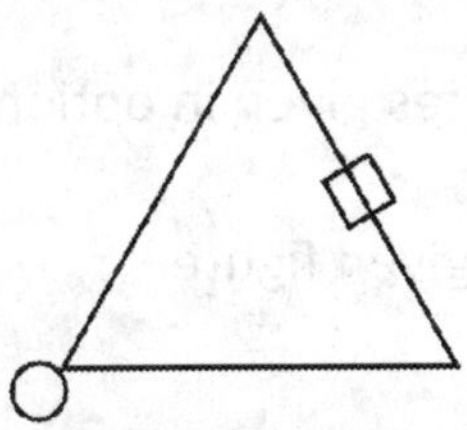

(D)

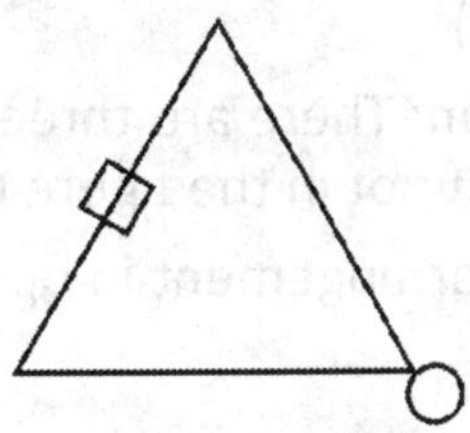

(E) None of these

Answer (B)

Explanation:

Check Number: Each option has one triangle, one circle and one square box. Thus, there is no odd one out.

Check Location: In options (A), (C) and (D), the circle is outside the triangle while in option (B), it is inside.

Hence, the figure given in option (B) is the odd one out.

Example:

Which one of the following is similar to Figure (X) given below:

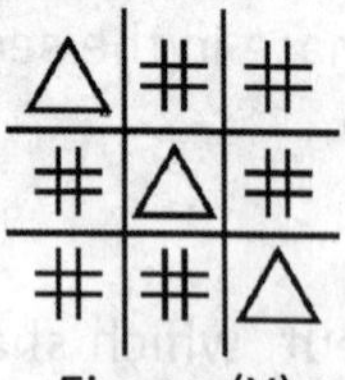

Figure (X)

(A) 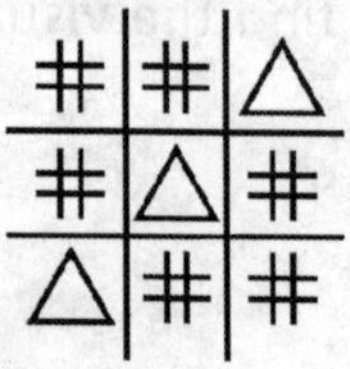

(B) 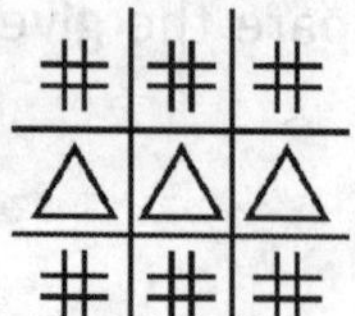

(C) 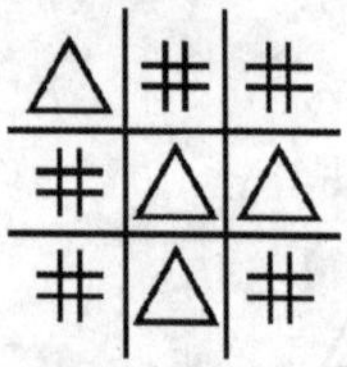

(D) 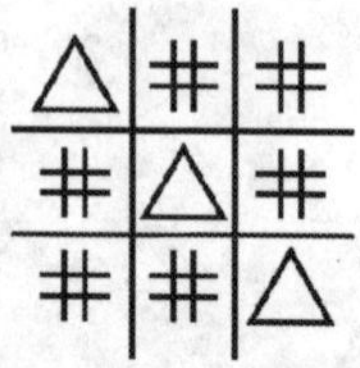

(E) None of these

Answer (D)

Explanation: There are three triangles in the figures given in options (A), (B) and (D) but not in the figure given in option (C).

Here, the arrangement in option (D) is similar to given figure.

Example:

What comes next in the figure pattern given below?

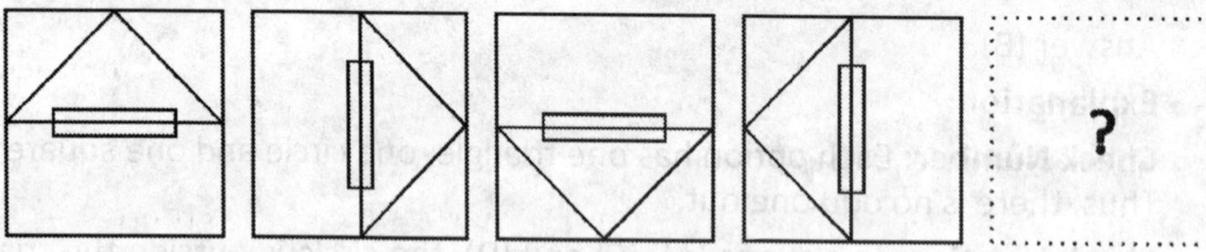

(A) 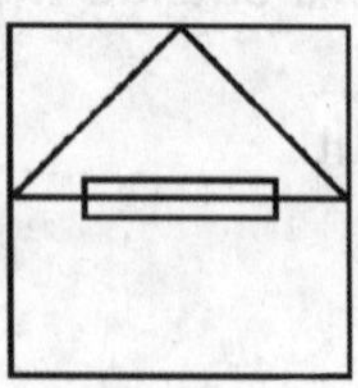

(B) 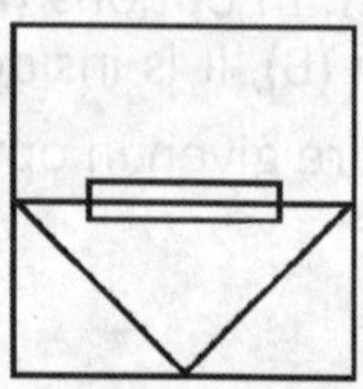

(C) 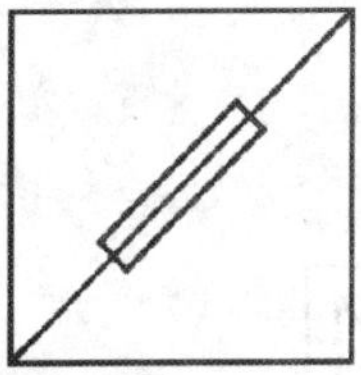

(D) 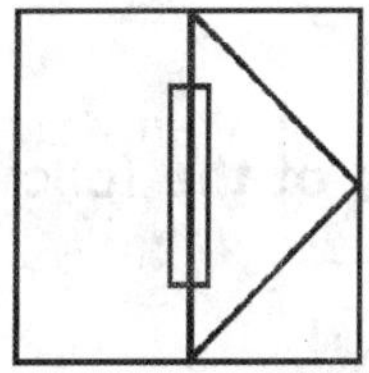

(E) None of these

Answer (A)

Explanation:

Shape: There is a triangle in each box and a rectangular strip is on its one side.

Position: Vertex opposite to rectangular strip is moving by 90° $\frac{1}{4}$ turn if we go to right side from left. Hence, the figure given in option (A) is correct.

Example:

On the basis of number and its digits, choose the pencil that does *not* belong to the group.

(A) 

(B) 

(C) 

(D) 

(E) 

Answer (C)

Explanation: In option (A): 645; 6 + 4 + 5 = 15

In option (B): 456; 4 + 5 + 6 = 15

In option (C): 478; 4 + 7 + 8 = 19

In option (D): 663; 6 + 6 + 3 = 15

In option (E): 276; 2 + 7 + 6 = 15

Hence, the pencil given in option (C) does not belong to the group.

Grouping of Figures

Reasoning based on grouping tests our understanding and recognition of the shapes and patterns. In these types of questions, we are required to analyze the given set of figures, numbers and classify them into groups.

Example:

 **belongs to which of the following groups?**

(A) 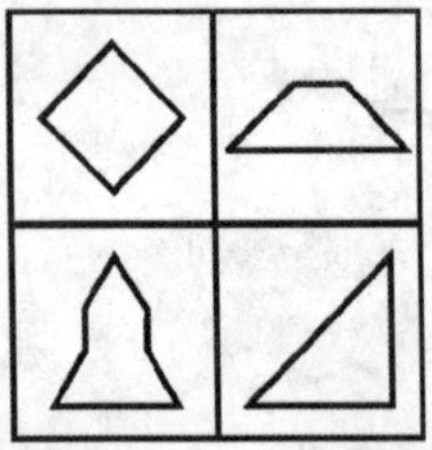

(B) 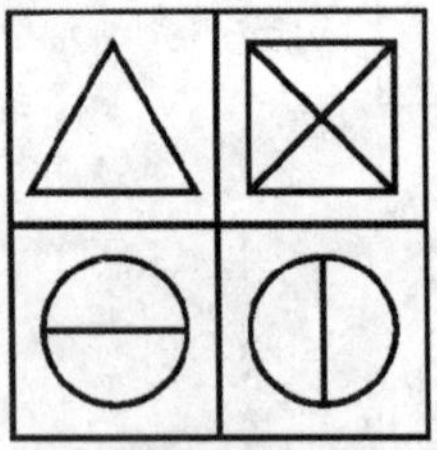

(C) 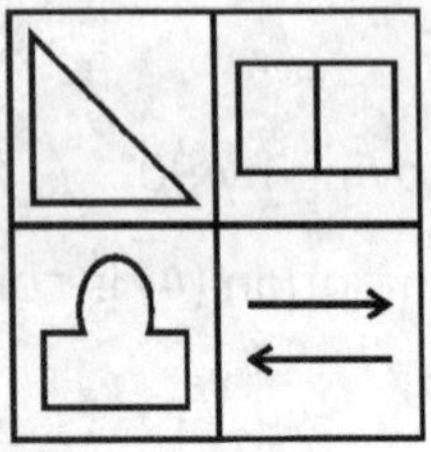

(D) 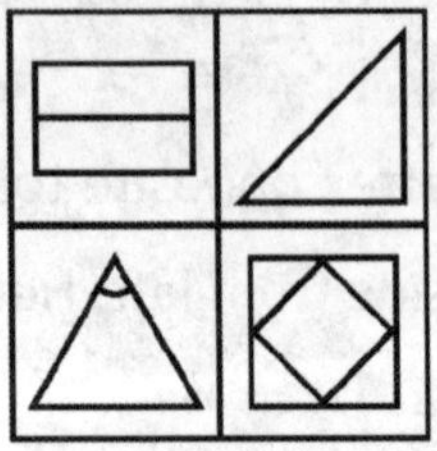

(E) None of these

Answer (B)

Explanation: The shape  is a semi-circle or half of a circle. Clearly, this shape belongs to the group given in option (B).

Example:

In which group does the number 27 belongs to?

(A) 3, 6, 9, 12, ...

(B) 5, 10, 15, ...

(C) 6, 12, 18, 24 . . . . .

(D) 2, 4, 6, 8, ...

(E) None of these

Answer (A)

Explanation: 27 comes in the table of 3.

Possible Combinations

Consider the following example:

How many possible combinations of one boy and one girl can be formed from 2 boys and 3 girls?

Let us see if two boys are B_1 and B_2 and three girls are G_1, G_2 and G_3, then the possible combinations are: B_1G_1, B_1G_2, B_1G_3, B_2G_1, B_2G_2, B_2G_3 or the number of possible combinations = 2 × 3 = 6. Now we can say that the number of possible (1 - 1) combinations of (x - y) objects are x × y.

Example:

There were 4 guests in a guest house. Each guest shook hands once with each other. How many handshakes took place?

(A) 4

(B) 6

(C) 10

(D) 8

(E) None of these

Answer (B)

Explanation:

If 4 guests are A, B, C, D, then the possible combinations of handshakes = (A,B) (A,C) (A,D), (B,C), (B,D), (C,D)

Hence, 6 handshakes took place.

Geometrical Shapes

Geometrical shapes come from geometry, which is the math of shapes made of points and lines. Some shapes are simple such as triangle, square and circle while other shapes are so complex that it takes math in order to create them.

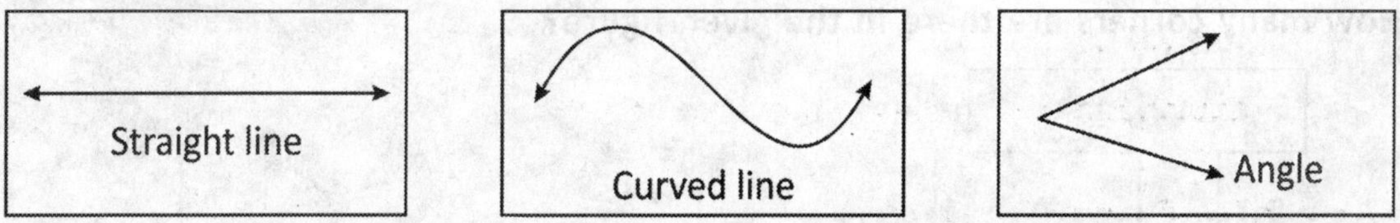

Following table shows different shapes and their properties:

Name	Shape	Properties
Rectangle		• Pair of opposite sides are equal • Four corners and four sides • Each angle is of 90° (right angle)
Square		• All four sides are equal • Four corners and four sides • Each angle is of 90° (right angle)
Circle		• No corner • Round in shape • Circle has a point in the centre from which each point on the circle is equidistant.
Oval	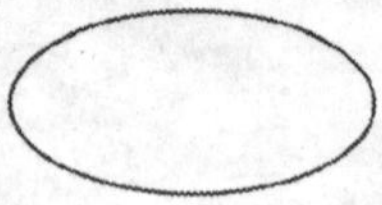	• No corner • Looks like an egg • Looks like an ellipse
Sphere		• No corner • Circular face • Shape of sphere is like a ball
Cone	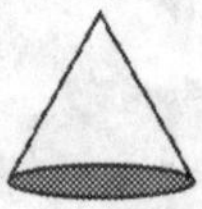	• Triangular and circular face • Has one vertex opposite to circular base
Cylinder	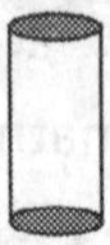	• Rectangular and circular faces • When unwrapped, the middle section and lay it flat, it is a rectangle

Example:

How many corners are there in the given figure?

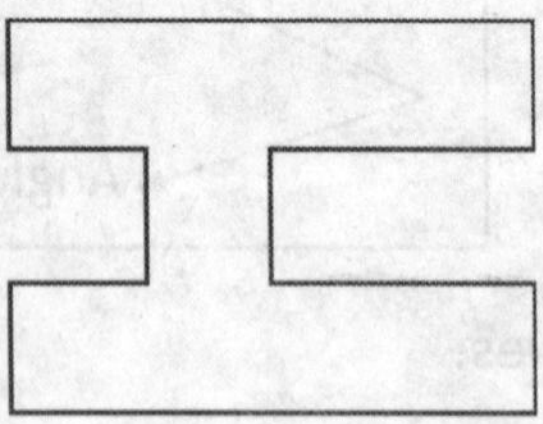

(A) 12 (B) 13 (C) 14 (D) 15

(E) None of these

Answer (A)

Explanation:

Here, the number of corners = 12

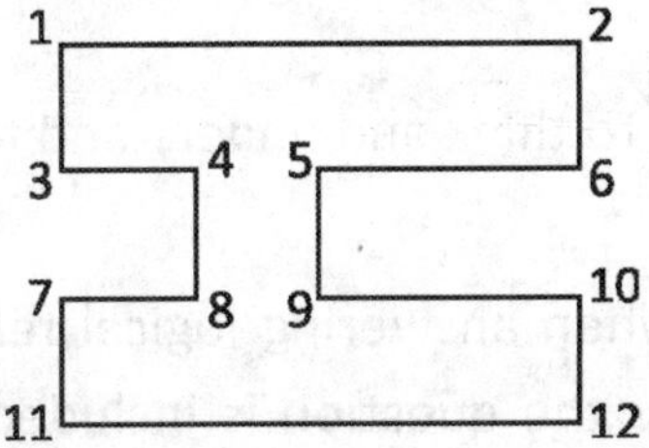

Example:

How many squares are there in the figure given below?

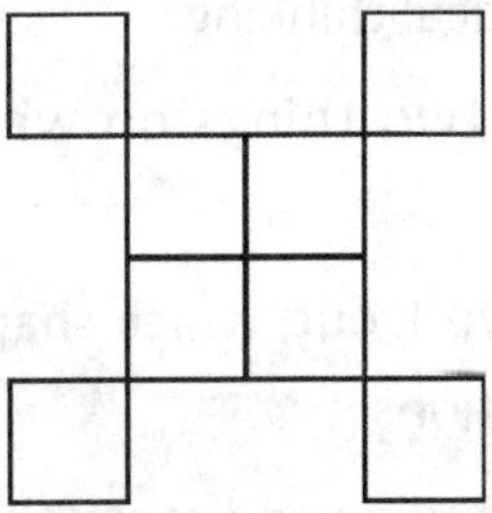

(A) 5
(B) 8
(C) 9
(D) 11
(E) None of these

Answer (C)

Explanation:

Here, the number of small squares = 8

Number of large square = 1; (ABCD)

Therefore, the total number of squares = 8 + 1 = 9

Summary

- The process of thinking about something in logical way in order to form a conclusion is called **Logical reasoning**.
- Logical reasoning is the ability of the mind to think and understand things in logical way.
- We do not use any general knowledge when answering logical reasoning questions. Everything we need to answer the question is included in the passage.
- While solving logical reasoning problems, we look at the problems with different perspectives through observation, explanation and critical thinking.
- **Analogy** is the similarity between like features of two things on which comparison may be based.
- **Classification** of figures or shapes tests our ability to work out, which shapes are similar and which are different in a given set of options.
- Logical reasoning based on grouping tests our understanding and recognition of shapes and patterns.
- The number of possible (1 - 1) combinations of (x - y) objects are x × y.

Solved Problems

1. **Which letter appears in the word TOMATO, but does *not* appear in the word POTATO?**

(A) P (B) T

(C) M (D) A

(E) None of these

Answer (C)

Explanation: The answer is M, because the letters T, O and A are in both the words TOMATO and POTATO, but M appears in the word TOMATO only.

2. Identify the new word that can be formed using the letters of the given word in capitals.

SPARROW

(A) Sapour (B) Prowar

(C) Parrot (D) Narrow

(E) None of these

Answer (B)

Explanation:

The answer is 'Prowar', because all the letters of the word 'Prowar' are given in the word SPARROW. The letters 'U', 'T' and 'N' are not in the given word SPARROW.

3. Pick the odd one out from the pair of letters given below.

(A) LO (B) NQ

(C) PS (D) RT

(E) EH

Answer (D)

Explanation: The pattern in options (A), (B), (C) and (E) between the two letters is to count forward in Threes where as in option (D), it is to count forward in Twos, which is, $L \xrightarrow[MN]{} O$, $N \xrightarrow[OP]{} Q$, $P \xrightarrow[QR]{} S$, $R \xrightarrow[S]{} T$, $E \xrightarrow[FG]{} H$

4. In the question given below, the letters are linked in someway. Identify the relation and complete the second pair.

CD	EF	GH	IJ	LM	NO	QR	?

(A) RS (B) ST

(C) TU (D) UV

(E) SU

Answer (B)

Explanation: CDEF, GHIJ and LMNO are consecutive letters. Hence, QRST is the next pattern.

5. Which one of the following pairs of letters will replace the question mark (?) in the letter series given below?

CM DN EO FP ?

(A) KR (B) GT (C) HQ (D) GQ

(E) None of these

Answer (D)

Explanation: The answer is GQ, because the pattern is to count towards in ones for both the first letter and the second letter as given below:

First letter: CM DN EO FP G

Second letter: CM DN EO FP GQ

6. Identify the letter which will end the first word and start the second word.

LIO ⬡ EST

(A) W (B) P (C) N (D) R

(E) None of these

Answer (C)

Explanation: The answer is N because it completes the first word LION and also begins the second word NEST.

7. Which number will replace the question mark (?) in the number pattern given below?

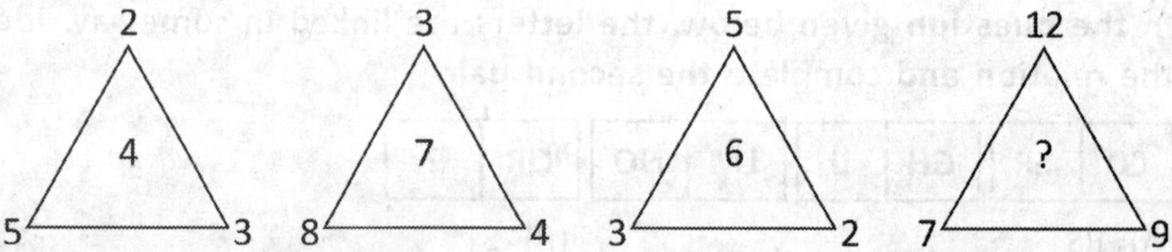

(A) 11 (B) 10 (C) 9 (D) 12

(E) 8

Answer (B)

Explanation: The number at the centre of each triangle equals the sum of two numbers left side, minus the right one.

Or, (5 + 2) – 3 = 4; (8 + 3) – 4 = 7; (3 + 5) – 2 = 6; (7 + 12) – 9 = (10)

8. In a certain code language, if 'REASONING' is written as 'abcdefgfh' then, 'SINGER' in this code of small letters will be:

(A) dgfhba (B) efgbad

(C) dabfgc (D) edcfga

(E) None of these

Answer (A)

Explanation: Here,

R	E	A	S	O	N	I	N	G
a	b	c	d	e	f	g	f	h

Therefore, 'SINGER' in this code will be 'dgfhba'.

9. If X is taller than Y and Y is taller than Z but shorter than P, then who is the shortest among all?

(A) X (B) Y (C) Z (D) P

(E) None of these

Answer (C)

Explanation: Here, $X > Y$, $Y > Z$, $Y < P$ or, $P > Y$

Therefore, $X > Y > Z$ and $P > Y > Z$. Hence, Z is shortest among all.

10. In a row of 13 boys, I am fifth from right. My position from left is:

(A) ninth (B) eleventh

(C) seventh (D) fifth

(E) None of these

Answer (A)

Explanation:

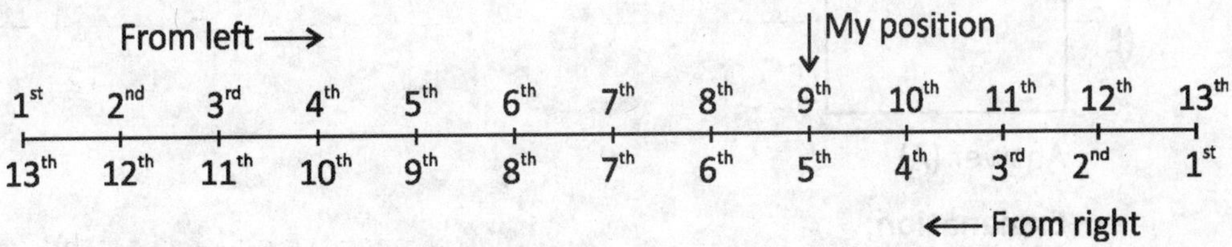

I am at fifth from right and ninth from left.

11. Which one of the following figures is different from the rest?

(A) 

(B) 

(C) 

(D) 

(E) 

Answer (D)

Explanation:

The shapes given in all options are same but in option (D), one circle is unfilled while in options (A), (B), (C) and (E), both circles are filled.

12. Find the odd one out.

(A) 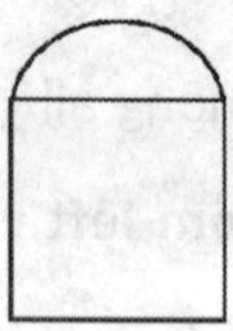

(B) 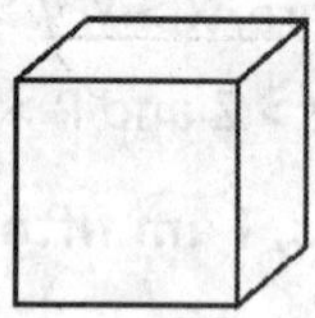

(C) 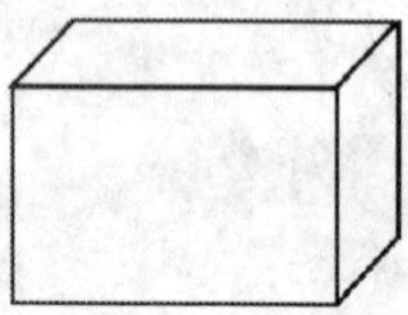

(D) 

(E) 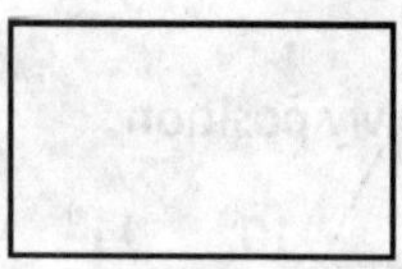

Answer (A)

Explanation:

All the figures given in options (B), (C), (D) and (E) have vertices and corners only. Figure given in option (A) has a circular top.

13. Keeping in mind the geometric shapes, find the odd one out.

(A) 

(B) 

(C) 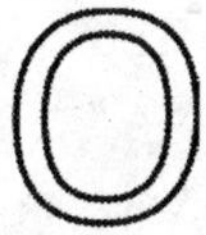

(D) 

(E) 

Answer (C)

Explanation: Figures given in options (A), (B), (D) and (E) are formed by straight lines. Figure given in option (C) is formed by curved lines.

14. Identify the relationship between the pair of figures given on either side of :: and then find the missing figure.

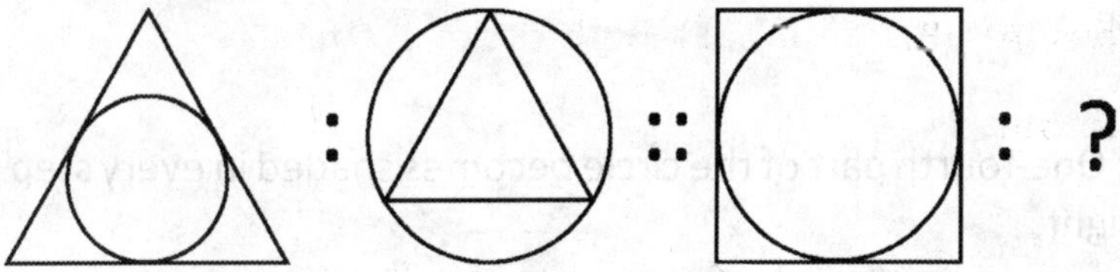

(A) 

(B) 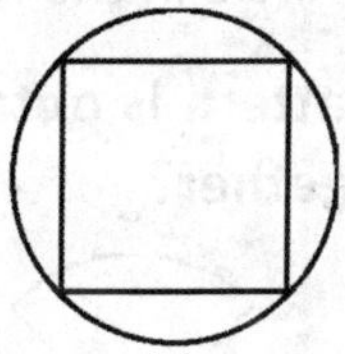

(C) 

(D) 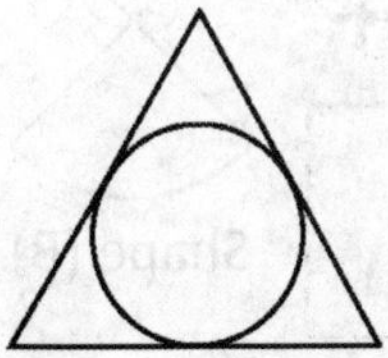

(E) None of these

Answer (B)

Explanation: Circle in a triangle became triangle in a circle. So, circle in a square should become square in a circle.

15. What comes next in the figure pattern given below?

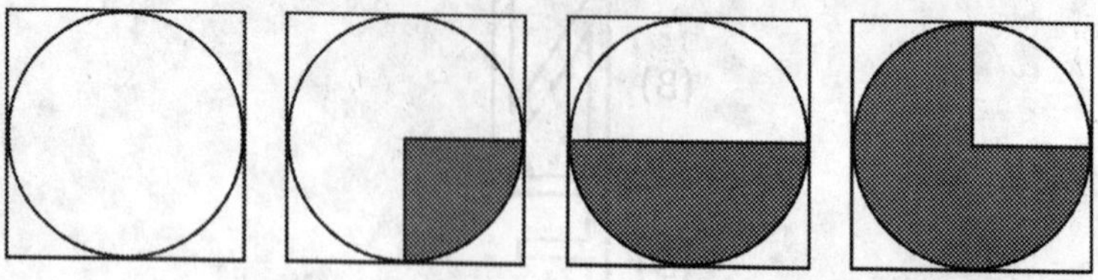

?

(A) 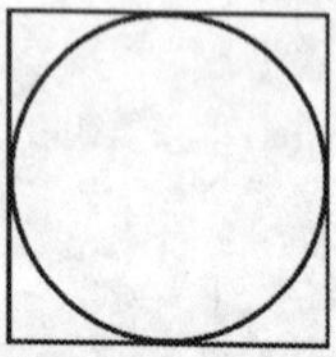

(B) 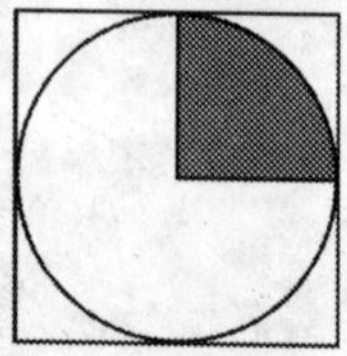

(C) 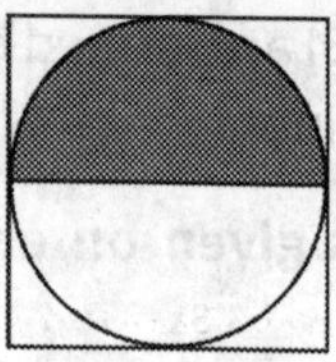

(D) 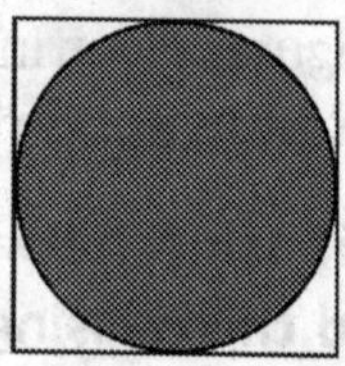

(E) None of these

Answer (D)

Explanation: One-fourth part of the circle becomes shaded in every step going from left to right.

Therefore, the circle in the required figure should become full shaded.

16. Which shape or pattern is obtained when the two shapes (A) and (B) given below are put together?

+

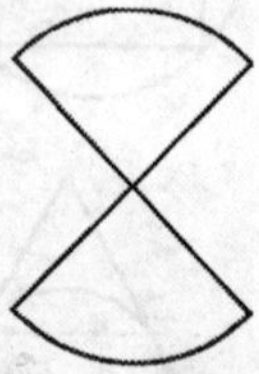

Shape (A) Shape (B)

(A) 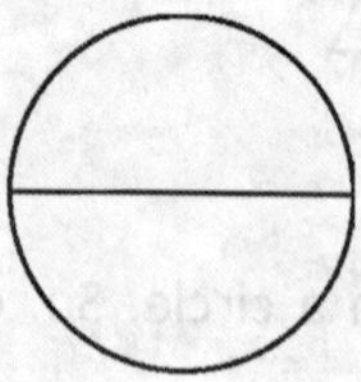

(B) 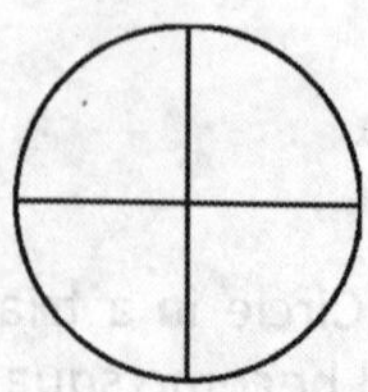

(C) 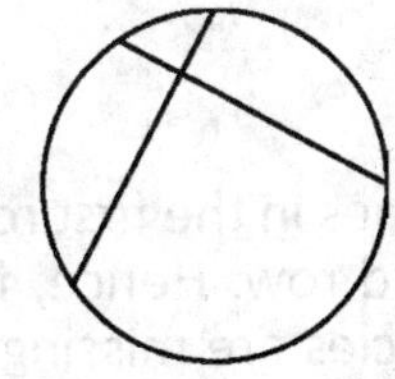

(D) 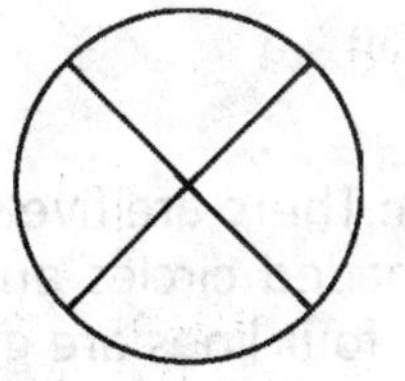

(E) None of these

Answer (D)

Explanation:

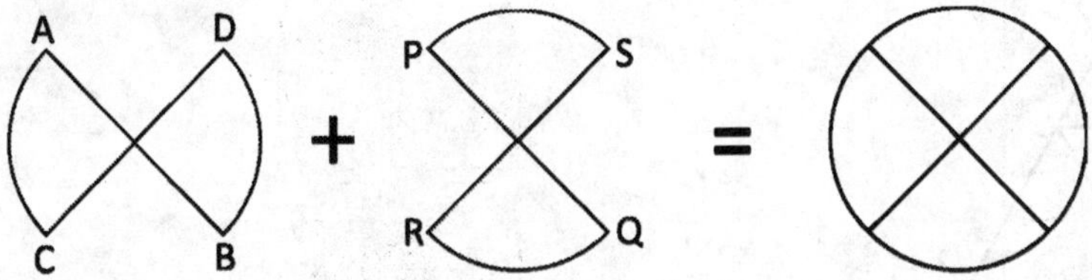

Here, when AB is on PQ and CD is on RS, the joint figure will become exactly the figure given in option (D).

17. Which one of the following figures will replace the question mark (?) in the figure pattern given below?

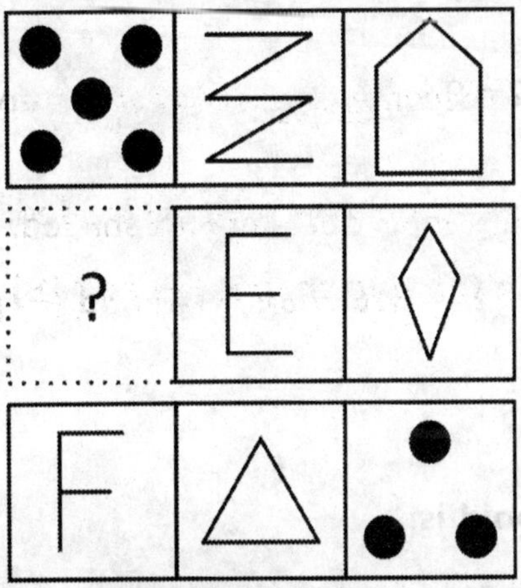

(A) 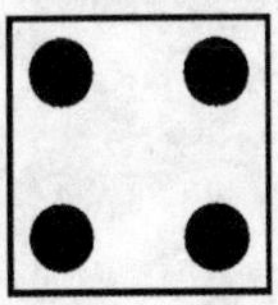

(B) 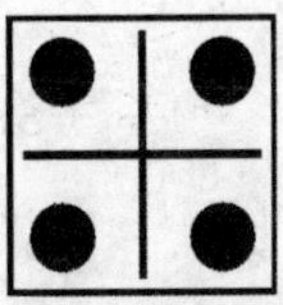

(C) 

(D) 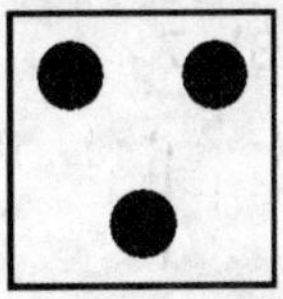

(E) None of these

Answer (A)

Explanation: There are five shaded circles and five lines in the first row. There are three shaded circles and three lines in the third row. Hence, figures in second row, four lines are given but four shaded circles are missing.

So, the figure given in option (A) is correct.

18. How many triangles are there in the figure given below?

(A) 7 (B) 8 (C) 9 (D) 11

(E) None of these

Answer (C)

Explanation: The number of smaller triangles = 7

Other two triangles are ABC and DEF.

So, the total number of triangles = 7 + 2 = 9

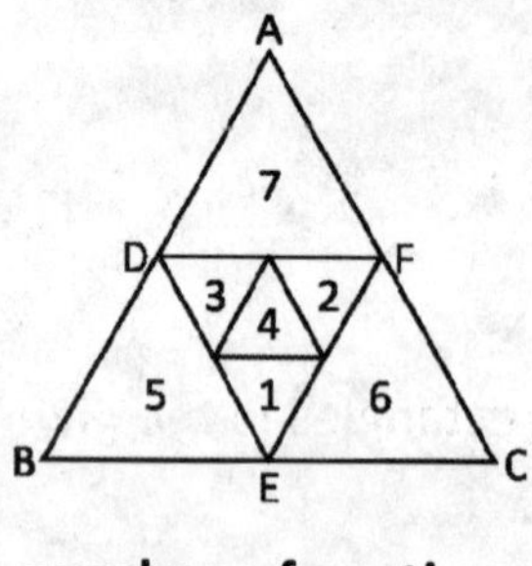

19. The number of vertices in the given cuboid is:

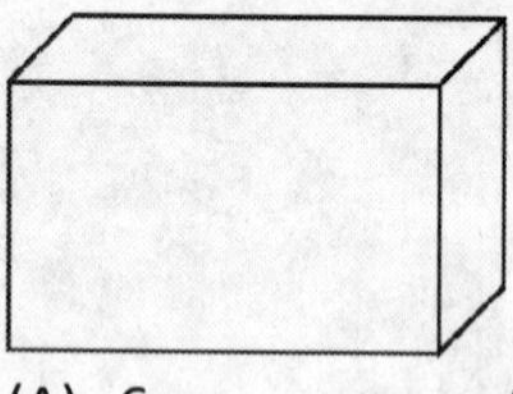

(A) 6 (B) 7 (C) 10 (D) 8

(E) None of these

Answer (D)

Explanation: There are 8 vertices in a cuboid.

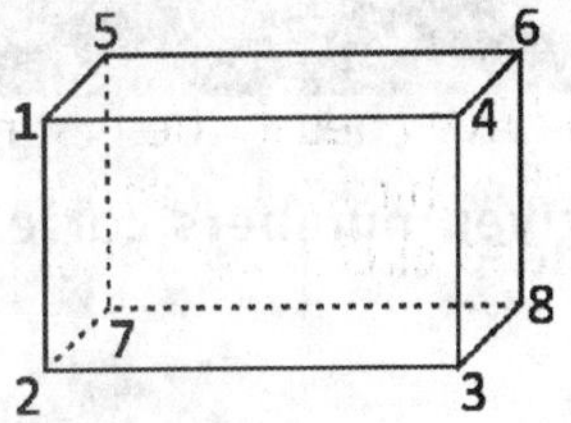

20. There are _______ more circles than rectangles.

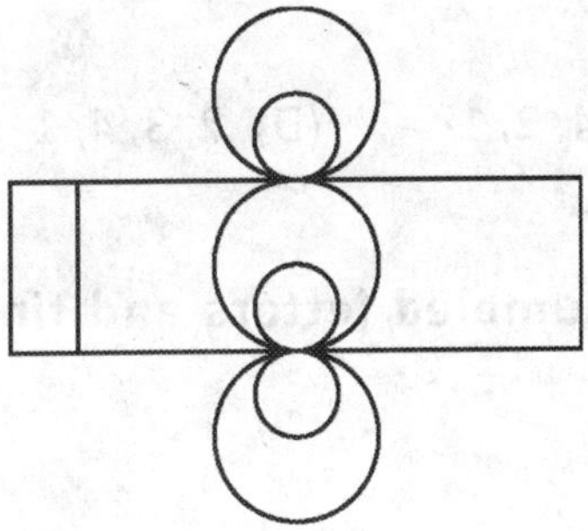

(A) 1
(B) 2
(C) 3
(D) 4
(E) None of these

Answer (C)

Explanation: Here, the number of circles = 6

Rectangles are ABCD, AEFD and BCFE.

Hence, there are 6 – 3 = 3 more circles than rectangles in the given figure.

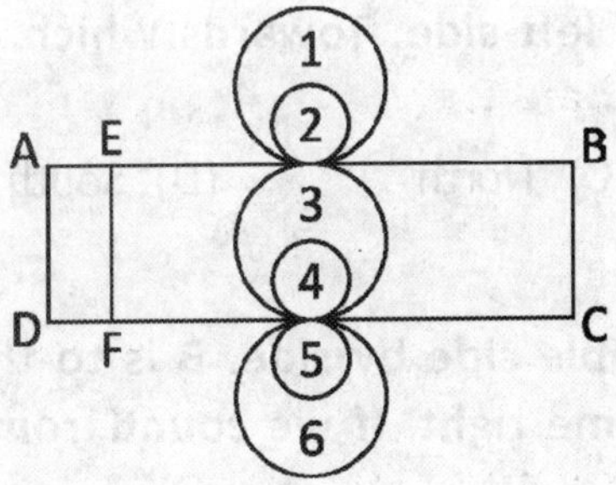

Practice Exercise 11

1. Form a meaningful word by arranging the given numbers corresponding the letters given below:

K	U	L	C
1	2	3	4

(A) 4, 3, 2, 1 (B) 3, 2, 4, 1 (C) 3, 4, 2, 1 (D) 2, 3, 4, 1
(E) None of these

2. Form a meaningful word from the given jumbled letters and find its category.

LRIZAB

(A) Grains (B) Animal
(C) Country (D) Game
(E) None of these

3. Find the next letter in the series given below:

X U R O L ?

(A) Z (B) K (C) J (D) I
(E) None of these

4. One morning after sunrise, I was standing facing an electric pole. The shadow of the pole felt exactly to my left side. Towards which direction was I facing?

(A) East (B) West (C) North (D) South
(E) None of these

5. Four children A, B, C and D sit on a table side by side. B is to the left of D and A is right to D. C is at the extreme right. If we count from the left then, who is in the first place?

(A) D (B) C (C) A (D) B
(E) None of these

6. **Find the odd one out.**

(A) Room (B) Chair (C) Seat (D) Sofa
(E) Bench

7. **Find the next pair of letters in the series given below:**

(OC) (QE) (SG) (UI) (?)

(A) PD (B) WK (C) TH (D) XM
(E) None of these

8. **Which one of the following numbers will replace the question mark (?) in the number pattern given below?**

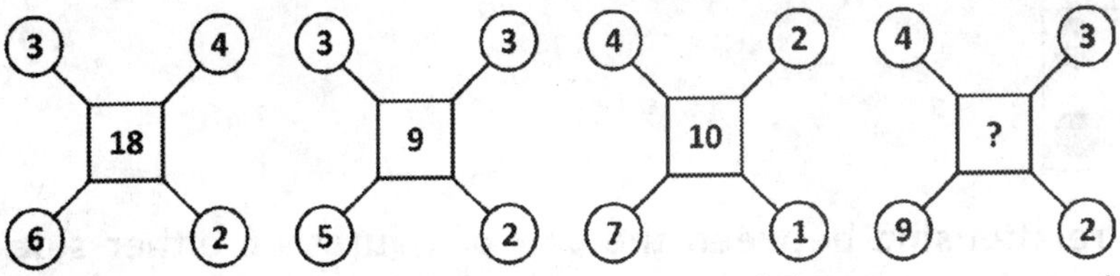

(A) 19 (B) 17 (C) 15 (D) 13
(E) None of these

9. **In a certain code language, if BEGIN is coded as CFHJO, then how LEAST be coded in that language?**

(A) KDBRS (B) MGCUV (C) NGCUV (D) MFBTU
(E) None of these

10. **Pick the odd one out.**

(A) ACE (B) DFH (C) GJL (D) JLN
(E) PRT

11. **Find the odd one out.**

(A) 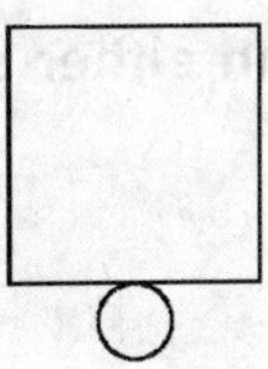 (B) 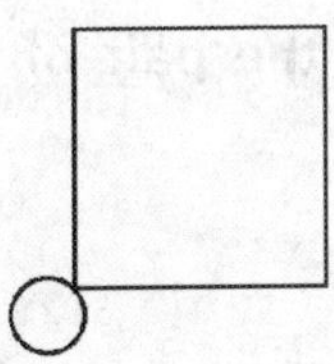 (C) 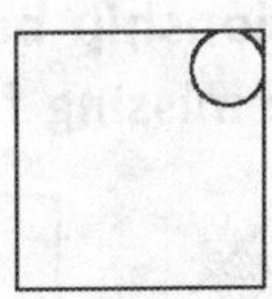 (D) 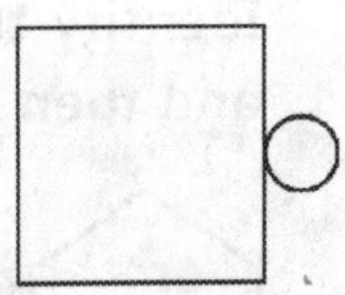

(E) 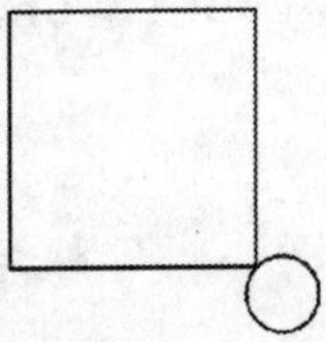

12. Find the odd one out.

(A) 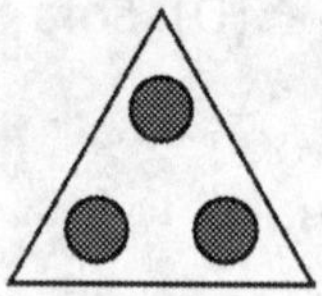

(B) 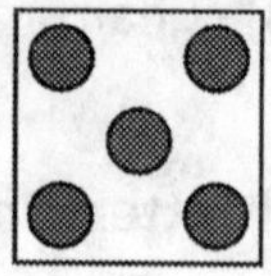

(C) 

(D) 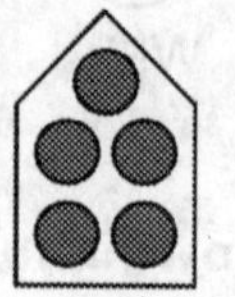

(E) 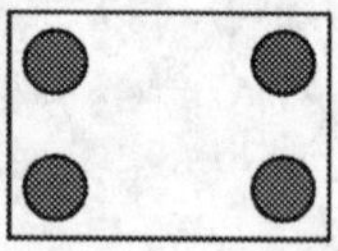

13. Identify the relationship between the pair of figures on either side of :: and then find the missing figure.

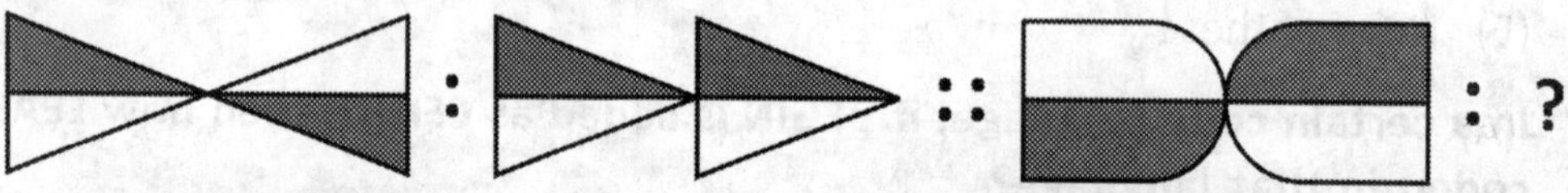

(A) 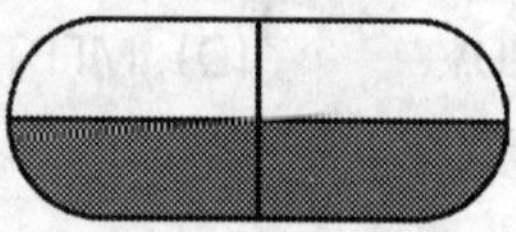

(B) 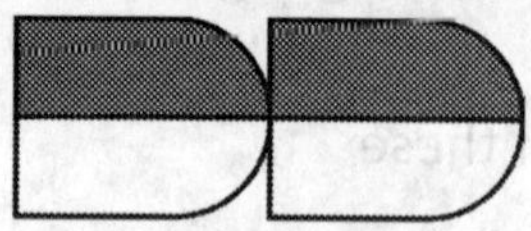

(C) 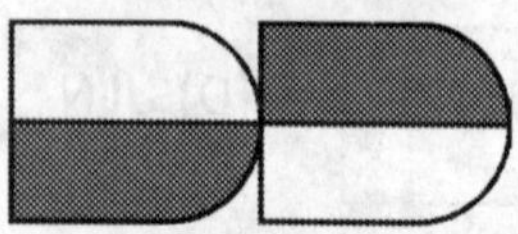

(D) 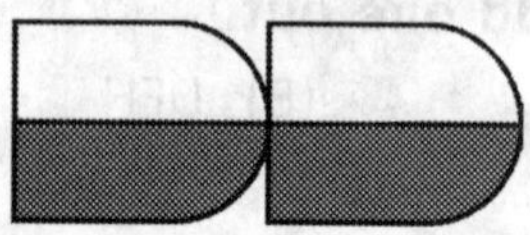

(E) None of these

14. Identify the relationship between the pair of figures on either side of :: and then find the missing figure.

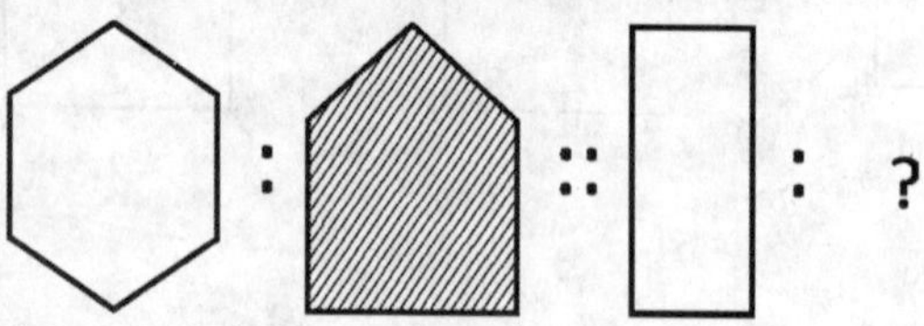

(A) 

(B) 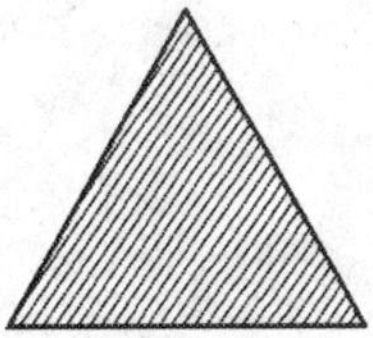

(C) 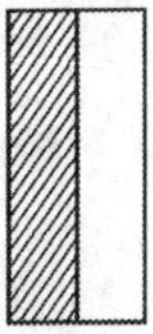

(D) 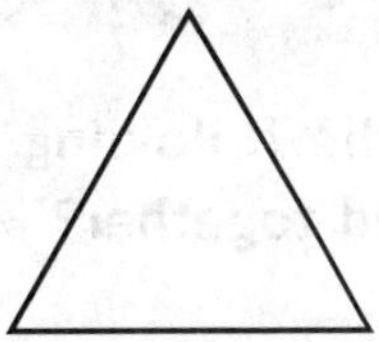

(E) None of these

15. What comes next in the figure pattern given below?

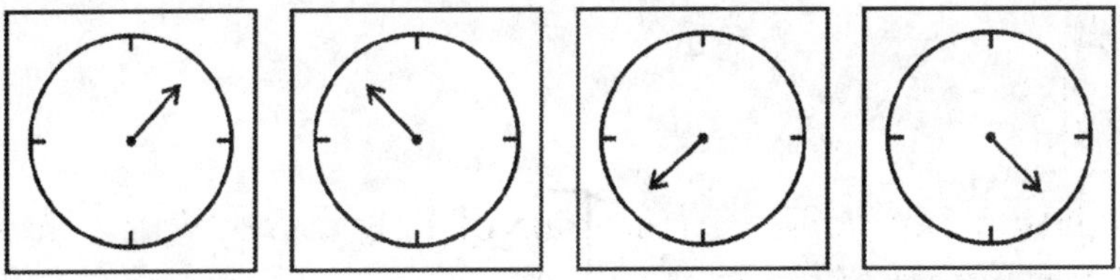

?

(A) 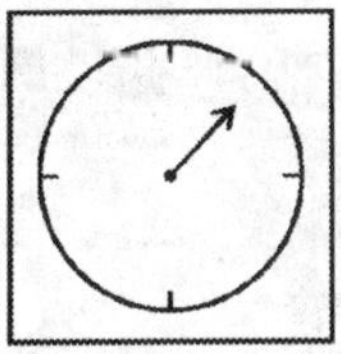

(B) 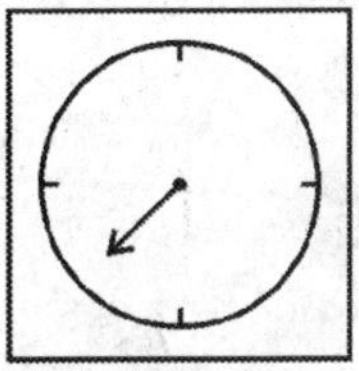

(C) 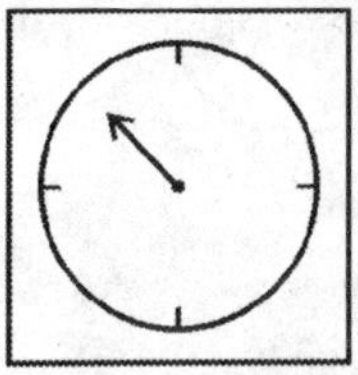

(D) 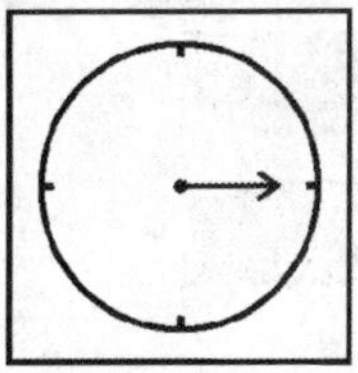

(E) None of these

16. What comes next in the figure pattern given below?

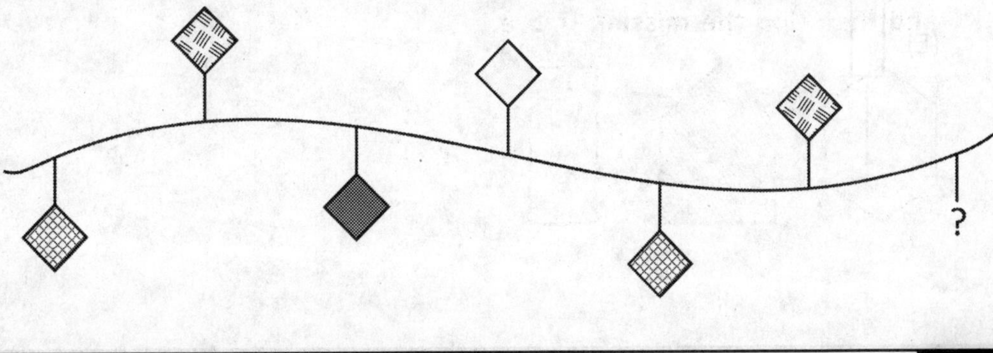

(A) 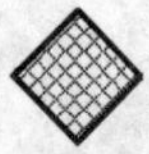   (B) 

(C)    (D) 

(E) None of these

17. Which one of the following shapes is obtained when two shapes given below are joined together?

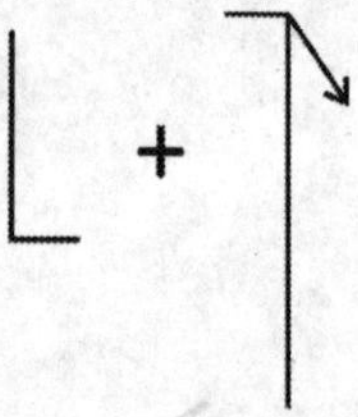

(A) 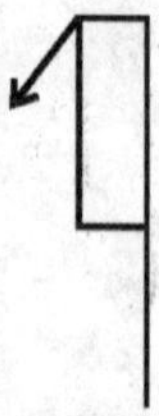   (B) 

(C)    (D) 

(E) 

18. Identify the option with which the figure given below is formed.

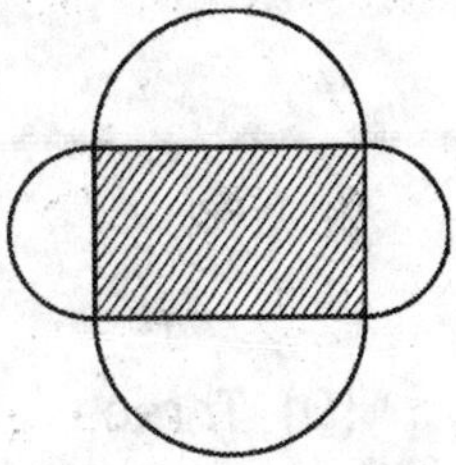

(A) 4 semicircles and 2 squares
(B) 4 semicircles and 1 rectangle
(C) 4 semicircles and 1 square
(D) 4 semicircles and 2 rectangles
(E) None of these

19. How many triangles are there in the given figure?

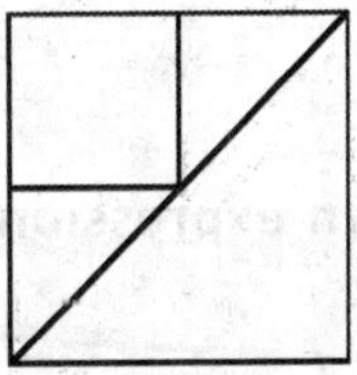

(A) 6 (B) 3
(C) 4 (D) 5
(E) None of these

20. How many circles are there in the given figure?

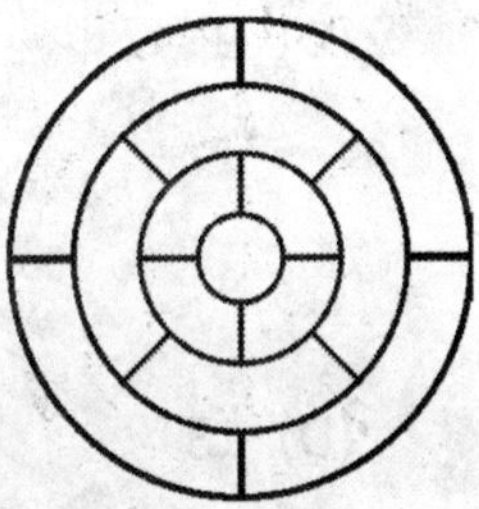

(A) 6 (B) 4
(C) 5 (D) 3
(E) None of these

Model Test Paper-1

1. **How many hundreds are there in 5309?**
   (A) Zero (B) Nine (C) Five (D) Three
   (E) None of these

2. **I had ₹4132. Which of the following in the correct number name for 4132?**
   (A) Four thousand three hundred twelve
   (B) Four thousand one hundred thirty two
   (C) Two thousand three hundred forty one
   (D) Four thousand two hundred thirteen
   (E) None of these

3. **What is the predecessor of resulting number of the given expression?**
   $$\frac{6+7+8}{7}$$
   (A) 2 (B) 3 (C) 6 (D) 4
   (E) None of these

4. **If 12 × 7 = 12 × a, where 'a' stands for a number then the value of 'a' is:**
   (A) 6 (B) 7 (C) 8 (D) 9
   (E) None of these

5. **Which number is missing from this sequence?**
   45, 39, 33, 27, 21, _______
   (A) 14 (B) 15 (C) 16 (D) 13
   (E) None of these

6. **What is the difference of the greatest prime number and the smallest prime number below 20?**
   (A) 14 (B) 13 (C) 17 (D) 15
   (E) None of these

7. Difference of the face value and the place value of 3 in the number 54321 is:

(A) 297 (B) 303 (C) 318 (D) 324

(E) None of these

8. When two-third of 27 is added in one-third of 27, the resulting number will be:

(A) 30 (B) 18 (C) 27 (D) 33

(E) None of these

9. Two-seventh of a circle is shaded as shown below. The *unshaded* part of the circle is:

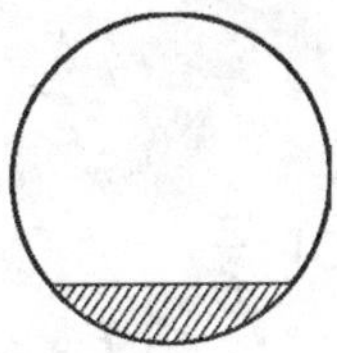

(A) $\frac{5}{7}$ (B) $\frac{4}{7}$ (C) $\frac{3}{7}$ (D) $\frac{2}{7}$

(E) None of these

10. Find the fraction represented by *unshaded* parts in the figure given below.

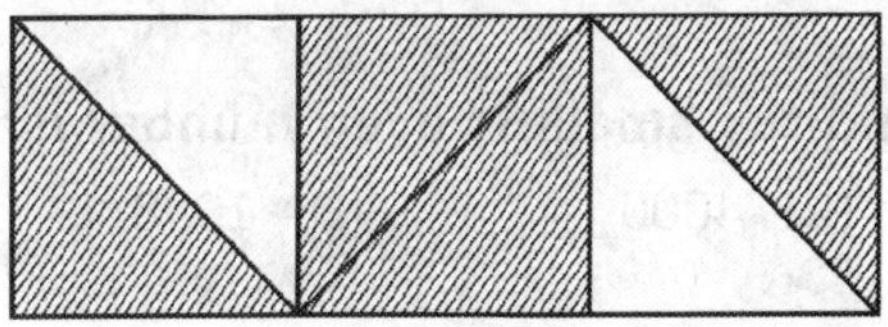

(A) $\frac{2}{3}$ (B) $\frac{1}{2}$ (C) $\frac{1}{3}$ (D) $\frac{2}{3}$

(E) None of these

11. When the 2-digit smallest number is divided by the smallest prime number, the quotient will be:

(A) 5 (B) 2 (C) 3 (D) 39

(E) None of these

12. How many centimetres are there in 43.50 metres?

(A) 435 cm (B) 43500 cm (C) 4350 cm (D) 4.35 cm

(E) None of these

13. Total rotation of second hand of a watch in 1 hour 30 minutes will be:

(A) 90 (B) 60 (C) 120 (D) 150

(E) None of these

14. Sum of the successor and the predecessor of 19 is:

(A) 39 (B) 37 (C) 21 (D) 19

(E) None of these

15. Find the fraction represented by *unshaded* parts in the figure given below.

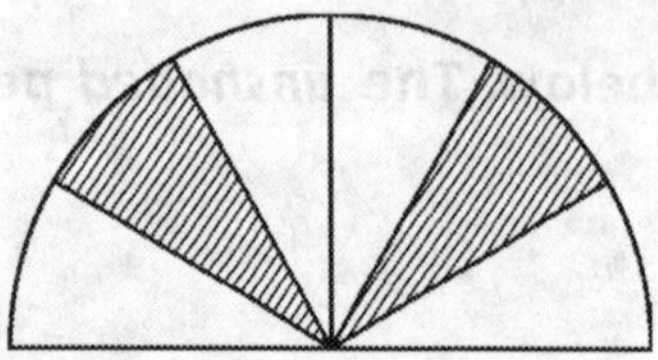

(A) $\frac{1}{3}$ (B) $\frac{1}{2}$ (C) $\frac{2}{3}$ (D) $\frac{1}{6}$

(E) None of these

16. Twice the value of ₹7.50 in paise is:

(A) 1500 paise (B) 750 paise

(C) 3000 paise (D) 375 paise

(E) None of these

17. Product of 3-digit smallest number and the smallest even number is:

(A) 3000 (B) 2000 (C) 4000 (D) 1098

(E) None of these

18. What should be added to 10 ml to make 10 L?

(A) 9090 ml (B) 9990 ml

(C) 10010 ml (D) 9900 ml

(E) None of these

19. Number of triangles in the given figure is:

(A) 10 (B) 9 (C) 8 (D) 11
(E) None of these

20. When three times of the smallest even prime number is subtracted from two times of the smallest odd prime number, the result is:

(A) 1 (B) 2 (C) 0 (D) 3
(E) None of these

21. Thirty times of 150 grams in kilograms will be:

(A) 4.5 kg (B) 45 kg
(C) 0.45 kg (D) 450 kg
(E) None of these

22. Sum of the numbers of days of February in 2008 and 2009 is:

(A) 56 (B) 57 (C) 58 (D) 60
(E) None of these

23. Number of triangles in the given figure is:

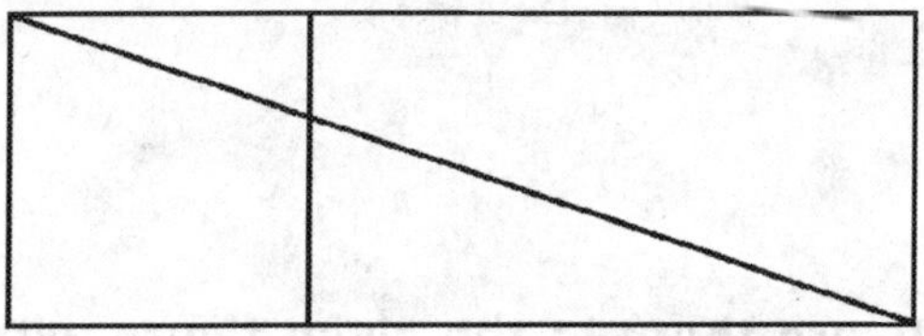

(A) 6 (B) 3 (C) 4 (D) 5
(E) None of these

24. The measures of A to B, B to C, C to D and D to E are in sequence which are mentioned on the given number line. The value of x will be:

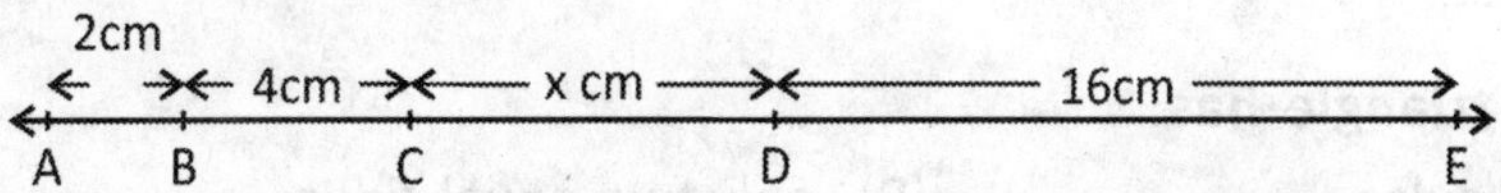

(A) 2 cm (B) 4 cm (C) 6 cm (D) 8 cm
(E) None of these

25. Which one of the following operations gives a prime number as result?

(A) 42×6 (B) $42 \div 6$
(C) $42 + 6$ (D) $42 - 6$
(E) None of these

26. How many straight lines can be drawn through two given points?

(A) Exactly two
(B) Exactly one
(C) Exactly three
(D) Uncountable
(E) None of these

27. How many vertices are three in given figure?

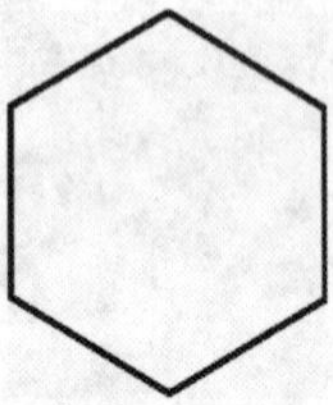

(A) 4
(B) 5
(C) 6
(D) 8
(E) None of these

28. A point has:

(A) position but not length.
(B) length but not position.
(C) both length and position.
(D) neither length nor position.
(E) None of these

29. How many different line segments are there in the given figure with the points P, Q and R ?

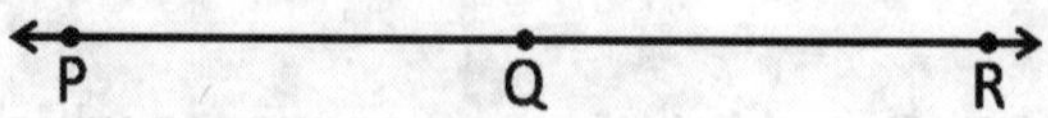

(A) 2
(B) 3
(C) 1
(D) 4
(E) None of these

30. An equilateral trlangle has:

(A) three equal sides
(B) only two equal sides
(C) no equal sides
(D) one side twice the other
(E) None of these

31. We measure the distance of two cities in:

(A) metres
(B) kilometres
(C) centimetres
(D) millimetres
(E) None of these

32. If we cut a 91 metres long wire into 7 parts of equal length, the measure of each part of the wire will be:

(A) 7 metres (B) 11 metres
(C) 13 metres (D) 17 metres
(E) None of these

33. If the cost of 8 magazines is ₹ 96, then the cost of 7 such magazines will be:

(A) ₹ 96 (B) ₹ 70
(C) ₹ 77 (D) ₹ 63
(E) None of these

34. The difference of the $\frac{4}{5}$th and $\frac{9}{5}$th part of a number is:

(A) more than the number
(B) less than the number
(C) the number itself
(D) equal to zero
(E) None of these

35. What time does the given clock show?

(A) 10 : 05 (B) 10 : 35
(C) 1 : 50 (D) 7 : 05
(E) None of these

36. How many coins of 50 paise make a sum amount ₹ 35?

(A) 35 (B) 140
(C) 100 (D) 70
(E) None of these

37. Distribution of students in different sections of a school is given below. If one symbol represents 50 students, then the sum of the numbers of students in section B and section C is:

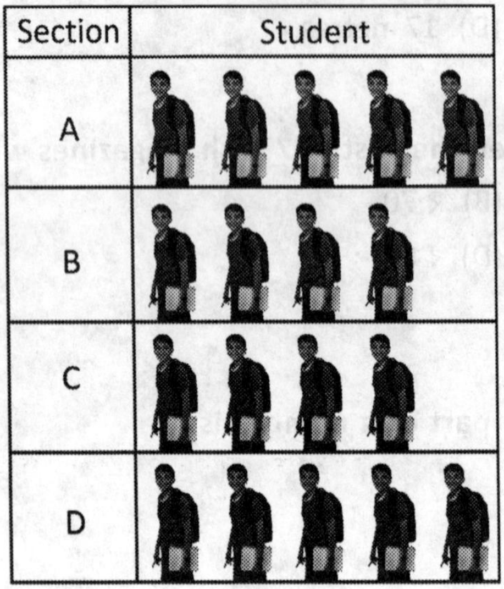

(A) 450
(B) 200
(C) 400
(D) 500
(E) None of these

38. A newspaper took a survey among the readers on their favorite type of music. The result was publish in the newspaper as shown below:

Rock	Pop	Classic	Country	Jazz
1700	4500	335	475	125

How many people voted for 'Rock', 'Classic' and 'Country' altogether?

(A) 6535
(B) 2510
(C) 4960
(D) 5310
(E) None of these

39. Given bar graph shows the saving of four children.

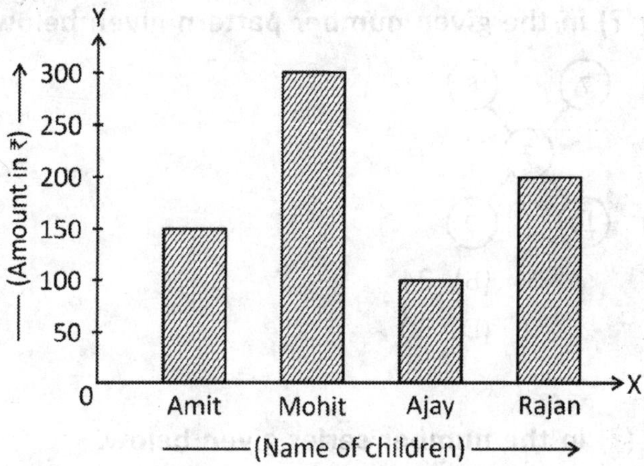

How much more money does Ajay need to save so that he has twice as much money as Amit does save?

(A) ₹ 100 (B) ₹ 150 (C) ₹ 200 (D) ₹ 250

(E) None of these

40. Given bar graph shows the marks obtained by Susan in her first term examination.

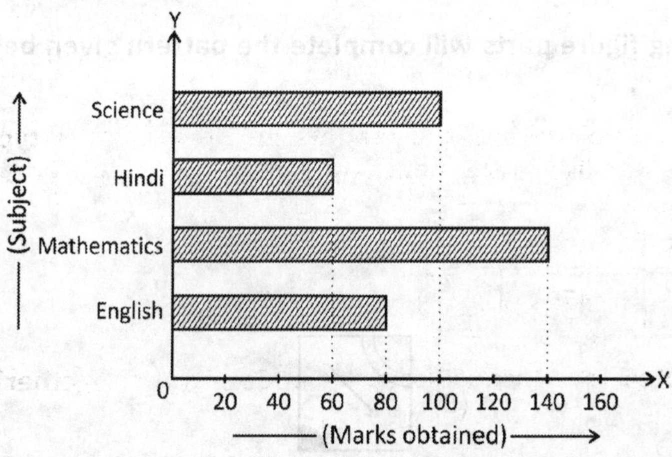

If 150 was the maximum marks for each paper, then the marks obtained by Susan in all four subjects out of 600 is:

(A) 390 (B) 380 (C) 450 (D) 370

(E) None of these

Direction (41 – 50): Reasoning and Aptitude

41. Find the missing number (?) in the given number pattern given below.

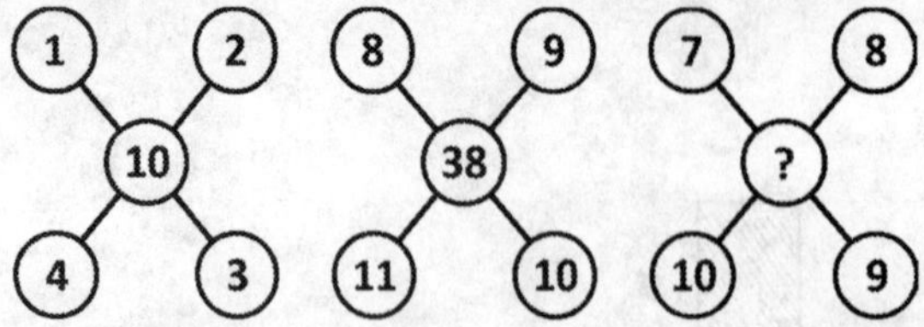

(A) 34
(B) 24
(C) 36
(D) 30
(E) None of these

42. Find the missing number (?) in the number series given below.

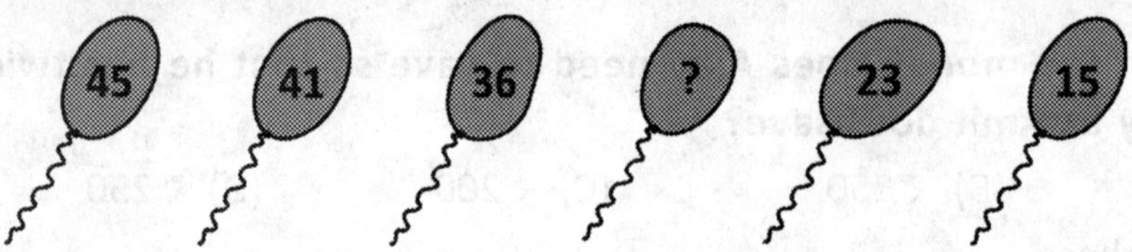

(A) 24
(B) 27
(C) 30
(D) 28
(E) None of these

43. Which of the following figure parts will complete the pattern given below?

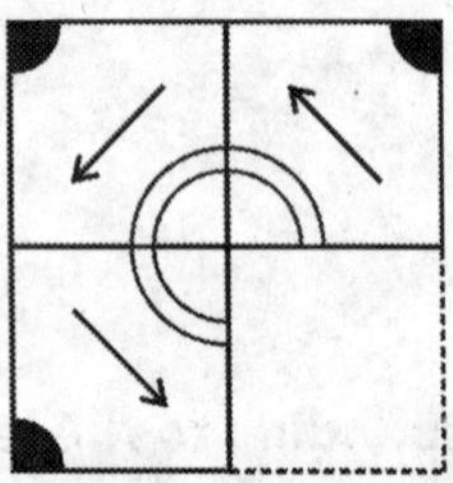

(A) 

(B) 

(C) 

(D) 

(E) None of these

44. Find the missing number (?) in the table given below, if a certain rule is applied row-wise or column-wise.

8	6	8
2	2	?
4	3	2

(A) 2 (B) 3 (C) 4 (D) 1

(E) None of these

45. Find the odd one out.

(A) A

(B) B

(C) R

(D) D

(E) P

46. Find the next term of the given series.

(E + P), (G + R), (I + T), (K + V), ?

(A) (L + W) (B) (N + Y)

(C) (M + X) (D) (W + Y)

(E) None of these

47. A meaningful word by arranging given numbers corresponding to the letters given below is:

L	A	C	F
1	2	3	4

(A) 4, 2, 3, 1 (B) 2, 4, 1, 3

(C) 3, 1, 4, 2 (D) 3, 2, 1, 4

(E) None of these

48. If M = 13, ME = 18 and MON = 42, then MONEY = _______?

(A) 71 (B) 72

(C) 68 (D) 78

(E) None of these

49. In a row of 8 girls, Rita is fifth from the right end. Her position from left end is:

(A) Fifth (B) Fourth

(C) Third (D) Second

(E) None of these

50. Minimum number of line segments to draw the given figure is:

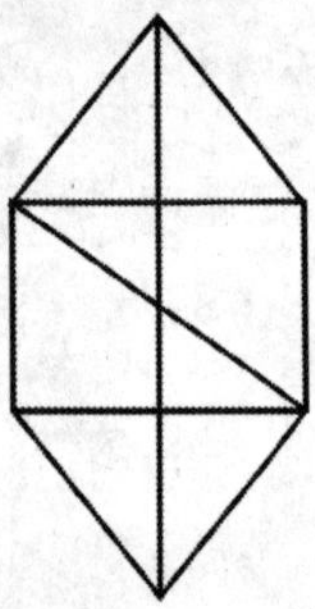

(A) 12 (B) 11

(C) 14 (D) 10

(E) None of these

Model Test Paper-2

1. **The product of 3-digit smallest number and the smallest even number is:**
(A) 1000 (B) 2000
(C) 4000 (D) 1980
(E) None of these

2. **One-fourth of the successor of 111 is:**
(A) 28 (B) 26 (C) 27 (D) 29
(E) None of these

3. **If 2 × 3 × a = 3 × 4 × 5, where 'a' stands for a number, then the value of 'a' will be:**
(A) 4 (B) 10 (C) 5 (D) 6
(E) None of these

4. **The product of the face value and place value of 3 in 54321 will be:**
(A) 300 (B) 900
(C) 1035 (D) 303
(E) None of these

5. **In a division, remainder is always less than:**
(A) quotient (B) divisor
(C) both quotient and divisor (D) one
(E) None of these

6. **The sum of two numbers is 43. If one of them is 22 then their difference will be:**
(A) 1 (B) 2 (C) 21 (D) 25
(E) None of these

7. **Multiplication of any two prime numbers is always:**
(A) a prime number (B) a composite
(C) an odd number (D) an even number
(E) None of these

8. **The predecessor of sum of the smallest prime number and the smallest composite number is:**
(A) 6 (B) 7 (C) 5 (D) 8
(E) None of these

9. **The sum of any two even numbers is always:**
(A) an odd number (B) an even number
(C) a prime number (D) a multiple of 10
(E) None of these

10. **If half of a number is 3, then twice the number will be:**
(A) 6 (B) 15 (C) 12 (D) 3
(E) None of these

11. **The value of 5 × 4 × 3 × 2 × 1 × 0 is:**
(A) 1200 (B) 120 (C) 240 (D) 0
(E) None of these

12. **Which one of the following is *not* divisible by 5?**
(A) 54320 (B) 54324 (C) 54325 (D) 23450
(E) None of these

13. **Which one of the following abacuses shows the number equal to 3241?**

(A) 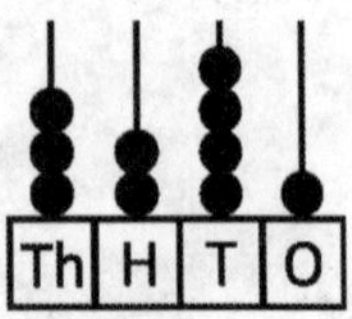

(B) 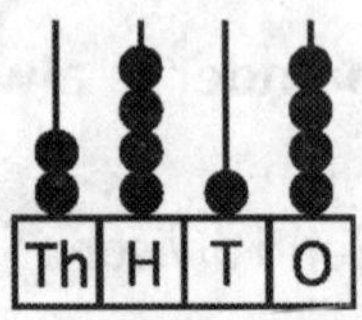

(C) 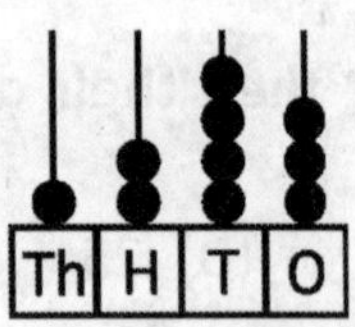

(D) 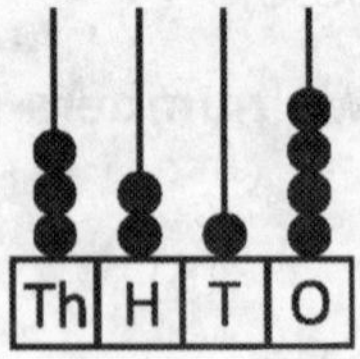

(E) None of these

14. **How many hundreds are there in 9257?**
(A) Zero (B) Two (C) Five (D) Nine
(E) None of these

15. 9602 is same as:

(A) 9000 + 600 + 20
(B) 9000 + 60 + 2
(C) 9000 + 600 + 2
(D) 900 + 600 + 2
(E) None of these

16 Find the sum of the missing digits A and B in the addition given below.

	2	0	1	3
+	A	5	0	9
	5	5	B	2

(A) 4
(B) 5
(C) 7
(D) 6
(E) None of these

17. Arrange the following erasers in the groups in such a way that each group contains 4 erasers and then find the number of groups.

(A) 6
(B) 8
(C) 5
(D) 4
(E) None of these

18. The sum of 15 and 45 is equal to the value of:

(A) 50 + 20
(B) 15 + 15 + 15 + 15
(C) 30 + 30 + 30
(D) 30 + 15 + 15 + 15
(E) None of these

19. The correct statement among the following is:

(A) $\frac{6}{7} > 1 > \frac{8}{7}$
(B) $\frac{6}{7} = 1 = \frac{8}{7}$
(C) $\frac{6}{7} < 1 < \frac{8}{7}$
(D) $\frac{8}{7} < 1 < \frac{6}{7}$
(E) None of these

20. $\frac{1}{3}+\frac{2}{3}+\frac{3}{3}$ **is equal to:**

(A) 2 (B) 1 (C) 6 (D) 3

(E) None of these

21. Which one of the following is a proper fraction?

(A) $\frac{2}{3}$ (B) $\frac{3}{2}$ (C) $\frac{5}{2}$ (D) $\frac{5}{3}$

(E) None of these

22. Time difference between 8 : 40 am and 12 : 30 pm is:

(A) 3 hours 50 minutes (B) 4 hours 10 minutes

(C) 3 hours 10 minutes (D) 4 hour 50 minutes

(E) None of these

23. What time does the clock shows in the given figure?

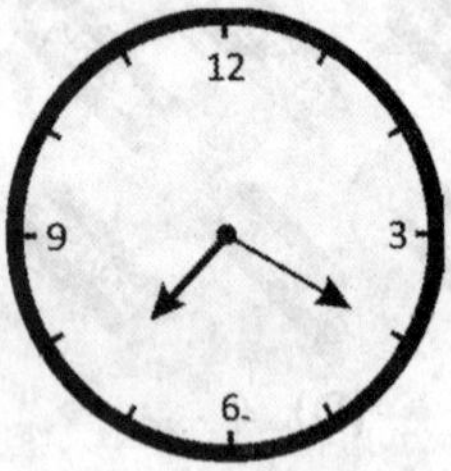

(A) 7 : 30 (B) 7 : 50

(C) 7 : 20 (D) 6 : 40

(E) None of these

24. In which one of the following years, number of days in February was more than 28 days?

(A) 1996 (B) 1995

(C) 1994 (D) 1998

(E) None of these

25. How many coins of 50 paise make a sum amount ₹ 25?

(A) 13 (B) 140 (C) 100 (D) 50

(E) None of these

26. Observe the following rate list:

Item	Price
Tea	₹ 35
Coffee	₹ 75
Juice	₹ 90
Curd	₹ 70

What is the cost difference of 3 cups of coffee and 2 glasses of Juice?

(A) ₹ 35 (B) ₹ 45 (C) ₹ 65 (D) ₹ 25

(E) None of these

27. If the cost of 8 magazines is ₹ 48, then the cost of 48 such magazines is:

(A) ₹ 288 (B) ₹ 248 (C) ₹ 276 (D) ₹ 312

(E) None of these

28. A pipe takes 90 minutes to empty a tank. What part of tank will empty in 1 hour?

(A) $\frac{1}{3}$ (B) $\frac{2}{3}$ (C) $\frac{3}{4}$ (D) $\frac{1}{4}$

(E) None of these

29. If a cat catches 4 rates in the morning and 7 rats in the evening, how many rats does the cat catch in a week?

(A) 77 (B) 71 (C) 28 (D) 84

(E) None of these

30. I am a 5-digit number. I have a 8 in the hundreds place. I have a 3 in the tens place. I have a 7 in the ones place. I have a 4 in the thousands place. I have a 8 in the ten thousands place. What number am I ?

(A) 84837 (B) 88437

(C) 83847 (D) 84387

(E) None of these

31. If a pair of scissors costs ₹75, then how many coins of 50 paise do you need to buy it?

(A) 25 (B) 150
(C) 100 (D) 125
(E) None of these

32. How many triangles are there in the given figure?

(A) 9 (B) 8 (C) 7 (D) 6
(E) None of these

33. A sheep weighs about 643 kilograms less than the weight of a buffalo. If the buffalo weigh about 715 kilograms, about how much does the sheep weigh?

(A) 78 kg (B) 68 kg
(C) 72 kg (D) 1358 kg
(E) None of these

34. The distance covered by a bus in 18 minutes is 6 km. Time taken by the bus to cover the distance 18 km will be:

(A) 36 minutes (B) 54 minutes
(C) 72 minutes (D) 45 minutes
(E) None of these

35. The weight of A is 30 kg and the weight of B is 45 kg. If the weight of C is twice the weight difference of A and B, then the weight of C will be:

(A) 30 kg (B) 35 kg
(C) 15 kg (D) 45 kg
(E) None of these

36. At a cycle parking, a board shows the following information:

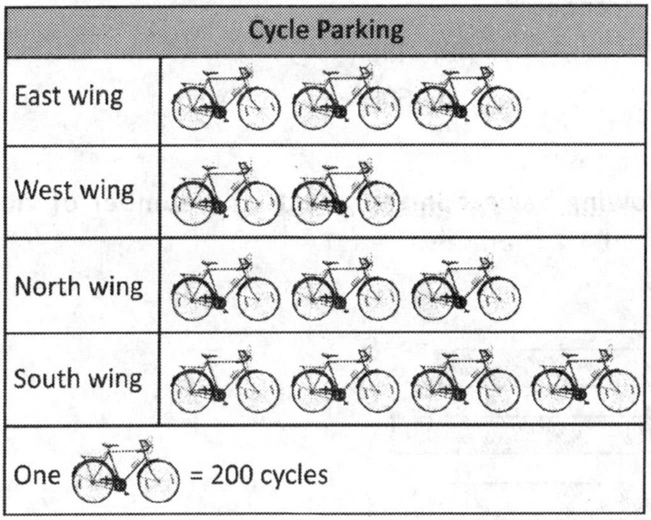

What is the total strength of cycle parking?

(A) 2600 (B) 2400 (C) 2800 (D) 3000
(E) None of these

37. Observe the following information newspaper readers which is obtalned during the survey.

What is the difference between the numbers of English newspaper readers and Punjabi newspaper readers?

(A) 400 (B) 450

(C) 350 (D) 500

(E) None of these

***Direction (38 – 40)*: The following bar graph represents the number of viewers who watched the five different TV channels.**

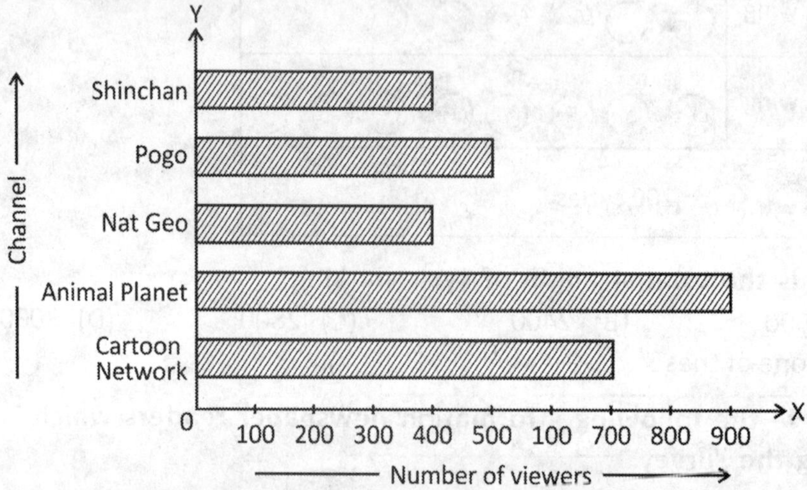

Study the graph and answer the following questions:

38. How many more viewers watched the Cartoon Network than Nat Geo?

(A) 400 (B) 300 (C) 500 (D) 200

(E) None of these

39. How many viewers watched Nat Geo and Animal Planet?

(A) 1400 (B) 1200

(C) 1500 (D) 1300

(E) None of these

40. How many viewers watched Shinchan, Pogo and Cartoon Network?

(A) 1600 (B) 1800

(C) 1400 (D) 1500

(E) None of these

Direction (41 – 50): Reasoning and Aptitude

41. Which one of the following numbers will replace the question mark (?) in the number pattern given below?

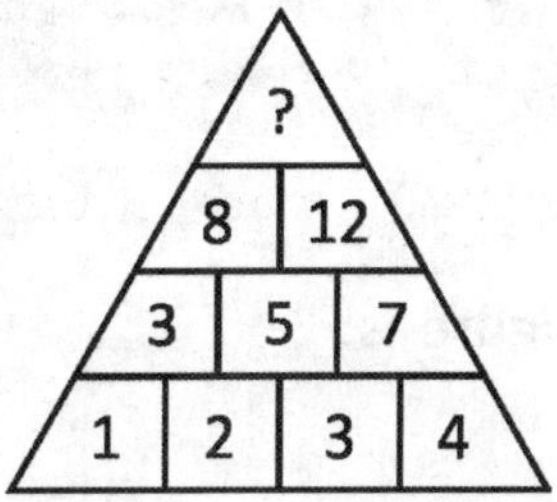

(A) 15 (B) 10 (C) 20 (D) 24
(E) None of these

42. Diya is making this calendar for the bulletin board. Which day of the week should be on 27th February 20XX?

February 20XX						
Sun	**Mon**	**Tue**	**Wed**	**Thu**	**Fri**	**Sat**
			1	2	3	4
5	6	7	8	9	10	11

(A) Sunday (B) Monday
(C) Saturday (D) Wednesday
(E) None of these

43. A part of land is ABCD covered with square tiles as shown below. How many more tiles are required to cover the land?

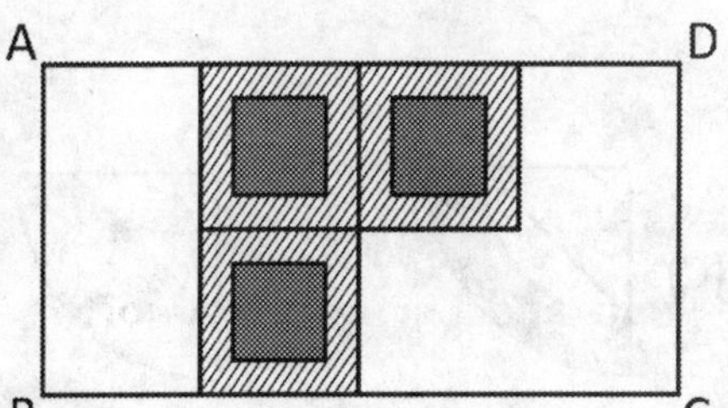

(A) 3 (B) 4 (C) 5 (D) 6
(E) None of these

44. Which of the following shapes has two circular ends?

(A) 

(B) 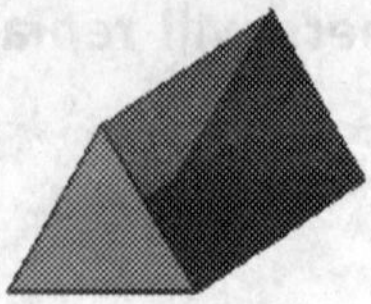

(C) 

(D) 

(E) None of these

45. Minimum number of line segments in the given figure is:

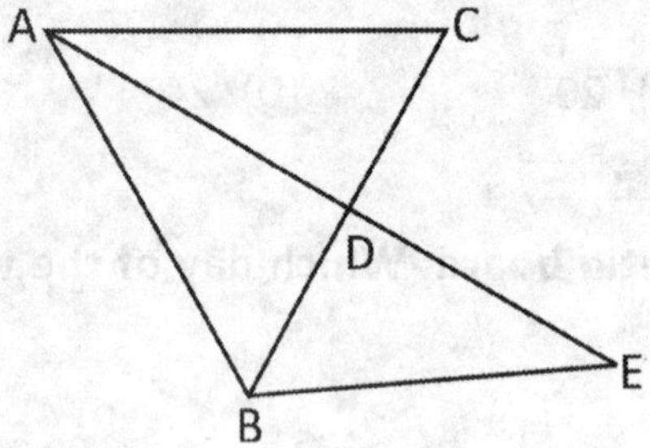

(A) 6 (B) 5 (C) 7 (D) 8

(E) None of these

46. Which one of the following figure parts will complete the figure pattern given below?

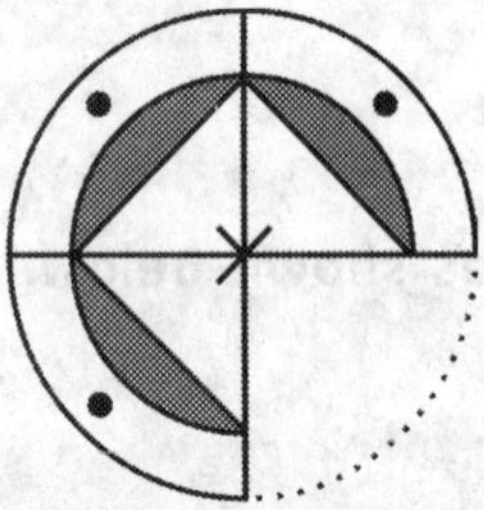

(A) 

(B) 

(C) 

(D) 

(E) None of these

47. How many triangles are there in the given figure?

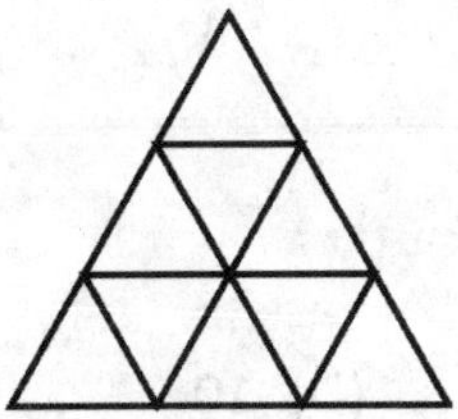

(A) 12 (B) 13 (C) 14 (D) 15

(E) None of these

48. Find the odd one out.

(A) 

(B) 

(C) 

(D) 

(E) 

49. If 'Tie' is called 'Handkerchief', 'Handkerchief' is called 'Sweater', 'Sweater' is called 'Hat' and 'Hat' is called 'Watch', then what you need to stay warm in freezing winter?

(A) Sweater (B) Handkerchief

(C) Hat (D) Watch

(E) None of these

50. Which one of the following numbers will replace the question mark (?) in the number series given below?

97, 88, 79, 70, 61, ?

(A) 51 (B) 53 (C) 54 (D) 50

(E) None of these

Model Test Paper-3

1. **All even numbers are divisible by:**

(A) 3 (B) 2 (C) 4 (D) 10

(E) None of these

2. **When the greatest 2-digit number is divided by the smallest odd prime number, the result is:**

(A) 9 (B) 11 (C) 33 (D) 50

(E) None of these

3. **The number 1 is:**

(A) a prime number

(B) a composite

(C) both a prime and a composite number

(D) neither a prime nor a composite number

(E) None of these

4. **The sum of the smallest natural number and the smallest whole number is:**

(A) 1 (B) 0 (C) 2 (D) 3

(E) None of these

5. **In a division, 9 is the quotient and 3 is remainder. If the divisor is 8, then the dividend will be:**

(A) 33 (B) 35 (C) 75 (D) 51

(E) None of these

6. **The predecessor of a number is 437, the successor of that number will be:**

(A) 439 (B) 438 (C) 437 (D) 436

(E) None of these

7. **If the sum and difference of digits of a number is 1 then the number is:**

(A) 11 (B) 20 (C) 10 (D) 21

(E) None of these

8. If we round 468 to the nearest ten and then multiply it by 7, the result is:

(A) 3276 (B) 3290 (C) 3220 (D) 3360

(E) None of these

9. The product of all the prime numbers below 10 is:

(A) 945 (B) 105 (C) 1890 (D) 210

(E) None of these

10. The sum of any two odd numbers is always:

(A) a prime number (B) a multiple of 4

(C) an even number (D) an odd number

(E) None of these

11. The smallest 4-digit number we can write by using the digits 0, 4, 7, 1 is:

(A) 1047 (B) 7410 (C) 4017 (D) 1470

(E) None of these

12. Which one of the following is correct?

(A) $(1 \times 2) + (3 \times 4) = 15$ (B) $(1 + 2) + (3 \times 4) = 15$

(C) $(1 \times 2) + (3 + 4) = 15$ (D) $(1 + 2) + (3 + 4) = 15$

(E) None of these

13. How many 4's are there in 36?

(A) 7 (B) 8 (C) 9 (D) 6

(E) None of these

14. Which one of the following abacuses shows the number 4314?

(A) 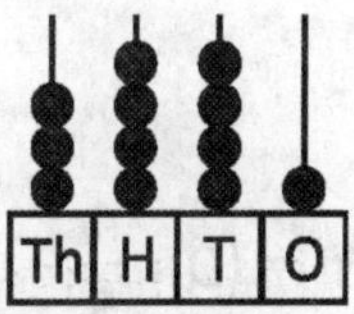

(B) 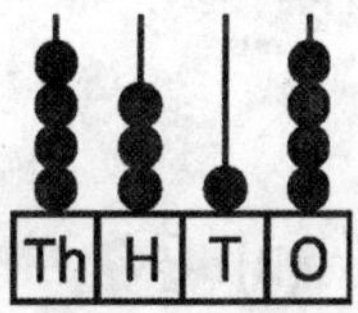

(C) 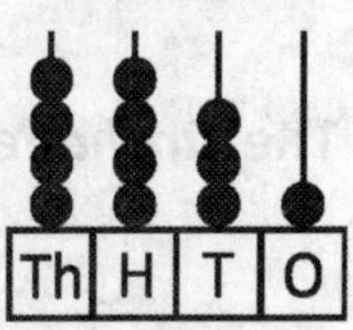

(D) 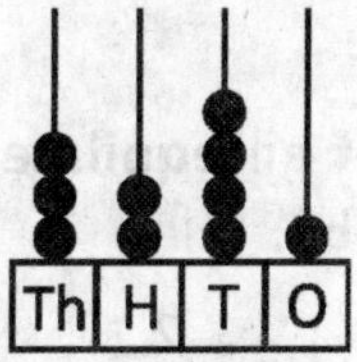

(E) None of these

15. Find the next two missing numbers in the number pattern given below.

4, 11, 18, 25, ___?___, ___?___

(A) 31, 38 (B) 32, 39 (C) 30, 37 (D) 37, 44

(E) None of these

16. Which of the following sets of numbers is in descending order?

(A) 474, 478, 470, 415 (B) 4480, 4417, 4074, 4704

(C) 1810, 1783, 1737, 1728 (D) 6245, 6425, 6524, 6625

(E) None of these

17. The value of ▲ is 3 times as much as the value of ●. What is the value of ▲ + ● if ● + 14 is 24?

(A) 30 (B) 40 (C) 38 (D) 42

(E) None of these

18. Find the missing digit [?] in the multiplication given below.

```
 4 ? 1 2
     × 3
---------
1 4 1 3 6
```

(A) 6 (B) 5 (C) 8 (D) 7

(E) None of these

19. The fraction represented by shaded parts in the given figure is:

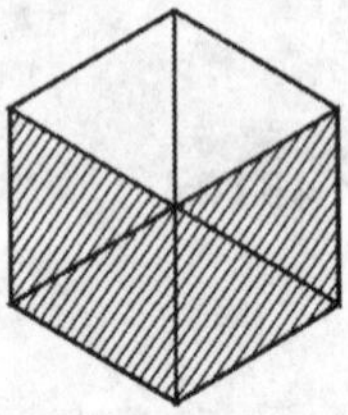

(A) $\frac{2}{3}$ (B) $\frac{1}{2}$ (C) $\frac{1}{3}$ (D) $\frac{4}{5}$

(E) None of these

20. One-third part of an equilateral triangle is shaded. The *unshaded* part of the triangle will be:

(A) $\frac{1}{3}$ (B) $\frac{2}{3}$ (C) $\frac{1}{4}$ (D) $\frac{5}{6}$

(E) None of these

21. Which one of the following fraction is equivalent to $\frac{2}{3}$?

(A) $\frac{10}{3}$ (B) $\frac{2}{30}$ (C) $\frac{10}{30}$ (D) $\frac{3}{2}$

(E) None of these

22. February of 29 days will be in the year:

(A) 2022 (B) 2026 (C) 2032 (D) 2038

(E) None of these

23. In the afternoon, Peter is staying at home because it is raining. His watch shows the time as shown below. What time is it?

(A) 3 : 12 pm (B) 3 : 12 am

(C) 3 : 12 mid-night (D) 3 : 12 hours

(E) None of these

24. Tommy played computer games from 11 : 50 am to 12 : 55 pm. How long did he play?

(A) 1 hour 5 minutes (B) 55 minutes

(C) 11 hours 5 minutes (D) 1 hour 55 minutes

(E) None of these

25. Kareena has a ₹500 note with her. Which of the following items she can buy?

(A)  Doll (₹515) (B)  Frock (₹625)

(C)  Car toy (₹495) (D)  Rackets (₹510)

(E) None of these

26. If the cost of one dozen eggs is ₹72, then the cost of one egg is:

(A) ₹6 (B) ₹5 (C) ₹4 (D) ₹3

(E) None of these

27. How many pieces of electric wires measuring 30 cm each can cut from a 27 m long electric wire?

(A) 36 (B) 45 (C) 90 (D) 180

(E) None of these

28. In an equilateral triangle, the sum of lengths of any two sides is:

(A) half of the third side (B) equal to the third side

(C) less than the third side (D) twice the third side

(E) None of these

29. A tray can hold 117 eggs. If there are 9 rows in the tray, then how many columns are there in the tray?

(A) 9 (B) 11 (C) 17 (D) 13

(E) None of these

30. What amount should be paid after a discount of ₹30.50 if the cost of an article is ₹100?

(A) ₹130.50 (B) ₹69.50

(C) ₹70.50 (D) ₹68.50

(E) None of these

31. An oil-can hold 5 L of oil. How much oil is left in the oil-can if 3 L 125 ml of oil is used?

(A) 1 L 875 ml (B) 2 L 125 ml

(C) 1 L 750 ml (D) 2 L 875 ml

(E) None of these

32. A peak is 47 m high. Amit has climbed 26 m 40 cm. How much more does he have to climb to reach the peak?

(A) 20 m 60 cm (B) 21 m 87 cm

(C) 20 m 47 cm (D) 21 m 60 cm

(E) None of these

33. It takes peter 35 minutes to walk to the car park and 55 minutes to drive to work. At what time should peter get out of the home in order to get to work at 10 : 00 am?

(A) 8 : 00 am (B) 8 : 30 am (C) 7 : 30 am (D) 7 : 00 am

(E) None of these

34. How many centimetres make the half of a kilometre?

(A) 50 cm (B) 50000 cm (C) 5000 cm (D) 10000 cm

(E) None of these

35. How many triangles are there in the given figure?

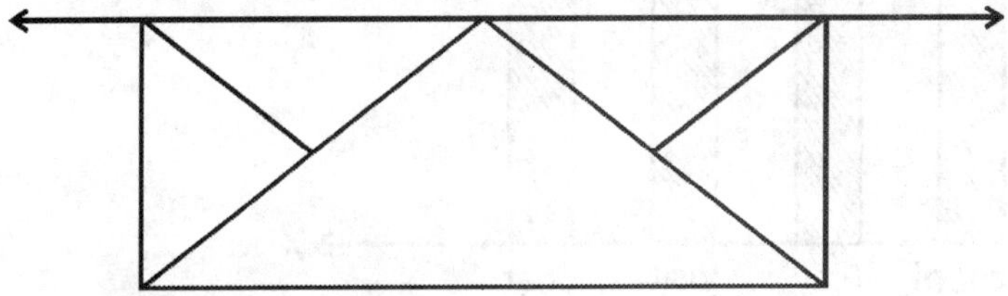

(A) 6 (B) 9 (C) 5 (D) 7

(E) None of these

36. If one  **represents 9 toys, then**  **will represent:**

(A) 7 toys (B) 78 toys (C) 72 toys (D) 63 toys

(E) None of these

37. The table given below shows the number of children in four different sections of a class in a school. Each child donates ₹5 to the foundation for the children in need. How much did they donate altogether?

Class	**4A**	**4B**	**4C**	**4D**
Number of Children	**80**	**65**	**45**	**40**

(A) ₹1350 (B) ₹1150 (C) ₹1200 (D) ₹1450

(E) None of these

***Direction (38 – 40)*: The given bar graph represents the favourite after-school activities of students.**

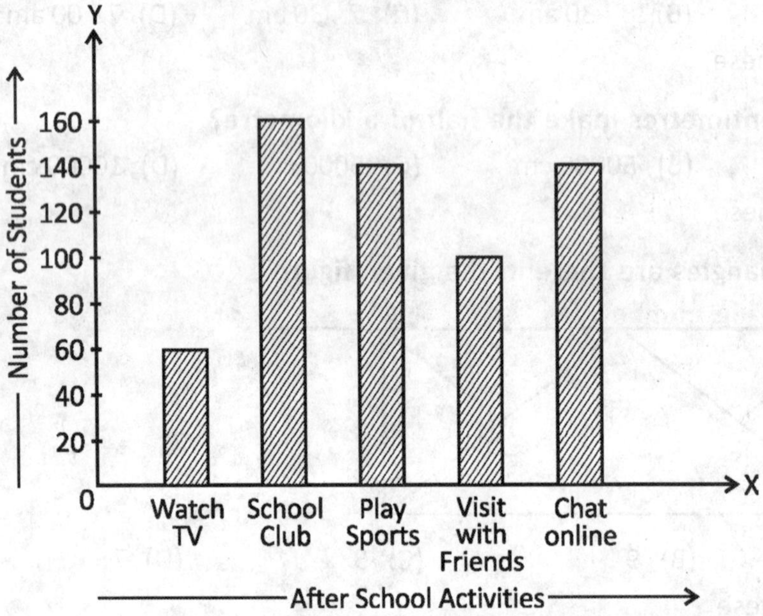

Study the bar graph and answer the following questions:

38. How many more students chat online than watched TV?

(A) 100 (B) 40 (C) 60 (D) 80

(E) None of these

39. Total number of students whose favourite after-School activities are 'visit with friends' and ______ is 260.

(A) Play sports (B) School Club

(C) Chat online (D) Watch TV

(E) None of these

40. In which two activities, there are equal number of students?

(A) Chat online and Watch TV

(B) Watch TV and School Club

(C) Play sports and Chat online

(D) Visit with friends and Play sports

(E) None of these

Direction (41 – 50)*: *Reasoning and Aptitude

41. How many squares are there in the given figure?

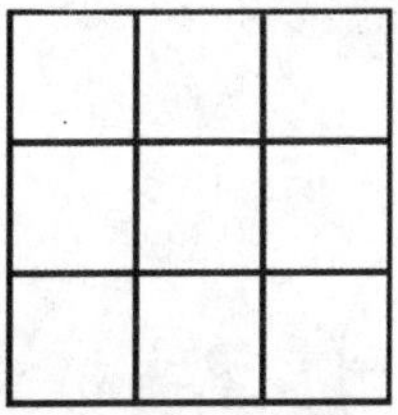

(A) 12 (C) 13 (C) 14 (D) 15

(E) None of these

42. Find the missing number.

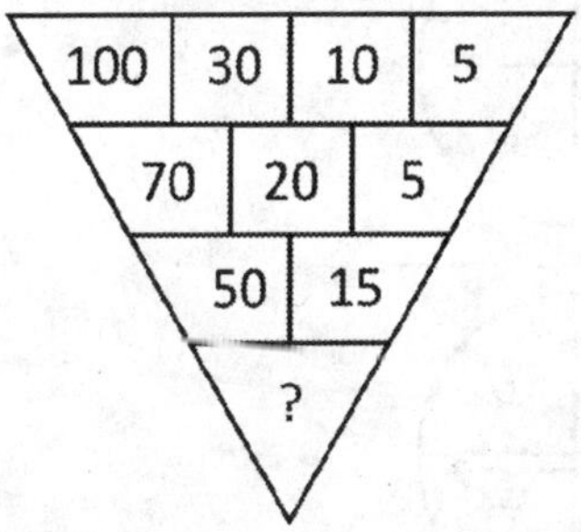

(A) 25 (B) 65 (C) 30 (D) 35

(E) None of these

43. Which letter occurs once in FROG, but twice in PROPER?

(A) P (B) R (C) O (D) F

(E) None of these

44. Identify the new word that can be formed using the letters of the given word in capital letters.

WEDNESDAY

(A) Scan (B) Send (C) Yard (D) Deep

(E) None of these

45. Find the next term of the given series.

(A + L), (C + N), (E + P), (G + R), ___?___

(A) (H + U) (B) (I + T) (C) (I + Q) (D) (J + V)

(E) None of these

46. If B = 2, BE = 7 and BEE = 12, then BEAK = _______ ?

(A) 19 (B) 15 (C) 17 (D) 16
(E) None of these

47. What comes next in the figure pattern given below?

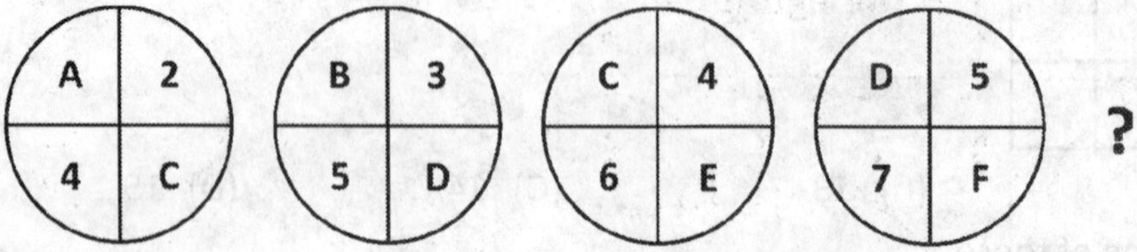

(A) 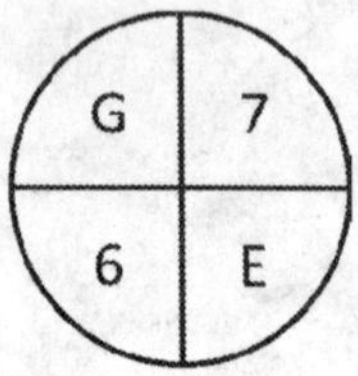

(B) 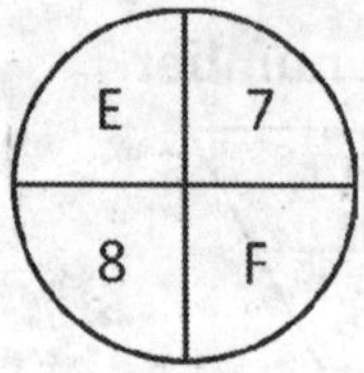

(C) 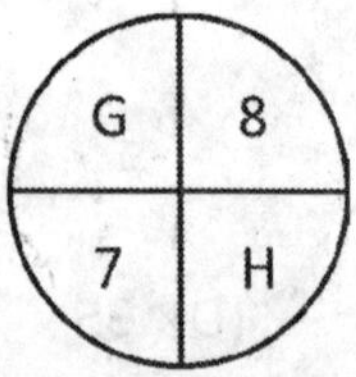

(D) 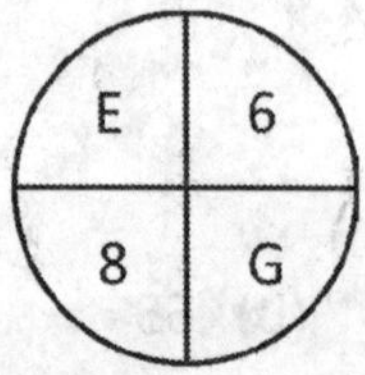

(E) None of these

48. Keeping in mind the number divisibility test, find the odd one out.

(A) 726 (B) 754
(C) 744 (D) 762
(E) 780

49. Identify the relationship between the pair of words on either side of :: and then find the missing figure.

(A) 

(B) 

(C)  (D) 

(E) None of these

50. What comes next in the figure pattern given below?

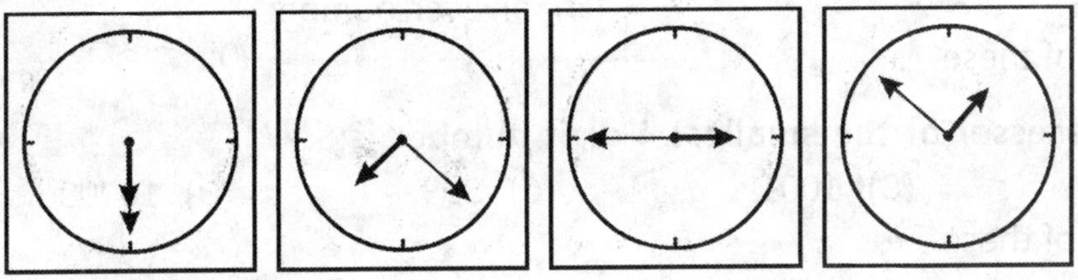 ?

(A) 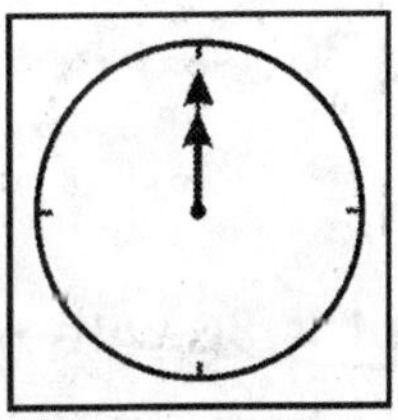 (B) 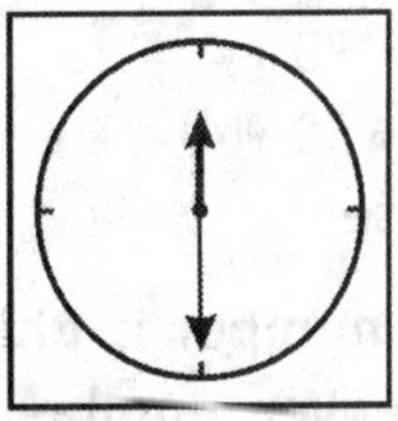

(C) 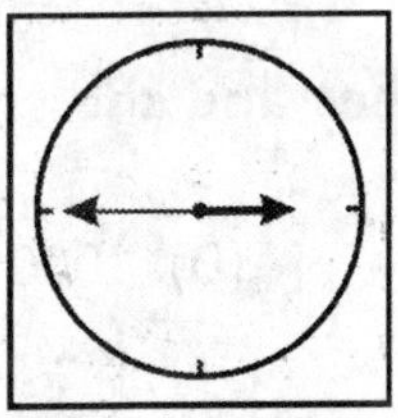 (D) 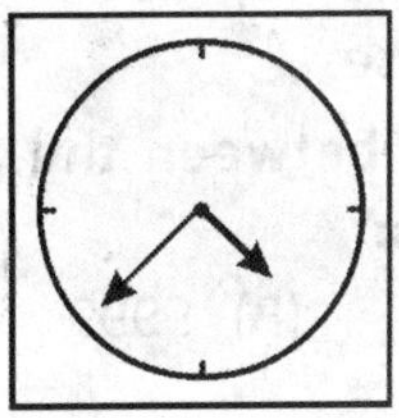

(E) None of these

Model Test Paper-4

1. **The division of an even number by 2 always leaves remainder:**
   (A) 0 (B) 1
   (C) 2 (D) an even number
   (E) None of these

2. **The predecessor of the smallest 4-digit number is:**
   (A) 1000 (B) 1001 (C) 999 (D) 10000
   (E) None of these

3. **Expanded form of 1234 is:**
   (A) 2000 + 100 + 30 + 4 (B) 3000 + 200 + 30 + 4
   (C) 1000 + 200 + 30 + 4 (D) 1000 + 2300 + 4
   (E) None of these

4. **When an even number is divided by 2 the quotient is 86 with remainder zero. The given even number is:**
   (A) 172 (B) 170 (C) 174 (D) 186
   (E) None of these

5. **The difference between the greatest 4-digit number and the smallest 4-digit number is:**
   (A) 9000 (B) 9999 (C) 8999 (D) 1000
   (E) None of these

6. **For counting the objects, we use:**
   (A) natural numbers (B) prime numbers
   (C) even numbers (D) odd numbers
   (E) None of these

7. **The sum of an even number and an odd number is always:**
   (A) an even number (B) an odd number
   (C) a prime number (D) a composite number
   (E) None of these

8. **Thirty times of 30 minus 30 will be:**
   (A) 930 (B) 900 (C) 870 (D) 830
   (E) None of these

9. **Difference of "5 taken away from 13" and "7 taken away from 11" is:**
(A) 4 (B) 8 (C) 2 (D) 6
(E) None of these

10. **Difference of place values of the digits 4 and 5 in the number 64527 will be:**
(A) 4600 (B) 3500 (C) 4000 (D) 500
(E) None of these

11. **Which one of the following abacuses shows the number more than 4000?**

(A) 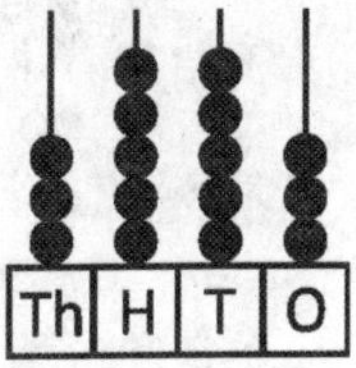

(B) 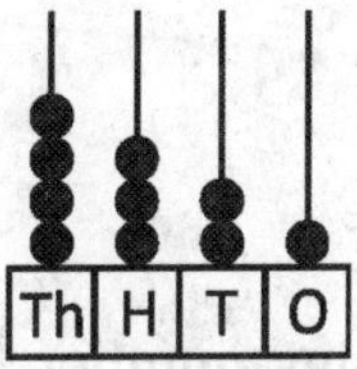

(C) 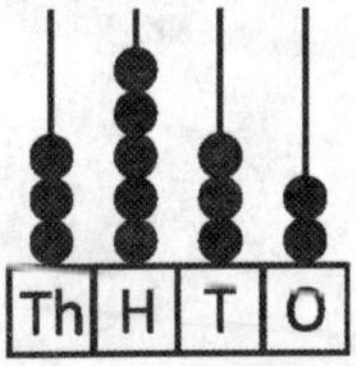

(D) 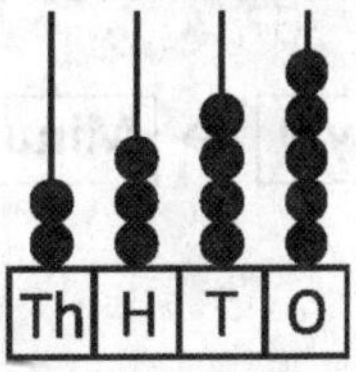

(E) None of these

12. **Find the next two missing numbers in the number pattern given below.**
100, 92, 84, 76, _?_, _?_
(A) 60, 56 (B) 64, 56 (C) 62, 54 (D) 68, 60
(E) None of these

13. **The smallest 4-digit number that can be formed by using the digits 6, 0, 2, 0, without repeating the digits is:**
(A) 6002 (B) 2006 (C) 2600 (D) 6200
(E) None of these

14. **If we interchange the hundreds place digit and ones place digit in each number given in options (A), (B), (C) and (D), which one will be an even number?**
(A) 6723 (B) 4277
(C) 6739 (D) 9178
(E) None of these

15. **If ■ + ● = 17, ● + ▲ = 14 and ▲ + ■ = 13, then the value of ■ + ● + ▲ will be:**

(A) 34 (B) 44

(C) 24 (D) 22

(E) None of these

16. **Difference of 82 and 28 is added to their sum. The result will be:**

(A) 192 (B) 162

(C) 164 (D) 102

(E) None of these

17. **What is the missing number [?] in the given box?**

[?] → [Divided by 9] → [Minus 4] = 3

(A) 52 (B) 63

(C) 48 (D) 93

(E) None of these

18. **Product of 11 and 5 is divided by their difference. The remainder will be:**

(A) 0 (B) 1 (C) 2 (D) 3

(E) None of these

19. **Find the fraction represented by *unshaded* parts in the figure given below.**

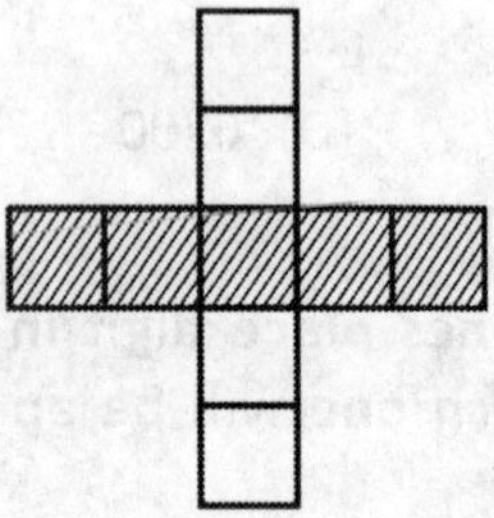

(A) $\frac{1}{2}$ (B) $\frac{4}{9}$ (C) $\frac{5}{9}$ (D) $\frac{4}{5}$

(E) None of these

20. If $\frac{28}{42} = \frac{a}{3}$, where 'a' stands for numerator, then the value of 'a' is:

(A) 4
(B) 3
(C) 2
(D) 1
(E) None of these

21. $\frac{3}{4}$ and $\frac{4}{5}$ are:

(A) equal fractions
(B) equivalent fractions
(C) like fractions
(D) unlike fractions
(E) None of these

22. If we interchange the numerator and denominator of the fraction $\frac{7}{2}$, the new fraction will be:

(A) an improper fraction
(B) a proper fraction
(C) a unit fraction
(D) an equivalent fraction of $\frac{7}{2}$
(E) None of these

23. The time shown by the given Roman numeral dial is:

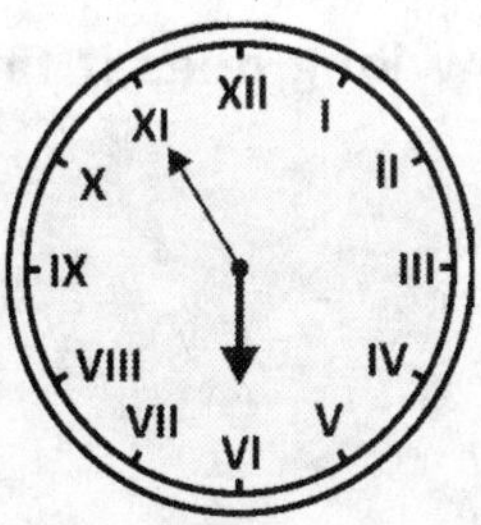

(A) 9 : 27
(B) 6 : 05
(C) 5 : 55
(D) 5 : 09
(E) None of these

24. I was born on February 29 in between 1981 to 1987. My birthday comes once in every four years. My birth year is:

(A) 1982 (B) 1984 (C) 1985 (D) 1986

(E) None of these

25. Raman has ₹255. He wants to buy a shirt that costs ₹374. How much more money does he need to buy the shirt?

(A) ₹119 (B) ₹117 (C) ₹127 (D) ₹129

(E) None of these

26. 40 coins of 50 paise is equal to ______ coins of ₹5.

(A) 8 (B) 2 (C) 4 (D) 6

(E) None of these

27. How many cups of 30 ml make an equivalent capacity of 1 L 500 ml?

(A) 5 (B) 100

(C) 500 (D) 50

(E) None of these

28. Which shape are the faces of a cube 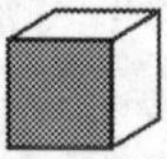 **?**

(A) Circle (B) Triangle

(C) Square (D) Hexagon

(E) None of these

29. A machine takes 22 hours to assemble 2 cars. How long does it take to assemble 22 such cars?

(A) 420 hours (B) 484 hours

(C) 242 hours (D) 176 hours

(E) None of these

30. The product of 91 and 9 is equal the sum of:

(A) 500 and 319 (B) 400 and 391

(C) 700 and 191 (D) 600 and 239

(E) None of these

31. There are 10 coins of 50 paise, 5 coins of ₹2 and 2 coins of ₹5. The value of sum of all coins is:

(A) ₹39 (B) ₹24 (C) ₹19 (D) ₹25

(E) None of these

32. How much length of the side BC of the given triangle ABC should be reduced to make it an isosceles triangle?

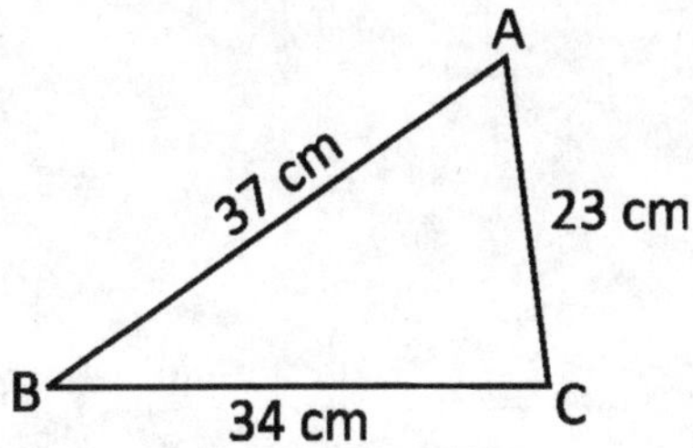

(A) 13 cm (B) 11 cm (C) 14 cm (D) 12 cm

(E) None of these

33. One-third of 6 L 123 ml is:

(A) 2 L 41 ml (B) 3 L 63 ml (C) 2 L 21 ml (D) 3 L 43 ml

(E) None of these

34. I can eat a quarter of a pizza in one minute. How long does it take me to eat one pizza?

(A) 2 minutes (B) 4 minutes

(C) 8 minutes (D) 6 minutes

(E) None of these

35. How many triangles are there in the given figure?

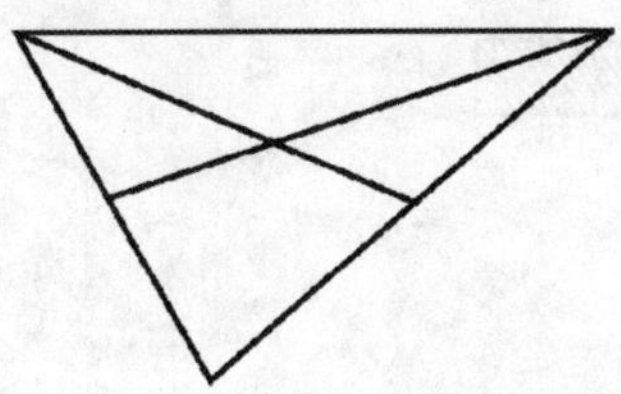

(A) 8 (B) 6 (C) 9 (D) 7

(E) None of these

36. Peter, Susan, Mariam and Codi received Christmas gifts from Santa Clause.

If one symbol  represents 6 gifts, then how many gifts did Peter and Mariam get altogether?

Christmas Gifts	
Name	Number of Gifts
Peter	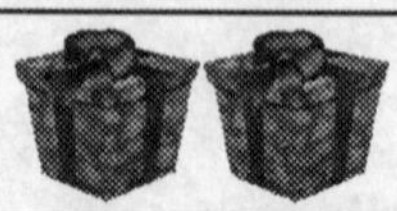
Susan	
Mariam	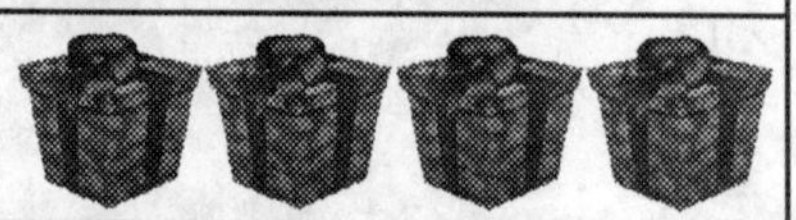
Codi	

(A) 24 (B) 30 (C) 42 (D) 36

(E) None of these

***Direction (37 – 40)*: The given bar represents the number of books sold at a bookstore during five months.**

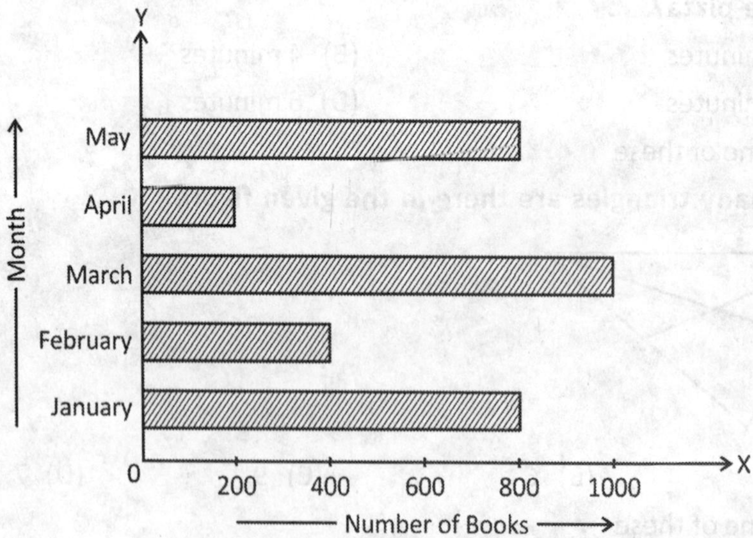

37. How many more books sold in March than February?

(A) 400 (B) 600 (C) 800 (D) 200

(E) None of these

38. 600 books were sold in the month of _______.

(A) April (B) February (C) May (D) January

(E) None of these

39. In which month the least number of books were sold?

(A) April (B) May

(C) January (D) February

(E) None of these

40. How many books were sold in all five months?

(A) 3000 (B) 3200

(C) 3400 (D) 2800

(E) None of these

Direction (41 – 50): Reasoning and Aptitude

41. Find the missing number ? in the number pattern given below:

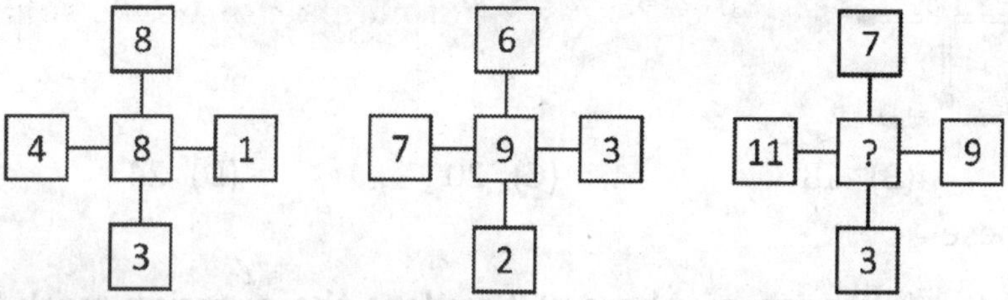

(A) 16 (B) 14

(C) 15 (D) 12

(E) 18

42. Find the two missing numbers (?) in the number series given below.

5, 9, 15, 23, ? , 45, 59, ?

(A) 31, 71 (B) 33, 75

(C) 27, 67 (D) 35, 79

(E) None of these

43. The difference between the numbers of matchsticks in pattern 1 and pattern 3 is:

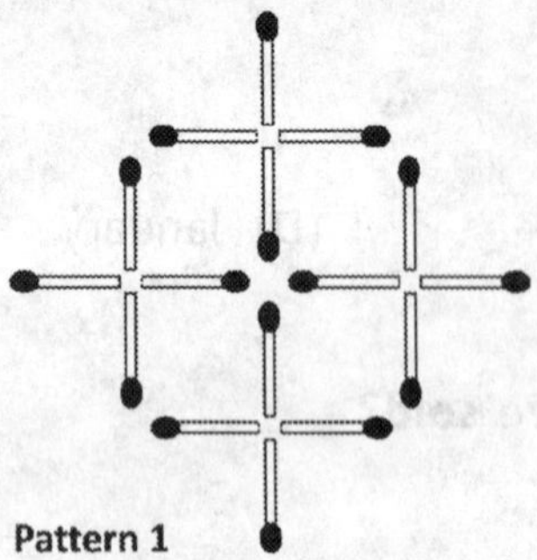

Pattern 1

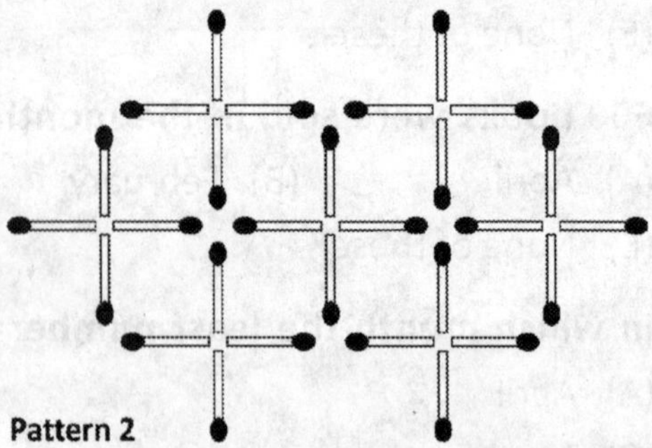

Pattern 2

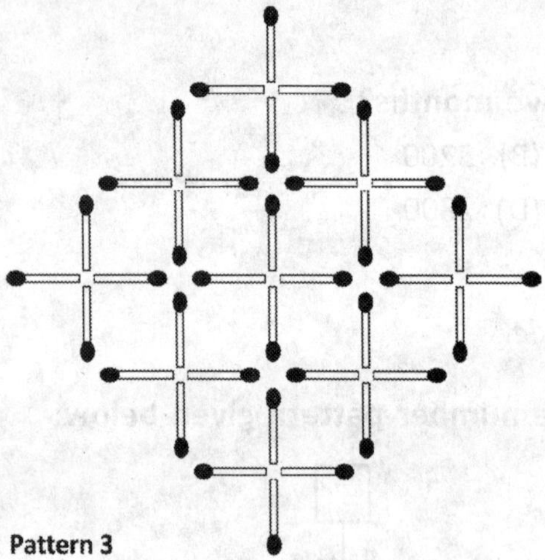

Pattern 3

(A) 5 (B) 18 (C) 20 (D) 24
(E) None of these

44. Which one of the following numbers will replace the question mark (?) in the number pattern given below?

99 90 81 72 ? 54

(A) 63 (B) 65 (C) 62 (D) 79
(E) None of these

45. Keeping in mind the types of numbers, select the odd one out.

(A) 19 (B) 15 (C) 13 (D) 11
(E) 17

46. Find the missing numbers x and y, respectively.

1	8	27	64	x	216
17	16	15	14	y	12

(A) 121, 11 (B) 100, 13 (C) 125, 13 (D) 243, 14
(E) None of these

47. Find the missing number (?), if a certain rule is applied row-wise or column-wise.

7	3	10
5	2	7
2	?	8

(A) 3 (B) 6 (C) 4 (D) 1
(E) None of these

48. Find the meaningful combination of numbers so that letters are arranged accordingly to form a meaning word.

R	M	T	I
1	2	3	4

(A) 2, 1, 4, 3 (B) 3, 4, 2, 1 (C) 3, 1, 4, 2 (D) 2, 1, 4, 3
(E) None of these

49. In a row of 11 girls, Susan is third from right end. What is her position from the left end?

(A) Eight (B) Ninth (C) Sixth (D) Seventh
(E) None of these

50. Minimum number of line segments in figure given below is:

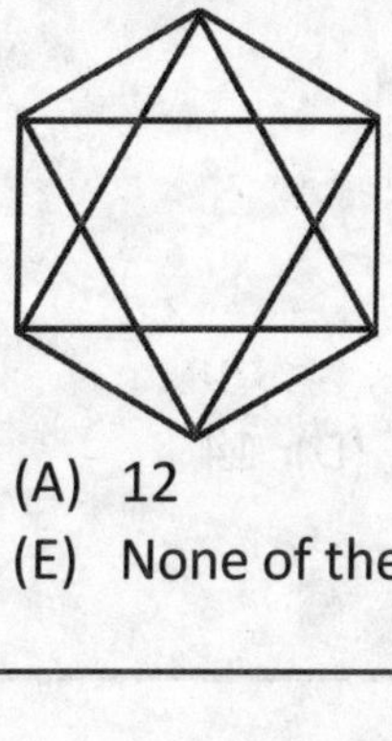

(A) 12 (B) 14 (C) 16 (D) 18
(E) None of these

Model Test Paper-5

1. How many prime numbers are there in between 10 to 20?

(A) 5 (B) 4 (C) 6 (D) 3

(E) None of these

2. The predecessor of the largest 4-digit number is:

(A) 1000 (B) 9998

(C) 9999 (D) 10001

(E) None of these

3. If you round off 654 to the nearest hundred and 546 to the nearest ten and then add them, the result is:

(A) 1250

(B) 1240

(C) 1150

(D) 1140

(E) None of these

4. Round the number 364 to the nearest 10.

(A) 365 (B) 360 (C) 370 (D) 300

(E) None of these

5. How many composite numbers are there in between 1 to 17?

(A) 6 (B) 7 (C) 8 (D) 9

(E) None of these

6. Multiplication means:

(A) repeated subtraction (B) repeated addition

(C) repeated multiplication (D) repeated division

(E) None of these

7. How many times 9 can be taken away from 135?

(A) 13 (B) 15 (C) 17 (D) 14

(E) None of these

8. A number is divided by itself. The quotient Q and the remainder R will be:

(A) Q = 0, R = 1 (B) Q = 1, R = 1
(C) Q = 1, R = 0 (D) Q = 0, R = 0
(E) None of these

9. The sum of the smallest composite number and the smallest prime number is:

(A) 4 (B) 6 (C) 2 (D) 8
(E) None of these

10. The largest number we can write by using the digits 0, 4, 7, 1 is:

(A) 1047 (B) 7410 (C) 7401 (D) 4710
(E) None of these

11. The number comes before 19 is:

(A) a prime number
(B) an odd number
(C) an even number
(D) a single digit number
(E) None of these

12. The number 12345 is divisible by:

(A) 6 (B) 2 (C) 4 (D) 10
(E) None of these

13. Which one of the following abacuses shows the number less than 2000?

(A)
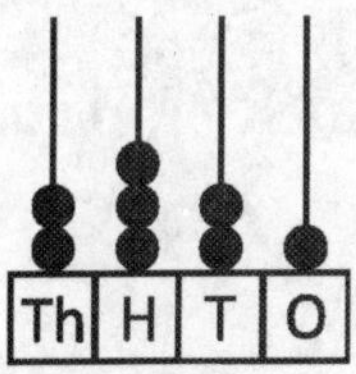

(B)
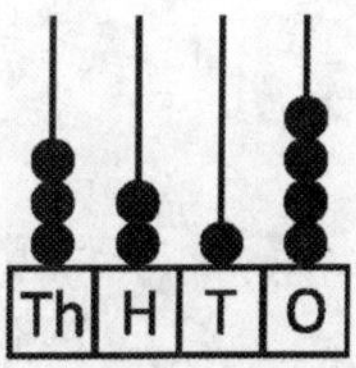

(C)
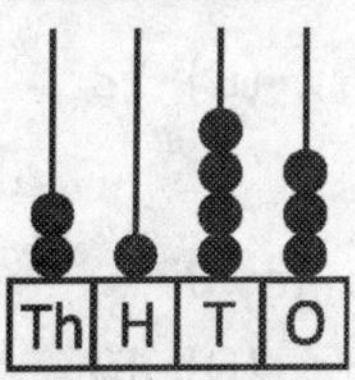

(D)
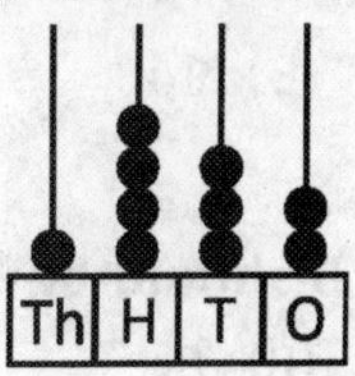

(E) None of these

14. The greatest 4-digit number that can be formed by using the digits 8, 0, 9, 6, without repeating the digits is:

(A) 9860 (B) 9806 (C) 9068 (D) 9860
(E) None of these

15. Which place value will determine the larger number among the given two numbers?
7521, 7659

(A) Ones place (B) Tens place
(C) Hundreds place (D) Thousands place
(E) None of these

16. Find the missing number which will come in place of ? in the subtraction given below.

	7	**5**	**3**	**4**
−	**3**	**?**	**8**	**1**
	3	**6**	**5**	**3**

(A) 9 (B) 8 (C) 7 (D) 6
(E) None of these

17. In the given magic square, the three numbers in each row, each column and each diagonal add up to the same total. Find the sum of all three missing digits.

1	**?**	**5**
?	**4**	**0**
3	**?**	**7**

(A) 16 (B) 14 (C) 12 (D) 18
(E) None of these

18. How many times 9 should be subtracted from 108 to get 0?

(A) 9 (B) 8 (C) 12 (D) 13
(E) None of these

19. If we divide the largest 3-digit number by the smallest 2-digit number, the remainder is:

(A) a prime number (B) an even number

(C) an odd number (D) zero

(E) None of these

20. Simplest form of $\frac{18}{30}$ is:

(A) $\frac{3}{5}$ (B) $\frac{6}{10}$ (C) $\frac{2}{5}$ (D) $\frac{3}{10}$

(E) None of these

21. Fraction represented by *unshaded* parts in the figure given below is:

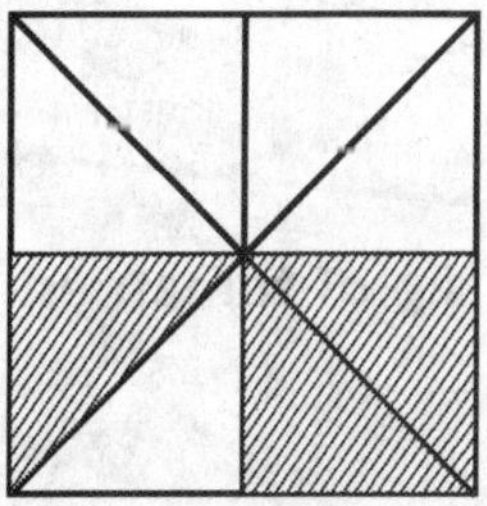

(A) $\frac{3}{8}$ (B) $\frac{1}{2}$ (C) $\frac{5}{8}$ (D) $\frac{3}{5}$

(E) None of these

22. What fraction is 5 days of two weeks?

(A) $\frac{3}{14}$ (B) $\frac{5}{14}$ (C) $\frac{1}{7}$ (D) $\frac{2}{7}$

(E) None of these

23. We can write (3 + 3 + 3 + 3 + 3 + 3 + 3) as:

(A) 3 × 3 × 3 × 3 × 3 × 3 × 3 (B) 3 × 7

(C) 3 + 7 (D) $\frac{3}{7}$

(E) None of these

24. A day of the month April in 2016 was Sunday. Just after 41 days, the day was:

(A) Friday (B) Saturday

(C) Sunday (D) Monday

(E) None of these

25. The maximum time for a mathematics test paper is 1 hour 30 minutes. If the test starts at 10 : 35 am, then the test end at:

(A) 11 : 30 am (B) 12 : 05 pm

(C) 11 : 55 am (D) 13 : 35 pm

(E) None of these

26. How many Sundays can be possible in the month of December?

(A) up to 4 (B) up to 5

(C) up to 6 (D) up to 7

(E) None of these

27. Aman buys 1 kg of onions, 1 kg of potatoes and 1 kg of tomatoes. How much money he has to pay?

Onion 1 kg	**₹ 45**
Potato 1 kg	**₹ 35**
Tomato 1 kg	**₹ 60**
Carrot 1 kg	**₹ 85**

(A) ₹ 145 (B) ₹ 155

(C) ₹ 130 (D) ₹ 140

(E) None of these

28. Weight of 6 bricks is 72 kg. Number of bricks in 48 kg of bricks is:

(A) 6 (B) 5

(C) 4 (D) 3

(E) None of these

29. The sum of the numbers of vertices in Figure (1) and Figure (2) is:

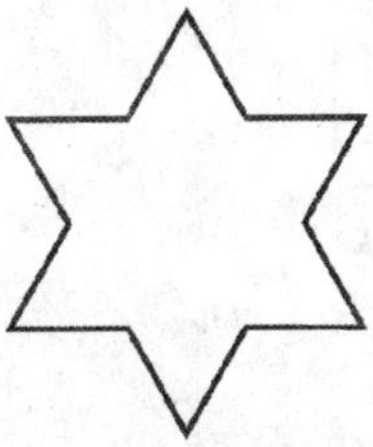

(Figure-1)

(Figure-2)

(A) 11 (B) 15
(C) 17 (D) 12
(E) None of these

30. If the cost of 2 bananas is ₹5, then the cost of 5 such bananas is:

(A) ₹ 15.50 (B) ₹ 16.50
(C) ₹ 12.50 (D) ₹ 18.50
(E) None of these

31. I consumed 15 L 200 ml of water in first 2 days of a week and 28 L 500 ml of water in the rest days of the week. How much water was I consumed in the week?

(A) 44 L 300 ml (B) 41 L 700 ml
(C) 43 L 700 ml (D) 42 L 700 ml
(E) None of these

32. If 24 chocolates are divide equally among 4 children, each child will get:

(A) 7 chocolates (B) 4 chocolates
(C) 6 chocolates (D) 8 chocolates
(E) None of these

33. A large box contains 16 small boxes and each small box contains 20 chocolate bars. The total number of chocolate bars in the large box is:

(A) 160 (B) 320
(C) 180 (D) 360
(E) None of these

34. Five times of 190 ml is:

(A) more than a litre.
(B) less than a litre.
(C) equal to a litre
(D) equal to 9 L 500 ml
(E) None of these

35. The sum of 436 grams and 634 grams in kilograms is:

(A) 10 kg 70 g
(B) 10 kg 700 g
(C) 1 kg 70 g
(D) 1 kg 700 g
(E) None of these

***Direction (36 – 37)*: Given pictograph shows the number of tally marks each student made.**

Student	Number of Tally Marks
Puja	||||| ||||| ||
Abhay	||||| ||||
Kanika	|||||
Rahul	||||| ||||| |||||	
Kirti	||||| ||||
Each symbol (|) represents 5 tally marks	

Read the pictograph carefully and answer the following questions:

36. How many less tally marks did kanika make than Abhay?

(A) 20
(B) 25
(C) 12
(D) 24
(E) None of these

37. How many more tally marks did Rahul make than Abhay and Kanika altogether?

(A) 5
(B) 10
(C) 15
(D) 20
(E) None of these

Direction (38 – 40): **The given bar graph represents the number of people of different villages who attended a village fair.**

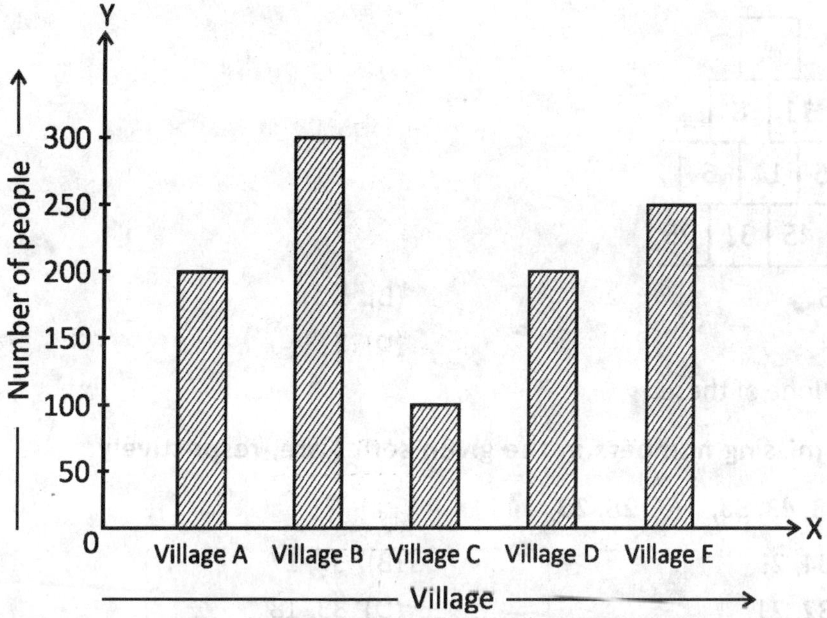

Observe the graph carefully and answer the following questions:

38. The number of people of Village C was three times the number of people of _______.

(A) Village A
(B) Village B
(C) Village D
(D) Village E
(E) None of these

39. People of which Village who attended the fair more than the people of Village C but less than people of Village E?

(A) Village D
(B) Village B
(C) Village A
(D) Both villages B and D
(E) None of these

40. How many people are attended the fair from all five villages?

(A) 1150
(B) 1050
(C) 950
(D) 1550
(E) None of these

Direction (41 – 50)*: *Reasoning and Aptitude

41. Find the missing number (?) in the number pattern given below.

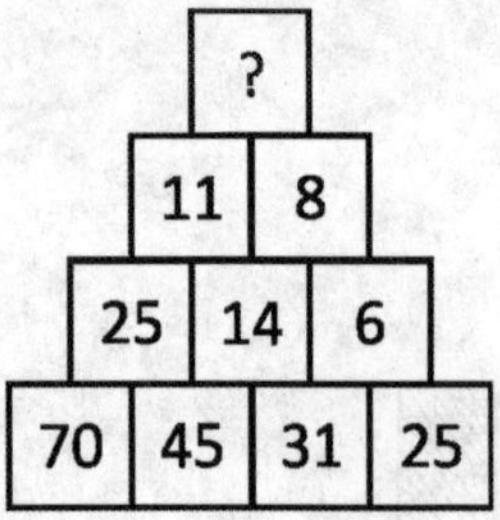

(A) 6 (B) 5

(C) 4 (D) 3

(E) None of these

42. Two missing numbers in the given series are, respectively:

53, 48, 43, 38, __?__ , 28, 23, __?__

(A) 34, 29 (B) 37, 17

(C) 32, 21 (D) 33, 18

(E) None of these

43. What comes next in the figure series given below?

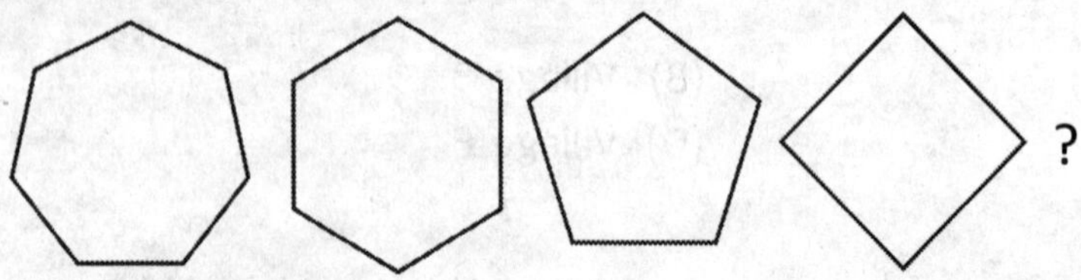

(A) 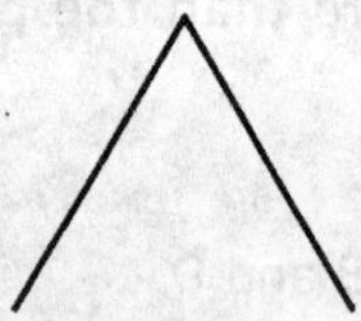

(B) 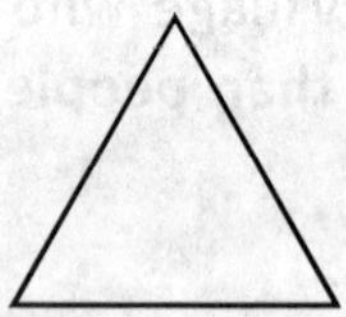

(C) 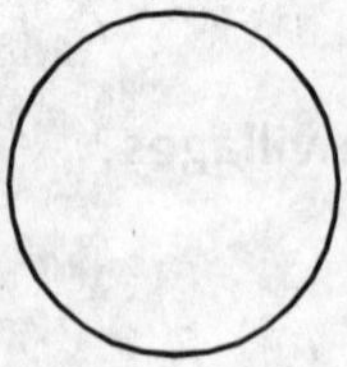

(D) 

(E) None of these

44. What comes next in the figure series given below?

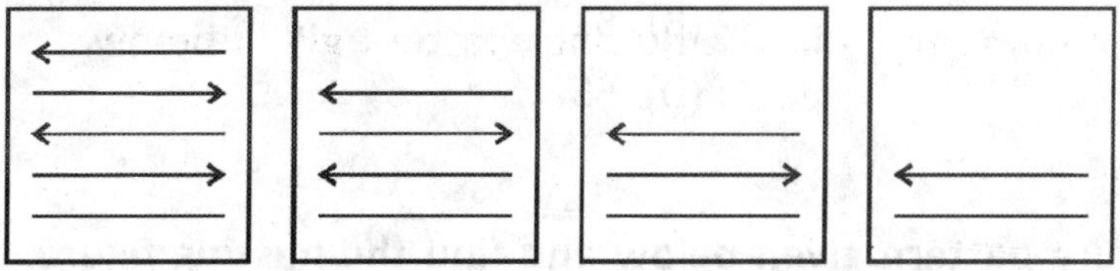

?

(A) 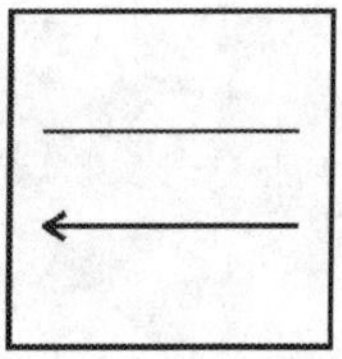

(B) 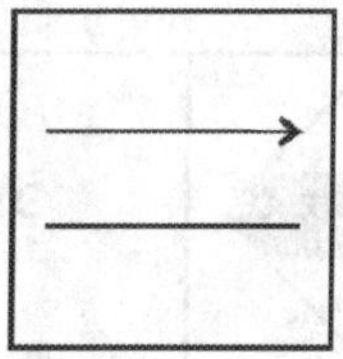

(C) 

(D) 

(E) None of these

45. Which shape is obtained when two shapes given below are put together?

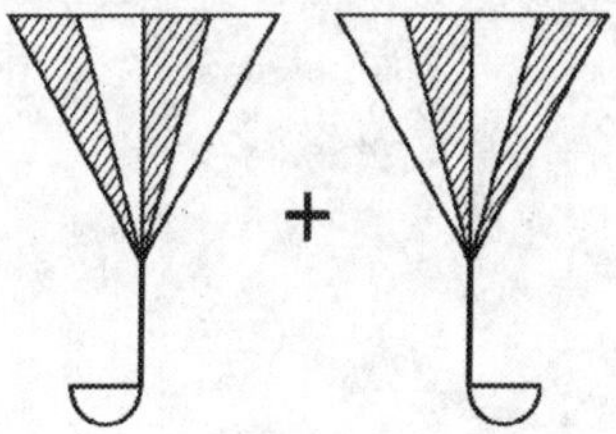

(A) 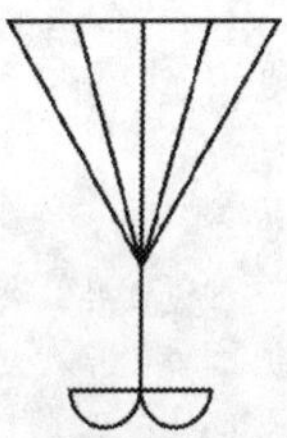

(B) 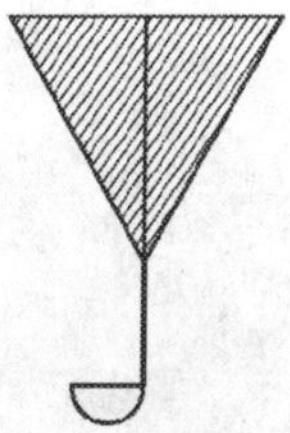

(C) 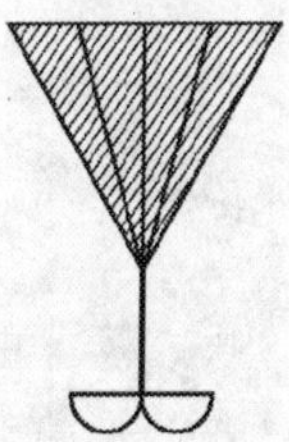

(D) 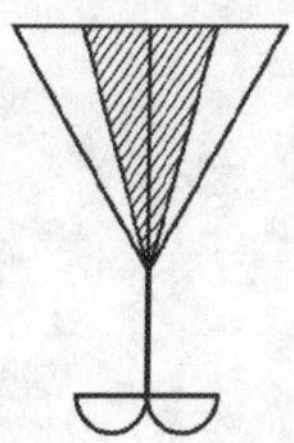

(E) None of these

46. If G = 7, GO = 22 and GOT = 42, then GOUT = _____?

(A) 59 (B) 61

(C) 63 (D) 65

(E) None of these

47. Observe the figure pattern given below and find the missing figure.

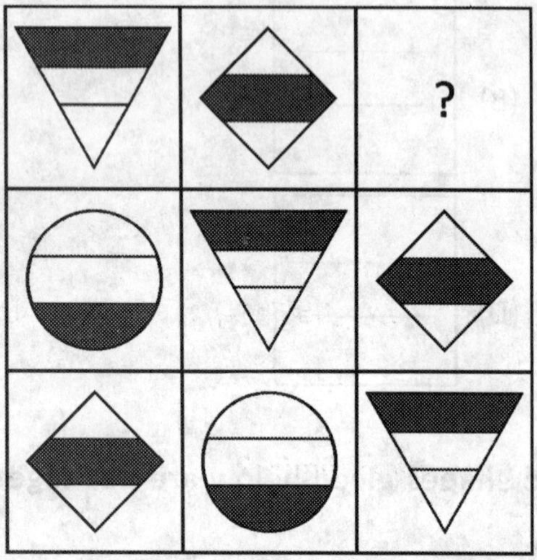

(A) 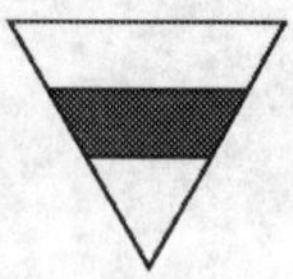

(B) 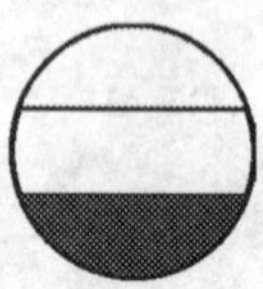

(C) 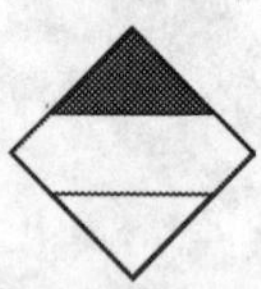

(D) 

(E) None of these

48. Group the following figures into three classes on the basis of their identical properties.

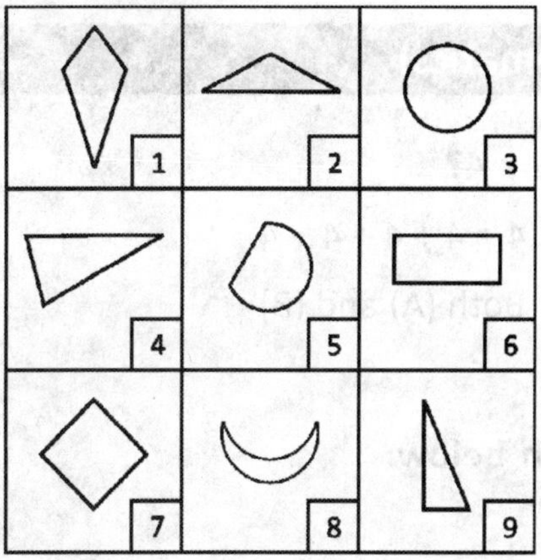

(A) [1, 4, 7]; [3, 5, 6]; [2, 8, 9]
(B) [3, 6, 9]; [5, 8, 4]; [1, 2, 7]
(C) [2, 5, 8]; [1, 3, 6]; [4, 7, 9]
(D) [3, 5, 8]; [1, 6, 7]; [2, 4, 9]
(E) None of these

49. How many curved lines are there in the given figure?

(A) 10
(B) 7
(C) 6
(D) 4
(E) None of these

50. Which one of the following numbers will replace the question mark (?) in the number pattern given below?

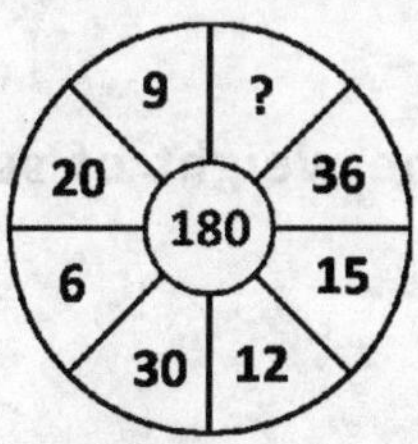

(A) 4
(B) 5
(C) 10
(D) 18
(E) None of these

Sample Question Paper

Section-A (Mathematics)

1. **Which one of the following is same as 5 × 4?**

   (A) 5 + 5 + 5 + 5 (B) 4 + 4 + 4 + 4 + 4

   (C) 5 + 4 (D) Both (A) and (B)

   (E) None of these

2. **Fill in the blank with the numbers given below:**

   380 + 20 = 10 × ________

   (A) 20 (B) 30 (C) 40 (D) 60

   (E) None of these

3. **Which one of the following numbers is a composite number?**

   (A) 1 (B) 3 (C) 2 (D) 4

   (E) None of these

4. **[12 + 9] is same as ______ more than 20.**

   (A) 1 (B) 2 (C) 4 (D) 3

   (E) None of these

5. **What number comes before 8 tens and 8 ones?**

   (A) 78 (B) 87

   (C) 89 (D) 90

   (E) None of these

6. **If 2 apples weigh 60 grams, then what would be the weight of such 5 apples?**

   (A) 105 grams (B) 501 grams

   (C) 150 grams (D) 300 grams

   (E) None of these

7. **In which way the numbers in column A is related to the numbers in column B in the following table?**

A	B
21	14
28	21
35	28

(A) A + 7 = B (B) B + 7 = A (C) A + 8 = B (D) B + 8 = A

(E) None of these

8. **If ▼▼ = 5, then ▼▼ + ▼▼ + ▼▼ + ▼▼ is equal to which of the following options?**

(A) 5 × 4 (B) 5 + 5 + 5 + 5

(C) 5 × 5 (D) Both (A) and (B)

(E) None of these

9. **What fraction of the given figure is unshaded?**

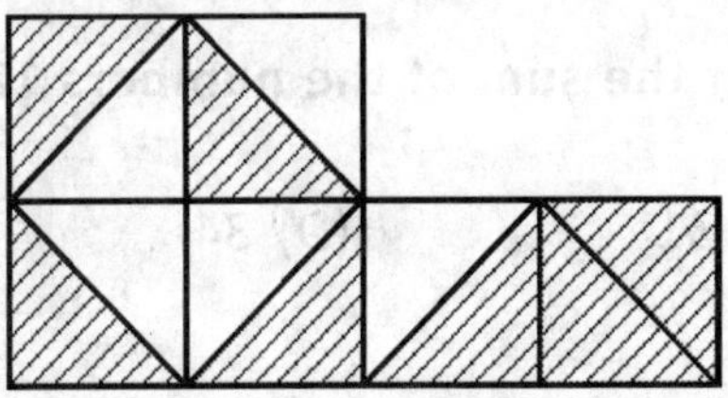

(A) $\frac{5}{12}$ (B) $\frac{7}{12}$ (C) $\frac{7}{13}$ (D) $\frac{5}{13}$

(E) None of these

10. **What is the missing number in the box?**

[?] [Multiplied by 4] [Reduced by 7] = [37]

(A) 8 (B) 9

(C) 11 (D) 18

(E) None of these

11. Find the values of A, B and C in the pattern given below.

(A) 

(B) 

(C) 

(D) 

(E) None of these

12. Find the correct match for the shaded part of the figure.

(A)  $= \frac{3}{4}$

(B) 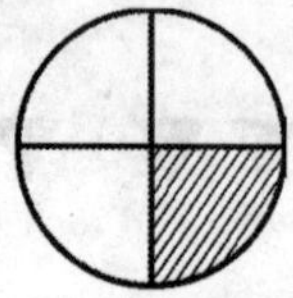 $= \frac{1}{3}$

(C) 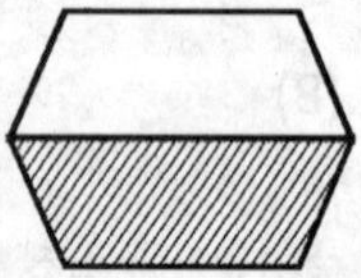 $= \frac{1}{2}$

(D) 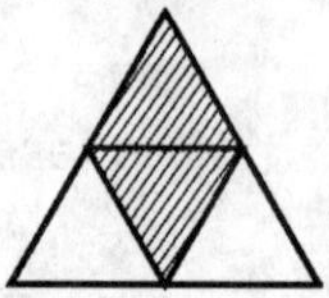 $= \frac{1}{4}$

(E) None of these

13. Which of the following is the successor of the sum of the numbers 12 and 21?

(A) 32 (B) 33 (C) 31 (D) 34

(E) None of these

14. Subtract $\frac{7}{8} - \frac{5}{8}$

(A) $\frac{12}{8}$ (B) $\frac{2}{8}$ (C) $\frac{3}{8}$ (D) $\frac{1}{8}$

(E) None of these

15. Find the difference between the place values of 5 and 9 in the number $\boxed{594}$.

(A) 140 (B) 401 (C) 410 (D) 144

(E) None of these

16. Find the predecessor of the number which will replace the question mark (?) in the following equation.

411 + 9 × 3 = ?

(A) 348 (B) 483 (C) 438 (D) 437

(E) None of these

17. How many tens make 120?

(A) 10 (B) 11 (C) 12 (D) 9

(E) None of these

18. Arrange the given numbers from smaller to greater.

112, 121, 211, 221

(A) 112 < 121 < 221 < 211 (B) 121 < 211 < 121 < 221

(C) 112 < 121 < 211 < 221 (D) 211 < 121 < 112 < 221

(E) None of these

19. Which of the following is less than 211 + 121 ?

(A) 332 (B) 333 (C) 334 (D) 331

(E) None of these

20. If  **= 1 whole, then** 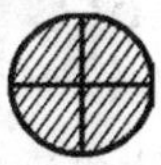 **+** 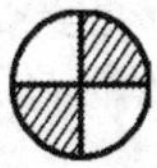 **+** 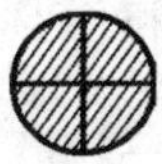 **is equal to which one of the following?**

(A) $3\frac{1}{2}$ (B) $5\frac{1}{2}$ (C) $2\frac{1}{2}$ (D) $2\frac{1}{4}$

(E) None of these

21. How many 8's are there in 64 ?

(A) 10 (B) 11 (C) 9 (D) 8

(E) None of these

22. 321 is divisible by which one of the following?

(A) 7 (B) 9 (C) 4 (D) 5

(E) None of these

23. Find the missing number in the blank box.

121 + 9 = ☐ + 11

(A) 111 (B) 119 (C) 121 (D) 122

(E) None of these

24. Which one of the following is not a prime number?

(A) 13 (B) 73 (C) 71 (D) 51

(E) None of these

25. If ▼ × ▲ = 15, then what could be the value of ▼ and ▲?

(A) ▼ = 5 and ▲ = 3 (B) ▼ = 3 and ▲ = 5

(C) ▼ = 7 and ▲ = 8 (D) Both (A) and (B)

(E) None of these

26. What should be added to 2 L 800 ml of water to get 3 L 300 ml of water?

(A) 1 L 500 ml (B) 1 L 800 ml (C) 800 ml (D) 500 ml

(E) None of these

27. According to the additive identity property which of the following represents additive identity property of 0?

(A) 1 + 0 = 10 (B) 29 + 18 = 18 + 29

(C) 14 + 0 = 14 (D) (2 + 3) + 4 = 2 + (3 + 4)

(E) None of these

28. What should be added to 800 grams to make it equal to 1 kg?

(A) 900 grams (B) 850 grams (C) 300 grams (D) 200 grams

(E) None of these

29. The measurement of an angle is 55°. What is the measurement of its complement?

(A) 23° (B) 25° (C) 35° (D) All of these

(E) None of these

30. Convert 85 m 55 cm into centimetres.

(A) 5585 cm (B) 5855 cm (C) 8555 cm (D) 5500 cm

(E) None of these

Section-B (Mental Ability and Reasoning)

31. How many triangles are there in the given figure?

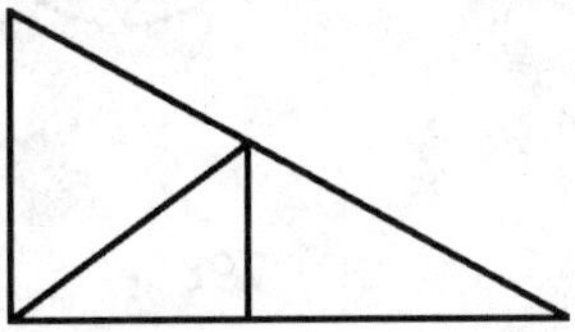

(A) 3 (B) 4 (C) 5 (D) 7
(E) None of these

32. Find the odd one out.

(A)  (B) 
(C)  (D) 
(E) None of these

33. Count the numbers in the figure given below that come into the table of 11.

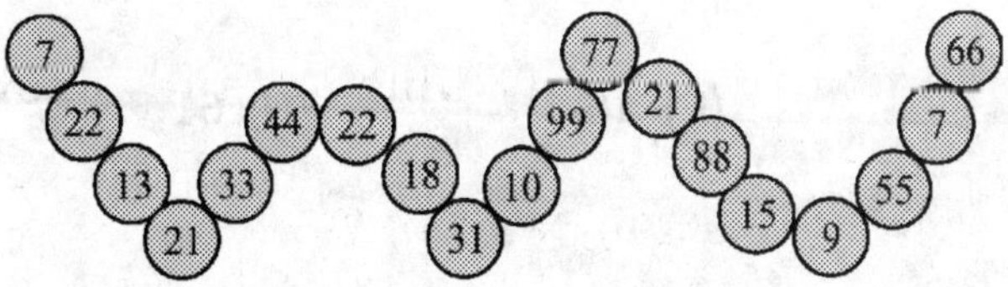

(A) 10 (B) 7 (C) 9 (D) 14
(E) None of these

34. If one more ball is added to the left of ball number 8 then how many balls are there to the right of ball number 6?

(A) 9 (B) 3 (C) 5 (D) 8
(E) None of these

35. Which of the following will be the next figure?

(A) 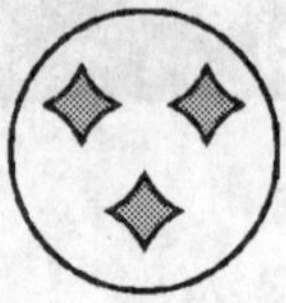 (B)  (C)  (D) 

(E) None of these

36. If BDC = 243 and DFE = 465, then find GIH.

(A) 879 (B) 789 (C) 978 (D) 798

(E) None of these

37. In the following figure, Alex multiplied the greatest and the smallest number and then he add rest of the numbers to the product. Find the result.

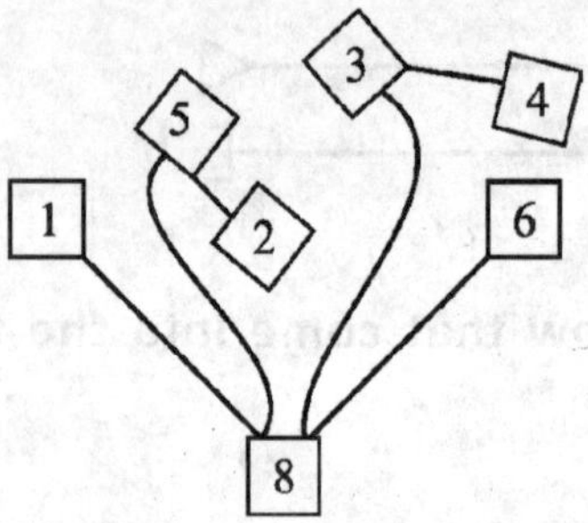

(A) 82 (B) 28 (C) 16 (D) 61

(E) None of these

38. Find the missing number.

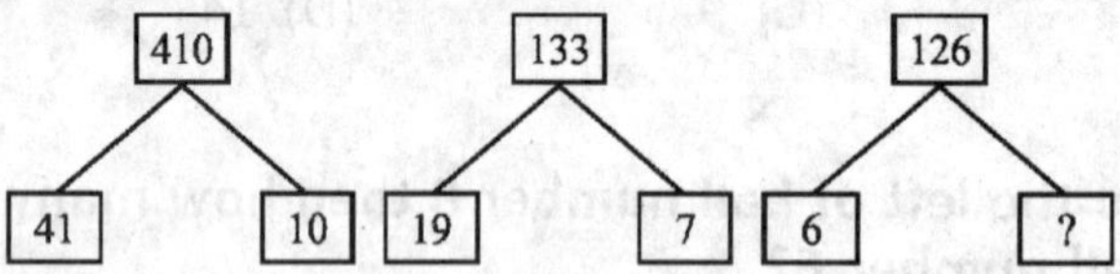

(A) 21 (B) 11 (C) 18 (D) 7

(E) None of these

39. Which letter appears in the word SEVEN, but not in the word NEVER?

(A) M (B) N (C) P (D) S

(E) None of these

40. Write the number that continues the sequence in the most sensible way.

(A) 27 (B) 32 (C) 29 (D) 36

(E) None of these

Section-C (Scholar's Zone)

41. What number does  **stand for?**

If  +  = 876 and  +  = 500

(A) 662 (B) 250 (C) 626 (D) 525
(E) None of these

42. Find the value of A and B respectively.

$$\begin{array}{r} 5\,A\,1\,2 \\ -\,2\,2\,1\,B \\ \hline 2\,8\,9\,6 \end{array}$$

(A) A = 6 and B = 1 (B) A = 1 and B = 6
(C) A = 5 and B = 3 (D) A = 3 and B = 5
(E) None of these

43. Following figure is made up of 3 squares. Find the length of each side of square X.

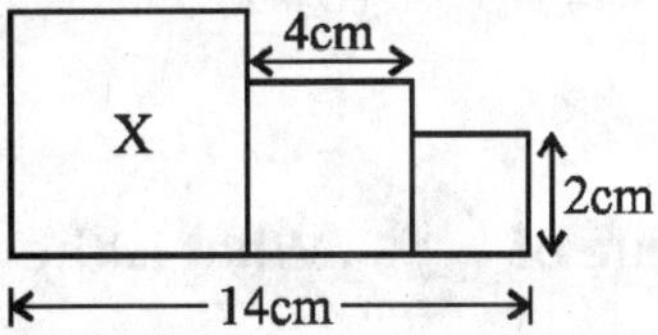

(A) 6 cm (B) 9 cm (C) 8 cm (D) 7 cm
(E) None of these

44. Which one of the following has the smallest value?

(A) 3 times of (8 × 8) (B) $\frac{1}{5}$ of 740
(C) 11 × 10 (D) 1000 × 1
(E) None of these

45. Find the difference between $\boxed{M}$ **and** $\boxed{N}$**.**

$$\begin{array}{r} 8\;\;7\;\;4 \\ -\,4\;\boxed{M}\;3 \\ \hline \boxed{N}\;8\;\;1 \end{array}$$

(A) 9 (B) 3 (C) 12 (D) 6
(E) None of these

46. All the blocks are identical. The height of the standing boy is 126 cm. Find the height of the tree.

(A) 42 cm (B) 162 cm (C) 126 cm (D) 168 cm
(E) None of these

47. Alex planted some trees along a straight road. Each tree was 4 cm apart. If the distance between the first tree and last tree is 40 cm, find the number of trees did he plant?

(A) 9 (B) 10 (C) 11 (D) 4
(E) None of these

48. The difference between 450 and ? is 339. What is the number in the box?

(A) 212 (B) 111 (C) 313 (D) 110
(E) None of these

49. The value of  is 4 times as much as the value of . What is the value of , if  – 37 is equal to 55?

(A) 638 (B) 368 (C) 836 (D) 336
(E) None of these

50. To follow the arrowhead how many different ways are there for the cat to reach its kittens?

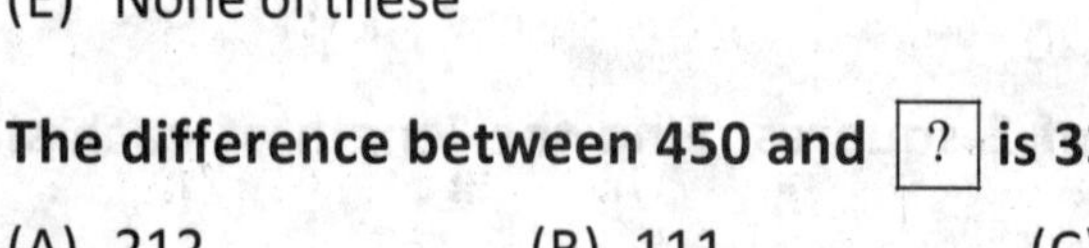

(A) 1 (B) 2 (C) 3 (D) 6
(E) None of these

Practice Exercise Answers and Explanation for Selected Questions

Practice Exercise 1
Number Sense and Numeration

1. (A)	2. (E)	3. (A)	4. (D)	5. (B)
6. (B)	7. (D)	8. (B)	9. (C)	10. (D)

Explanation for Selected Questions:

2. Place value of 9 in the number 4987 is 9 × 100 = 900
   Face value of 9 is 9. Therefore, the required sum = 900 + 9 = 909
3. Given number pattern is : 10, 30, 20, 40, 30, 50, ... Rule followed:
   10 + (20) = 30; 30 – 10 = 20; 20 + (20) = 40; 40 – 10 = 30; 30 + (20) = 50; 50 – 10 = 40
   Therefore, the required missing number = 40
4. Given digits are 2, 5, 0, 7. Here 7 > 5 > 2 > 0, or, 0 < 2 < 5 < 7
   Therefore, the smallest 4-digit number = 2057
5. Number shown by abacus given in option (A) = 3525
   Number shown by abacus given in option (B) = 4531
   Number shown by abacus given in option (C) = 1453
   Number shown by abacus given in option (D) = 2343
   Now, 4531 > 4000. Therefore, the abacus shown in the option (B) represents the number more than 4000.
8. Numbers formed by using the digits 7, 4, 1 are: 741, 714, 471, 417, 147, 174
   Therefore, 6 numbers are formed by using the digits 7, 4, 1.
9. Here, predecessor of 14 = 14 – 1 = 13. Therefore, the difference of 18 and 13 = 18 – 13 = 5. Hence, 5 should be subtracted from 18 to get the predecessor of 14.
10. The largest 4-digit number = 9999. Successor of 9999 = 9999 + 1 = 10000; which is the smallest 5-digit number.

Practice Exercise 2
Addition and Subtraction

1. (C)	2. (D)	3. (B)	4. (A)	5. (E)
6. (C)	7. (B)	8. (D)	9. (B)	10. (A)

Explanation for Selected Questions:

2. The largest 4-digit even number = 9998
   The largest 3-digit even number = 998
   Therefore, the required difference = 9998 – 998 = 9000
4. Here, the subtraction is as follow:

	8	7	[8]	5
–	7	[4]	3	4
	1	3	5	1

   Therefore, the required sum of missing digits = 4 + 8 = 12
5. 86 – [?] + 13 = 86 + 13 – [?] = 99 – [?]

   Now, 99 – [?] =27 Or, 99 – 27 = [?] Or, [?] = 72
6. Sum of 29 and 92 = 29 + 92 = 121
   Therefore, the required difference = 2992 – 121 = 2871
7. Here, sum of numbers in one diagonal = 4 + 5 + 6 = 15
   Now, missing number in first-column = 15 – (7 + 6) = 15 – 13 = 2
   And, missing number in second column = 15 – (9 + 5) = 15 – 14 = 1
   Now, missing number in third column = 15 – (4 + 8) = 15 – 12 = 3
   Therefore, the required sum of numbers = 2 + 1 + 3 = 6
   Also, it is a magic square of numbers from 1 to 9 in which three numbers 1, 2 and 3 are missing.

2	7	6	
9	5	1	
4	3	8	= 15

10. Here, 11 + 3 = 14, 3 + 5 = 8, 5 + 7 = 12, 14 + 8 = 22, 8 + 12 = 20

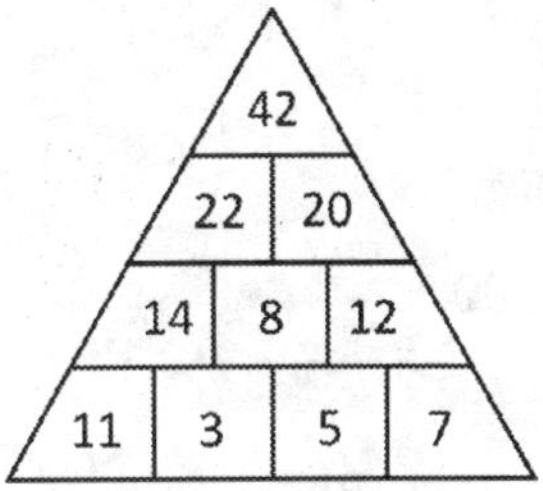

So, the required missing number = 22 + 20 = 42

Practice Exercise 3
Multiplication and Division

1. (D)	2. (A)	3. (B)	4. (E)	5. (A)
6. (D)	7. (B)	8. (C)	9. (D)	10. (B)

Explanation for Selected Questions:

1. 9998 = 9 × 1110 + 8

3. Given that 2[?]4[?] × 7 = 14301
   As we know, multiplication and division are the inverse process.
   Therefore, 14301 ÷ 7 = 2[?]4[?]. Division is as follow:

```
     2047
  7) 14301
    -14↓
     030
      28
       21
       21
        X
```

   So we have, 14301 ÷ 7 = 2[?]4[?]. Or, 2043 = 2[?]4[?]
   Or, the missing digits are 0 and 3. Therefore, the required sum = 0 + 3 = 3

4. Here, quotient = 1, remainder = 2 and divisor = 3
   Therefore, dividend = divisor × quotient + remainder = 3 × 1 + 2 = 3 + 2 = 5

5. The third multiple of 3 = 3 × 3 = 9. Therefore, the required product = 33 × 9 = 297

6. Given number are 12 and 4. Product of 12 and 4 = 12 × 4 = 48
   Sum of 12 + 4 = 16. So, 48 ÷ 16 = 3

8. Number of shuttles = 9 × 2 = 18. Cost of one shuttle = ₹ 11
   Total cost of 18 shuttles = ₹ (18 × 11) = ₹ 198

9. Here, 47 tens = 47 × 10 = 470 and 3 hundreds = 3 × 100 = 300
   Therefore, the required product = 470 × 300 = 141000

10. It is a multiplication pyramid.

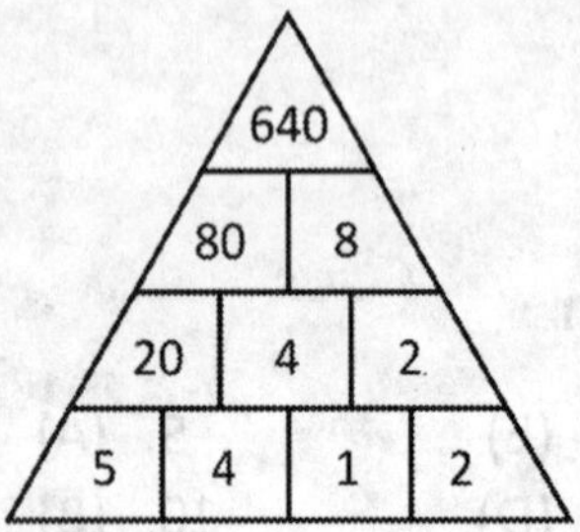

Clearly, 5 × 4 = 20; 4 × 1 = 4; 2 × 1 = 2. And, 20 × 4 = 80; 4 × 2 = 8
Therefore, the required missing number = 80 × 8 = 640

Practice Exercise 4
Fractions

1. (D)	2. (C)	3. (A)	4. (B)	5. (C)
6. (D)	7. (A)	8. (B)	9. (E)	10. (C)

Explanation for Selected Questions:

3. Whole part of the wall = 1. Painted part of the wall = $\frac{5}{8}$

   So, the unpainted part of the wall = $1 - \frac{5}{8} = = \frac{8}{8} - \frac{5}{8} = \frac{8-5}{8}$

5. Total number of squares = 8

   Fraction represented by unshaded parts = $\frac{3}{8}$

Number of unshaded squares = $\frac{3}{8} \times 8 = 3$

Therefore, the required number of shaded squares = 8 – 3 = 5

8. Here 49 ÷ 7 = 7 and 24 ÷ 3 = 8. Also, $\frac{3}{7} = \frac{3\times7}{7\times7} = \frac{21}{49}$ and $\frac{3}{7} = \frac{3\times8}{7\times8} = \frac{24}{56}$

We have, $\frac{\boxed{21}}{49} = \frac{3}{7} = \frac{24}{\boxed{56}}$. Therefore, the required sum = 21 + 56 = 77

9. Half of the number = 10. So, the number = 10 × 2 = 20

One-fourth of the number = $20 \times \frac{1}{4} = 5$

10. The portion of book that Codi read in the class = $\frac{3}{4}$

The portion of book that Codi read at home = $\frac{1}{4}$

Total portion of the book that Codi read = $\frac{3}{4} + \frac{1}{4} = \frac{3+1}{4} = \frac{4}{4} = \frac{4\div4}{4+4} = \frac{1}{1} = 1$

Therefore, Codi read whole of the book.

Practice Exercise 5
Time and Calendar

1. (C)	2. (B)	3. (A)	4. (C)	5. (E)
6. (B)	7. (D)	8. (B)	9. (A)	10. (C)

Explanation for Selected Questions:

1.

Yesterday	Thursday
Today	Friday
Tomorrow	Saturday
4th day after tomorrow	Wednesday

Therefore, 4th day after tomorrow will be Wednesday.

2. Date on 3rd Monday of the April 20XX is April 15, 20XX.
   Date one day before April 15, 20XX is April 14, 20XX.
   Therefore, Rahul's birthday falls on April 14, 20XX.

4. As we know, after seven days, the days repeat. Here, 17 = 7 + 7 + (3)
   Now, day on March 3, 20XX is Friday. And, day on March 10, 20XX is Friday.
   So, day on March 17, 20XX is also, Friday.

5. Number of days in one week = 7. Number of days in 7 weeks = 7 × 7 = 49

6. When 3 hours 45 minutes is added to 18 : 50 hours, the addition is as follow:

H : M
18 : 50
+ 3 : 45
21 : 95

   21 : 95 = 22 : 35 hours

   Now, 22 : 35 hours = (22 – 12) : 35 pm = 10 : 35 pm

8. The last three months in a year are October (31), November (30) and December (31).
   Therefore, the required number of days = 31 + 30 + 31 = 92

9. Starting time = 6 : 45 am. Time to reach = 10 : 20 am
   Time difference is as follow:

H	:	M
(9)		(80)
~~10~~	:	~~20~~
– 6	:	45
3	:	35

   Therefore, time taken by bus to reach from one town to another = 3 hours 35 minutes

10.

Monday	Date
First Monday	1
Second Monday	1 + 7 = 8
Third Monday	8 + 7 = 15
Fourth Monday	15 + 7 = 22
Fifth Monday	22 + 7 = 29

Hence, the required set of dates is 1, 8, 15, 22, 29.

Practice Exercise 6
Money

1. (B)	2. (B)	3. (C)	4. (A)	5. (D)
6. (A)	7. (B)	8. (E)	9. (C)	10. (B)

Explanation for Selected Questions:

3. Number of coins = 13. Type of coins = 50 paise.
   Therefore, the total amount = (13 × 50) paise = 650 paise = (600 + 50) paise
   = (600 ÷ 100) rupees and 50 paise = ₹ 6 and 50 paise.

4. As we know, subtraction is the inverse process of addition.
   Now, the difference in amounts = ₹ 500 – ₹ 130.90

```
  (4)(9)(9)  (10)
   5̸  0̸  0̸ :  0̸  0
 – 1  3  0 :  9  0
 ------------------
   3  6  9 :  1  0
```

   Therefore, ₹ 369.10 should be added to ₹ 130.90 to get ₹ 500.

6. Here, 5 pants is equal to 3 pants plus 2 pants.
   Cost of one pant = ₹ 600. Cost of 5 pants = ₹ 600 × 5 = ₹ 3000
   Cash back on 3 pants = ₹ 500. Cash back on 2 pants = ₹ 200
   Total cash back = ₹ 500 + ₹ 200 = ₹ 700
   Therefore, Sumit has to pay = ₹ 3000 – ₹ 700 = ₹ 2300

8. ₹ 180, ₹ 120, ₹ 190 and ₹ 205 have the values more than ₹ 175.

9. Total cost of the given four items = ₹ 850 + ₹ 110 + ₹ 190 + ₹ 450 = ₹ 1600

10. Cost of 1 chocolate = ₹80.50
    Cost of 2 jam bottles = ₹81.00
    Cost of 1 cherry knob = ₹50.50
    Cost of all items = ₹212.00

    Now, amount that Sangeeta got back = ₹ 500 – ₹ 212 = ₹ 288

Practice Exercise 7
Unitary Method

1. (C)	2. (B)	3. (C)	4. (A)	5. (E)
6. (C)	7. (A)	8. (D)	9. (D)	10. (A)

Explanation for Selected Questions:

2. Value of ● + ● + ● = 39, So, the value of ● = 39 ÷ 3 = 13
   Value of ■ + ■ + ■ + ■ = 48, So, the value of ■ = 48 ÷ 4 = 12
   Hence, the value of ● + ■ + ● = 13 + 12 + 13 = 38
4. Here, half dozen = 6. One and half dozen = 12 + 6 = 18
   Now, the cost of half dozen eggs = ₹ 24. Or, the cost of 6 eggs = ₹ 24
   Therefore, the cost of 1 egg = ₹ (24 ÷ 6) = ₹ 4
   So we have, the cost of one and half dozen eggs = ₹ (4 × 18) = ₹ 72
5. As we know, 1 hour = 60 minutes and 1 minute = 60 seconds
   Now, 2 hours = 2 × 60 minutes = 120 minutes = (120 × 60) seconds = 7200 seconds
6. Here, ⬢ represents 171 articles. Or, 1 symbol represents 171 articles
   Now, the number of given symbols = 8
   Therefore, 8 symbols represent (171 × 80) articles = 1368 articles
8. In 13 kg, number of books = 65. In 1 kg, number of books = 65 ÷ 13 = 5
   In 5 kg, number of books = 5 × 5 = 25. Hence, 25 books weigh 5 kg.
10. Half an hour = $\frac{1}{2}$ hours = 30 minutes. In half an hour, John types 360 words
    Or, in 30 minutes, John types 360 words.
    Therefore, in 1 minute, John types (360 ÷ 30) words = 12 words
    So we have, in 40 minutes, John types (12 × 40) words = 480 words

Practice Exercise 8
Measurement

1. (C)	2. (B)	3. (A)	4. (B)	5. (B)
6. (C)	7. (D)	8. (A)	9. (C)	10. (C)
11. (A)	12. (B)	13. (A)	14. (C)	15. (E)
16. (A)	17. (B)	18. (A)	19. (B)	20. (C)

Explanation for Selected Questions:

2. Here, the capacity of  = 750 ml
   So, the capacity of 4 such cups = (750 × 4) ml = 3000 ml. Now, 1000 ml = 1 L
   Or, 3000 ml = $\left(\frac{1}{1000} \times 3000\right)$ L = $\frac{3000}{1000}$ L = 3 L
3. Given that the weight of 5 balls = 180 grams
   Or, the weight of 1 ball = (180 ÷ 5) grams = 36 grams
   Therefore, the weight of 2 balls = (36 × 2) grams = 72 grams
4. Length of copper wire = 68 m. Number of equal pieces = 8
   Length of each piece = (68 ÷ 8) m = 8.5 m
11. Weight of 7 coins = 84 grams. Weight of 1 coin = (84 ÷ 7) grams = 12 grams
    Therefore, the weight of 6 coins = (12 × 6) grams = 72 grams
13. Length of Susan's rope = 3 m 350 cm. Length of Garima's rope = 4 m 650 cm
    The required length of both ropes = 3 m 35 cm + 4 m 65 cm = 800 cm = 8 m
14. Length of dining table = 7 m 50 cm. Breadth of dining table = 3 m 45 cm
    Difference of length and breadth = 7 m 50 cm – 3 m 45 cm = 4 m 5 cm
15. 3.7 kilometres = (3.7 × 1000) metres = 3700 metres
16. Distance covered by Peter in first hour = 7 km 70 m
    Distance covered by Peter in next hour = 6 km 77 m
    Total distance covered by Peter in 2 hours
    = 7 km 70 m + 6 km 77 m = 7070 m + 6077 m = 13 km 147 m.
18. Tea leaves in 1 tea bag = 1 g 760 mg
    Tea leaves in 6 tea bags = (1 g 760 mg) × 6 = 10 g 560 mg
    So, the pack of tea bag is of 10 g 560 mg.
19. 5 L of milk distributed equally among 8 boys.
    Each boy will get = 5 L ÷ 8 = (5000 ml) ÷ 8 = 625 ml
20. Wheat in first drum = 8 kg 500 g
    Wheat in second drum = 11 kg 800 g
    Total wheat in two drums = 8 kg 500 g + 11 kg 800 g = 20 kg 300 g

Practice Exercise 9
Geometrical Shapes

1. (B)	2. (D)	3. (C)	4. (B)	5. (C)
6. (B)	7. (D)	8. (E)	9. (D)	10. (D)

Explanation for Selected Questions:

3. An isosceles triangle has two sides of equal length.
Triangle given in option (C) has all sides unequal.

4. Given 3D shape is a shape of cuboid which has 12 edges.

5. 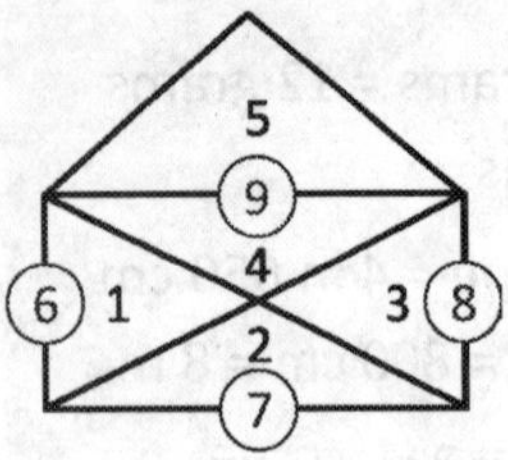

Clearly, there are 9 triangles in the given figure.

7. Here, the given rectilinear figure is as follow:

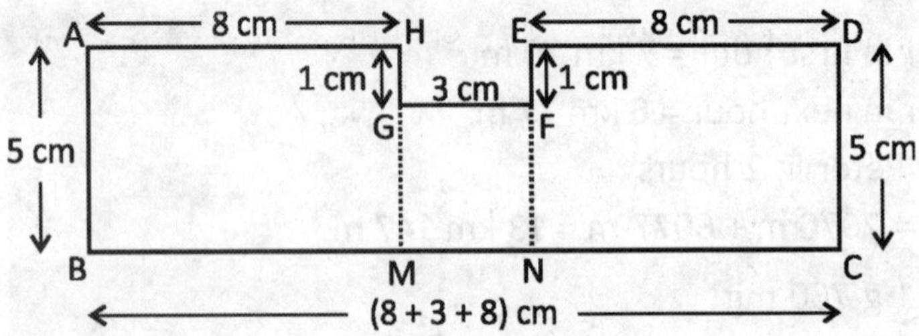

Now, BM = AH = 8 cm, MN = GF = 3 cm, NC = ED = 8 cm and AB = DC = 5 cm
So, the required perimeter = AH + GH + GF + EF + ED + DC + BC + AB
= 8 cm + 1 cm + 3 cm + 1 cm + 8 cm + 5 cm + (8 + 3 + 8) cm + 5 cm
= (31 + 19) cm = 50 cm

8. A line has no starting point and has no end point. There are only 4 lines in the given figure.

9. Side of square A = 7 cm. Perimeter of square = 28 cm
Length of rectangle B = 12 cm. Breadth of rectangle B = 4 cm
Perimeter of rectangle B = 2 × (12 + 4) cm = (2 × 16) cm = 32 cm

So, the required sum of perimeters = (28 + 32) cm = 60 cm

10. A cube has exactly 12 vertices or corners.

Practice Exercise 10
Data Handling

1. (B)	2. (B)	3. (C)	4. (A)	5. (C)
6. (B)	7. (D)	8. (A)	9. (C)	10. (C)

Explanation for Selected Questions:

6. Seeing the bar graph, we find that there were 15 people when the store opened at 10 am.
7. Seeing the bar graph, we find that there were 15 people when the store closed at 4 pm.
8. Seeing the bar graph, we find that the maximum number of people is 40 and at 1 pm, there were 40 people at the store. So the busiest time of the day at the store was 1 pm.
9. Seeing the bar graph, we find that at 1 pm, there were 30 people and at 2 pm, there were 40 people at the store. So, there were 30 to 40 people at the store in between 1 pm to 2 pm.
10. Seeing the bar graph, we find that at 10 am and 4 pm, there were same number of people, or 15 people at the store.

Practice Exercise 11
Reasoning and Aptitude

1. (B)	2. (C)	3. (D)	4. (C)	5. (D)
6. (A)	7. (B)	8. (A)	9. (D)	10. (C)
11. (C)	12. (B)	13. (D)	14. (B)	15. (A)
16. (C)	17. (D)	18. (B)	19. (C)	20. (B)

Explanation for Selected Questions:

1. Option (A); 4, 3, 2, 1 = CLUK. Option (B); 3, 2, 4, 1 = LUCK
   Option (C); 3, 4, 2, 1 = LCUK. Option (D); 2, 3, 4, 1 = ULCK
   So, the word given in option (B) is a meaningful word.

2. Word formed by using the letters of LRIZAB is BRAZIL which is the name of a country.
3. The answer is I, because the pattern is to count backward in three from the first given letter.

Ⓧ W V Ⓤ T S Ⓡ Q P Ⓞ N M Ⓛ K J Ⓘ

4. Sun rises in the East in the morning. Since my shadow falls to my left side. So, I was facing North.

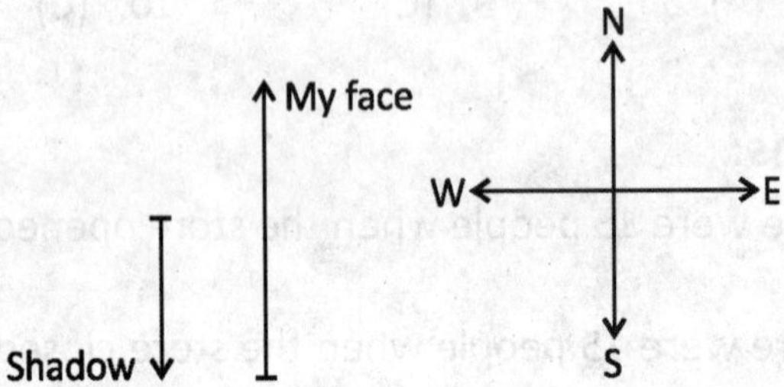

5. Here, B is in the first place.

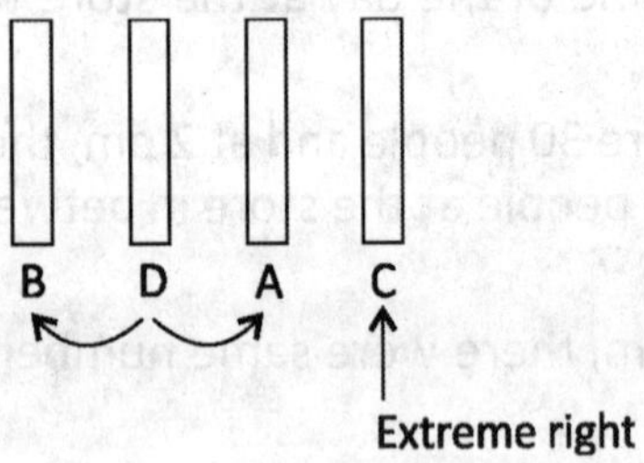

6. Room is the odd one out or it is different from the rest because it is not for sitting.
7. The answer is WK, because the pattern is to count towards in twos for both the first letter and the second letter as given below:

O	P	Q	R	S	T	U	V	W
C	D	E	E	G	H	I	J	K

8. Number in the box of the centre equals the difference of the products of opposite circled numbers.
   Or, 6 × 4 – 3 × 2 = 18; 5 × 3 – 3 × 2 = 9; 7 × 2 – 4 × 1 = 10, 9 × 3 – 4 × 2 = 19
9. Here, B + 1 = C; E + 1 = F; G + 1 = H; I + 1 = J; N + 1 = O
   Thus, L + 1 = M; E + 1 = F; A + 1 = B; S + 1 = T; T + 1 = U
   So, the required code is : MFBTU

10. Here

Ⓐ B Ⓒ D Ⓔ ⟹ ACF

Ⓓ E Ⓕ G Ⓗ ⟹ DFH

Ⓖ H I Ⓙ Ⓚ L ⟹ GJK

Ⓙ K Ⓛ M Ⓝ ⟹ JLN

Ⓟ Q Ⓡ S Ⓣ ⟹ PRT

11. In options (A), (B) and (D), circle is outside the square but in option (C), circle is inside the square. Therefore, figure in option (C) is the odd one out.

12. In option (A); a triangle (3 sides) has 3 shaded circles.
In option (B); a square (4 sides) has 5 shaded circles.
In option (C); a hexagon (6 sides) has 6 shaded circles.
In option (D); a pentagon (5 sides) has 5 shaded circles.
In option (E); a rectangle (4 sides) has 5 shaded circles.
Hence, the figure in option (B) is the odd one out.

13. 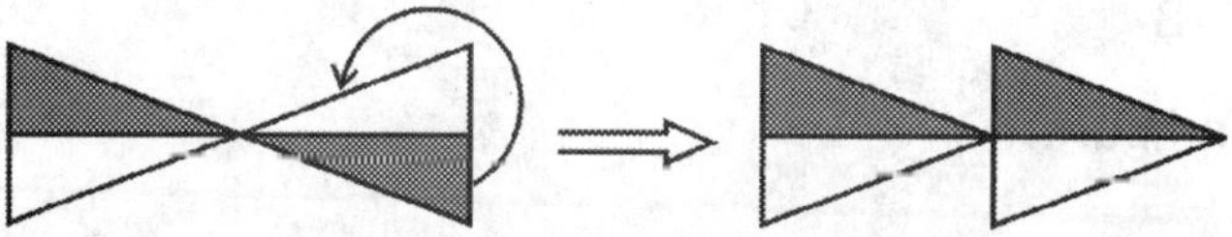

When direction change

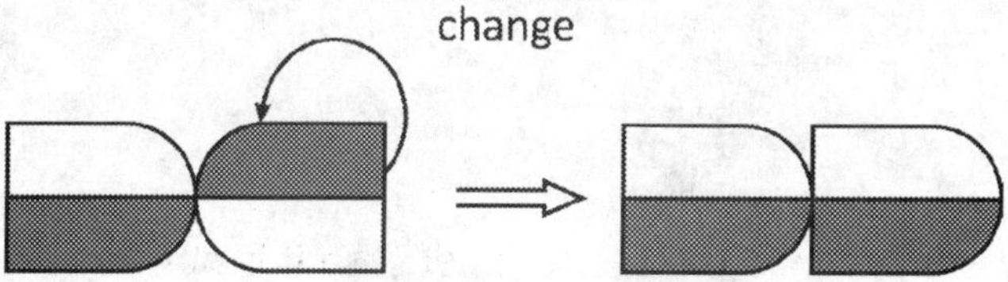

When direction change

14. Here, the unshaded hexagon (6 sides) is to shaded pentagon (5 sides).
So, the unshaded rectangle (4 sides) is to shaded triangle (3 sides).

15. There is a sequence related to the position. The hand of each clock moving by 90° anticlockwise $\frac{1}{4}$ turn left. Hence, the position of hand in the required step will be same as in the first position. So, the correct option is (A).

16. Here, figure pattern is as follow:

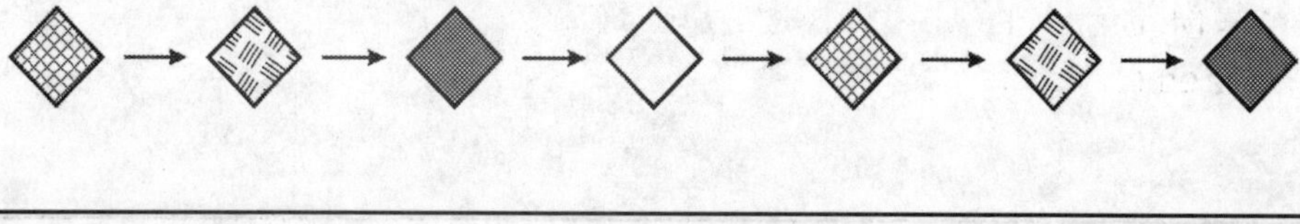

Hence, the figure given in option (C) will come in the place of the question mark (?).

17. 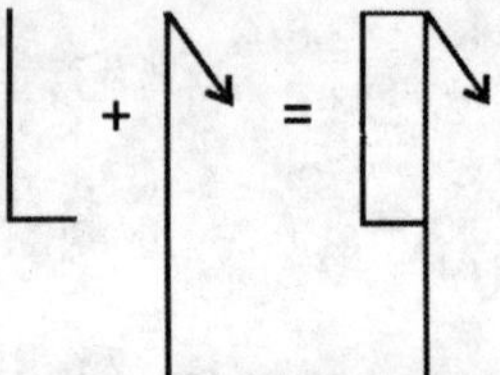

18. Here, four semicircles and 1 rectangle form the given figure: BEF, GFD, ABD, BCD.

19. There are 4 triangles in the given figure.

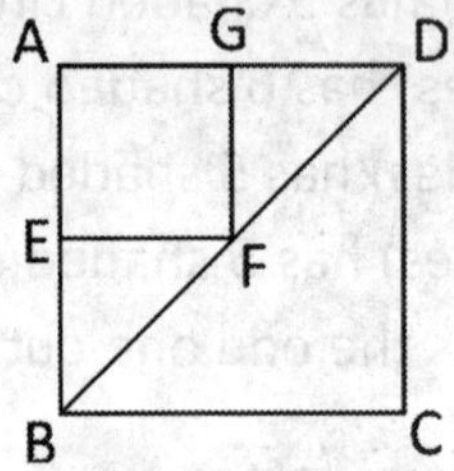

20. There are 4 circles in the given figure.

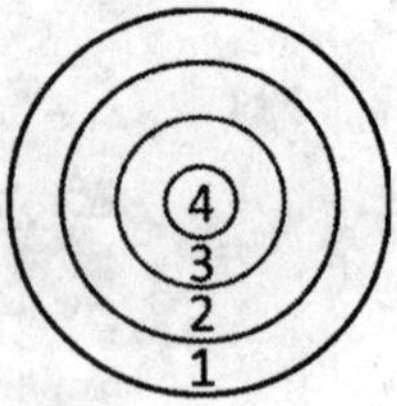

Model Test Paper Answer Keys

Model Test Paper - 1

1. (D)	2. (B)	3. (A)	4. (B)	5. (B)	6. (C)	7. (A)	8. (C)
9. (A)	10. (C)	11. (A)	12. (C)	13. (A)	14. (E)	15. (C)	16. (A)
17. (B)	18. (B)	19. (B)	20. (C)	21. (A)	22. (B)	23. (C)	24. (D)
25. (B)	26. (B)	27. (C)	28. (A)	29. (B)	30. (A)	31. (B)	32. (C)
33. (E)	34. (C)	35. (A)	36. (D)	37. (C)	38. (B)	39. (C)	40. (B)
41. (A)	42. (C)	43. (D)	44. (C)	45. (A)	46. (C)	47. (D)	48. (B)
49. (B)	50. (D)						

Model Test Paper - 2

1. (B)	2. (A)	3. (B)	4. (B)	5. (B)	6. (A)	7. (B)	8. (C)
9. (B)	10. (C)	11. (D)	12. (B)	13. (A)	14. (B)	15. (C)	16 (B)
17. (C)	18. (B)	19. (C)	20. (A)	21. (A)	22. (A)	23. (C)	24. (A)
25. (D)	26. (B)	27. (A)	28. (B)	29. (A)	30. (A)	31. (B)	32. (B)
33. (C)	34. (B)	35. (A)	36. (B)	37. (B)	38. (B)	39. (D)	40. (A)
41. (C)	42. (B)	43. (C)	44. (A)	45. (B)	46. (D)	47. (B)	48. (A)
49. (C)	50. (E)						

Model Test Paper - 3

1. (B)	2. (C)	3. (D)	4. (A)	5. (C)	6. (A)	7. (C)	8. (B)
9. (D)	10. (C)	11. (A)	12. (B)	13. (C)	14. (B)	15. (B)	16. (C)
17. (B)	18. (D)	19. (A)	20. (B)	21. (E)	22. (C)	23. (A)	24. (A)
25. (C)	26. (A)	27. (C)	28. (D)	29. (D)	30. (B)	31. (A)	32. (A)
33. (B)	34. (B)	35. (D)	36. (D)	37. (B)	38. (D)	39. (B)	40. (C)
41. (C)	42. (D)	43. (B)	44. (B)	45. (B)	46. (A)	47. (D)	48. (B)
49. (D)	50. (A)						

Model Test Paper - 4

1. (A)	2. (C)	3. (C)	4. (A)	5. (C)	6. (A)	7. (B)	8. (C)
9. (A)	10. (B)	11. (B)	12. (D)	13. (B)	14. (B)	15. (D)	16. (C)
17. (B)	18. (B)	19. (B)	20. (C)	21. (D)	22. (B)	23. (C)	24. (B)
25. (A)	26. (C)	27. (D)	28. (C)	29. (C)	30. (A)	31. (D)	32. (B)
33. (A)	34. (B)	35. (A)	36. (D)	37. (B)	38. (E)	39. (A)	40. (B)
41. (C)	42. (B)	43. (C)	44. (A)	45. (B)	46. (C)	47. (B)	48. (C)
49. (B)	50. (A)						

Model Test Paper - 5

1. (B)	2. (B)	3. (A)	4. (B)	5. (D)	6. (B)	7. (B)	8. (C)
9. (B)	10. (B)	11. (C)	12. (E)	13. (D)	14. (D)	15. (C)	16. (B)
17. (A)	18. (C)	19. (C)	20. (A)	21. (C)	22. (B)	23. (B)	24. (B)
25. (B)	26. (B)	27. (D)	28. (C)	29. (C)	30. (C)	31. (C)	32. (C)
33. (B)	34. (B)	35. (C)	36. (A)	37. (B)	38. (B)	39. (A)	40. (B)
41. (D)	42. (D)	43. (B)	44. (C)	45. (C)	46. (C)	47. (B)	48. (D)
49. (B)	50. (B)						

Sample Question Paper

1. (D)	2. (C)	3. (D)	4. (A)	5. (B)	6. (C)	7. (B)	8. (D)
9. (A)	10. (C)	11. (C)	12. (C)	13. (D)	14. (B)	15. (C)	16. (D)
17. (C)	18. (C)	19. (D)	20. (C)	21. (D)	22. (E)	23. (B)	24. (D)
25. (D)	26. (D)	27. (C)	28. (D)	29. (C)	30. (C)	31. (C)	32. (D)
33. (C)	34. (B)	35. (D)	36. (D)	37. (B)	38. (A)	39. (D)	40. (C)
41. (C)	42. (B)	43. (C)	44. (C)	45. (D)	46. (D)	47. (C)	48. (B)
49. (B)	50. (C)						